BEYOND DOGMATISM

Studies in Critical Social Sciences Book Series

Haymarket Books is proud to be working with Brill Academic Publishers (www.brill.nl) to republish the *Studies in Critical Social Sciences* book series in paperback editions. This peer-reviewed book series offers insights into our current reality by exploring the content and consequences of power relationships under capitalism, and by considering the spaces of opposition and resistance to these changes that have been defining our new age. Our full catalog of *SCSS* volumes can be viewed at https://www.haymarketbooks .org/series_collections/4-studies-in-critical-social-sciences.

BEYOND DOGMATISM

Studies in Historical Sociology

EDITED BY
ANDREA BORGHINI

Haymarket Books
Chicago, IL

First published in 2023 by Brill Academic Publishers, The Netherlands
© 2023 Koninklijke Brill NV, Leiden, The Netherlands

Published in paperback in 2024 by
Haymarket Books
P.O. Box 180165
Chicago, IL 60618
773-583-7884
www.haymarketbooks.org

ISBN: 979-8-88890-319-3

Distributed to the trade in the US through Consortium Book Sales and
Distribution (www.cbsd.com) and internationally through Ingram Publisher
Services International (www.ingramcontent.com).

This book was published with the generous support of Lannan Foundation,
Wallace Action Fund, and the Marguerite Casey Foundation.

Special discounts are available for bulk purchases by organizations and
institutions. Please call 773-583-7884 or email info@haymarketbooks.org for more
information.

Cover design by Jamie Kerry and Ragina Johnson.

Printed in the United States.

Library of Congress Cataloging-in-Publication data is available.

Contents

Preface

The Many Worlds of Historical Sociology

George Steinmetz

Pierre Bourdieu suggested that the history of sociology should be included in sociological methods training programs (Bourdieu 1990, 178), since it is an essential component of epistemic vigilance (Bourdieu and Heilbron 2022; Steinmetz 2023, Ch. 15). Yet one striking feature of historical sociology in the United States is its lack of interest in rigorous research on the history of sociology itself (Camic 1997: 229). The paucity of serious research by American sociologists on their own discipline is ironic in light of the fact that the first panels on "historical sociology" at the meetings of the American Sociological Society were actually focused on the history of sociology (Blumer 1933, 11). The "History of Sociology" section of the American Sociological Association issues regular warnings that its membership is in danger of falling below the threshold required to keep sections going. There is no dedicated journal for the history of sociology in the US. Indeed, the history of sociology is one of the rare sociological subfields in which there are more fulltime specialists in Austria, Britain, Denmark, France, and Germany than in the US.

Most writing on the history of historical sociology resembles the standard approach to writing the history of science before 1900, which sought to legitimate particular sciences and theories, celebrate particular geniuses, fight battles with scientific competitors, and emphasize the idea of inexorable scientific progress (Daston 2001; Steinmetz 2022). This is true of the three books that have tried to organize the subfield's self-understanding in the past four decades. The first is Theda Skocpol's *Vision and Method* (1984), a collection of essays on individual thinkers. This volume proposes a canon for historical sociology that includes Polanyi, Eisenstadt, Bendix, Perry Anderson, Charles Tilly, Wallerstein, Moore, and Skocpol herself, along with two historians, Marc Bloch and E.P. Thompson. From the standpoint of the present there seem to be two glaring absences here. The first is Max Weber and the entire network of historicist sociological thinkers around Weber or who oriented themselves to his legacy during the Weimar Republic, from Alfred Weber and Max Scheler to

Karl Mannheim, Norbert Elias, Otto Hinze, and Werner Sombart.[1] The second striking absence is Karl Marx and the entire western Marxist tradition of pro- cessual historical scholarship prior to Thompson, Anderson, and Wallerstein. As Dello Buono argues in this volume, the less reductionist tradition of west- ern Marxism that starts with Georg Lukàcs presents a very different approach to historical sociology. A third striking absence is Pierre Bourdieu, who had already moved from structuralism to processual practice theory in *Esquisse d'une théorie de la pratique* (1972) and published historical field-theoretical studies since the beginning of the 1970s (e.g., Bourdieu 1971; 1975; 1983; 1984).[2]

The second volume is Dennis Smith's *The Rise of Historical Sociology* (1991). Smith added Parsons, Smelser, Lipset, and T.H. Marshall to historical sociology's putative founders along with Runciman and Giddens as more contemporary practitioners, along with one historian who was mentioned in the chapters on Bloch and Wallerstein in the Skocpol volume, Fernand Braudel. Smith's book attempts to create a coherent tradition, a progressive intellectual history leading up to the present. He traces an ongoing concern throughout postwar historical sociology with questions about why the West is "different," and with the relations between capitalism and democracy. However, research on non- Western areas or guided by "non-Western" questions is marginalized. As I wrote in a review of the book at the time of its publication, "at the 1992 ASA meetings, the comparative-historical sessions included papers on Iraq, South Asia, the Caribbean, and Taiwan, with theoretical approaches ranging from 'subaltern studies' to rational choice theory," adding that *The Rise of Historical Sociology* "ultimately imposes an extremely narrow definition on an intellectual field increasingly characterized by its very heterogeneity" (Steinmetz 1993).

The third and most recent effort to take stock of historical sociology is Adams, Clemens and Orloff (2005), especially the editor's introduction (pp. 1–72), enti- tled "Social Theory, Modernity, and the Three Waves of Historical Sociology." Here, most of the historical sociologists discussed in the earlier overviews are characterized as members of a supposed "second wave" focused mainly on social structural causation and using a reductive "utilitarian model of action"

---

1 See the essays by Borghini, Dello Buono, and Iannone in this volume on Elias, Weber, and Sombart; see Steinmetz (2009, 2020) on the entire network of historicist sociologists in Weimar Germany and their epistemological distinctiveness.

2 The Anglophone reception of Bourdieu introduced delays and misperceptions of Bourdieu's work, inserting him into to American social scientific categories (e.g., sociology of educa- tion and stratification); see Bourdieu's (1991) comments on the US reception of his work and the general problem of the *circulation of texts without contexts*, which is basic problem overlooked by most if the literature on transnational, connected, and "croisé" approaches to historiography.

(Ibid.: 22, 8). This putative second wave emphasized grand epochal transitions (Ibid.: 16) and were oriented toward Marxism as an "overall regime of knowledge" (Ibid.: 20). Methodologically, they combined comparative design with a Humean logic of "constant conjunctions of events" (Ibid.: 23). The result was a body of work that elicited sharp criticism from historians and from "more conventional social scientists" (Ibid., 23).

What is wrong with this account? First, the Adams, Clemens and Orloff model relies on a generational model rather than a field model in characterizing historical sociology, which deemphasizes the differences within a given field at a given moment in time. As a generational model, it does not take into consideration the internal "nonsimultaneity" of intellectual generations, which had already been emphasized by Karl Mannheim in his classic essay on generations (Mannheim 1928) As Wolfgang Knöbl (2022, 114) points out, Mannheim's analysis of "generations" was used to undermine the supposed homogeneity of historical "epochs," raising questions about "whether the actions of a generation truly constitute something like a process, and how and if practices in such different contexts can be linked together in such a way that one can speak of a process" (Ibid., 115). It was Mannheim's generations essay, Knöbl argues, that realigned him with ongoing discussions of historical sociology in Central Europe at the time. Elsewhere Knöbl has also shown that even modernization theory, which is usually described as a uniformly reductionist formation of historical sociology, experienced growing disagreement among its practitioners as time went on (Knöbl 2003, 104).

This points to a second problem with the "three waves" model, which is its neglect of national contexts other than the American one. Borghini suggests (this volume) that there is a need to "provincialize America" in the discussion of historical sociology. This imperative becomes startlingly obvious once as we reexamine the actual history of professional historical sociology. The focus on the American (or Anglo-American) lineages obscures some of the most generative moments in historical sociological thought, such as those in Germany (ca. 1890–1933), France (ca. 1975-present), and, as the present volume suggests, in Italy.[3] Recent discussions of the history of sociology have emphasized the importance of reevaluating canons, and many have emphasized W.E.B. Du Bois' study of Black Reconstruction in United States after the Civil War (Du Bois 1935). I agree completely work by Du Bois should be included in the lineage of

---

3 On interactions between historians and sociologists in Germany before 1933 and in France since the 1970s, especially in the circles around Pierre Bourdieu and his Centre de sociologie européenne (now the Centre européen de sociologie et de science politique), see Steinmetz (2017).

historical sociology.[4] I would also agree with Andrea Borghini and other contributors to this volume on the importance of including non-American source-roots in reconstructing the genealogy of historical sociology. This means that a reconstruction of historical sociology's "canon" cannot be restricted to figures like Du Bois and Oliver C. Cox (1959), however important their inclusion is in other respects (Steinmetz 2019).[5]

A deprovicialized history of historical sociology could also include figures like the early Indian historical sociologists G.S. Ghurye, Ramakrishna Mukerjee, D. P. Mukerji, and Benoy Sarkar, who published historical-sociological works before Indian independence (Ghurye 1932; Mukerjee 1923; Mukerji 1945; Sarkar 1932). It might encompass Nguyễn Văn Huyên, the Vietnamese student of Marcel Mauss who wrote his doctoral thesis at the Sorbonne in 1935 with Lucien Lévy-Bruhl and was hired as a researcher at the French École française d'Extrême-Orient in Hanoi in 1940, published the historical-ethnological book Annamite Civilization in 1944, and then rallied to Ho Chi Minh and served as Education Minister in the Democratic Republic of Vietnam from 1946 until his death in 1975 (Nguyễn 1944). It should include the French Orientalist-cum-sociologist Jacques Berque, who became the leading historical sociologist of North Africa and published in the leading history journal Annales d'histoire économique et sociale (Berque 1937) before moving into sociology (Berque 1955; Steinmetz 2023, Ch. 12). Such a revised canon might include Abdoulaye Bara Diop, who wrote his first doctoral thesis at the University of Dakar on the historical sociology of migration and immigration of the Toucouleur people (Diop 1965) and his thèse d'état (second doctoral thesis) on social change in Wolof society (Diop 1978). It could include the Lebanese historian-turned-sociologist Toufic Touma, a student of Berque and author of a study of Druze and Maronite social and political institutions from the 17th century to 1914 (Touma 1971–1972). The canon should certainly include the foundational works on the historical sociology of slavery, including Gilberto Freyre's Casa-Grande & Senzala (The Masters and the Slaves, 1933), CLR James' The Black Jacobins (1938), through to Orlando Patterson's The Sociology of Slavery (1965/1967). None of these works were included in the above-mentioned overviews of historical sociology, even though Freyre was trained in the US, CLR James lived in the US from 1938 to 1953, and Patterson has taught in the United States at Harvard University

---

4 I would also urge that historical sociologists include in their lineage Du Bois' crucial work on World War One (Du Bois 1915; Williams 2023) and The Souls of Black Folk (1903), which is crucial for its genre experimentation and his famous concept of the "color line."
5 Of course, Du Bois lost his American passport due to the Cold War and ended his life in Ghana.

since 1969. There are many other examples, especially given the proliferation of historical sociological research by students of the French Africanist sociologist Georges Balandier and by students and colleagues of Pierre Bourdieu (Steinmetz 2018).

The present volume, edited by Andrea Borghini, also presents a unique chain of founders, continuers, concepts, and ideas for historical sociology. It shows how certain ideas were reworked and transformed over time – for example in Elena Gremigni's virtuosic account of the transformations of the *habitus* concept from Aristotle to Bourdieu. Historical sociology's new reference points, according to the authors in this collection, might begin with the familiar figures of Hegel, Marx, and Weber, but then continue with Lukàcs, Werner Sombart, Walter Benjamin, Norbert Elias, Carl Schmitt, Karl Polanyi, and Antonio Gramsci, and then move forward to the present with Christopher Chase-Dunn, Michael Mann, and Pierre Bourdieu. These proposals sketch out an entirely different set of intellectual lineages than the previous volumes mentioned above. Perhaps the most prominent of the genealogical pathways suggested by this volume begins with Hegel's historicizing critique of Kant and moves forward through various historical approaches that foreground process, dialectics, and becoming rather than statics and being (see the chapters by Pastore on Gramsci, and Dello Buono). The present collection lies outside the neo-positivist lineage of "comparative historical sociology (2005) characterized by Adams, Clemens, and Orloff as "second wave," and reaffirms the importance of non-dogmatic Marxist traditions (essays by Pastore, Dello Buono, Maddaloni, Campo and Iacono), critiques of unilinear theories of social evolution and positivist social science (essays by Borghini, Blad, and Iannone), and approaches that refuse the rigid separation of science and urge a critical historical sociology or a sociology of judgments (essays by Ferrara, Pastore, and Dello Buono).

The keywords, central topoi, and master thinkers discussed here diverge from those in the American-centric histories of historical sociology discussed above. In the present volume, interdisciplinarity, contingency, heterogeneity, critique, the history of concepts, *anti-dogmatism*, are seen as core elements of historical sociology and not as demons to be slain or embarrassments to be shunted aside.

References

Adams, Julia, Elisabeth Clemens, and Ann Orloff, eds. 2005. *Remaking Modernity: Politics, Processes and History in Sociology*. Durham, NC: Duke University Press.

Berque, Jacques. 1937. "Sur un coin de terre marocaine: seigneur terrien et paysans." *Annales d'histoire économique et sociale* 45: 227–235.

Berque, Jacques. 1955. "Les sociétés nord-africaines vues du Haut-Atlas." *Cahiers internationaux de sociologie* 19: 59–65.

Blumer, Herbert, ed. 1933. *Publication of the American Sociological Society*, vol. 27, no. 1, *February 1933, Proceedings*. Chicago: American Sociological Society.

Bourdieu, Jérôme and Johan Heilbron. 2022. "Introduction. De la vigilance épistémologique à la réflexivité." In Pierre Bourdieu, *Retour sur la réflexivité*. Paris: EHESS, pp. 9–28.

Bourdieu, Pierre, 1971. "Genèse et structure du champ religieux." *Revue française de sociologie* 12(3): 295–334.

Bourdieu, Pierre. 1972. *Esquisse d'une théorie de la pratique, précédé de trois études d'ethnologie kabyle*. Genéve: Librairie Droz.

Bourdieu, Pierre. 1975. "L'ontologie politique de Martin Heidegger." *Actes de la recherche en sciences sociales* 5/6: 109–156.

Bourdieu, Pierre. 1983. "The Field of Cultural Production or the Economic World Reversed." *Poetics* 12 (4/5): 311–356.

Bourdieu, Pierre. 1984. *Homo academicus*. Paris: Les Éditions de Minuit.

Bourdieu, Pierre. 1991. "On the Possibility of a Field of World Sociology." In Pierre Bourdieu and James S. Coleman, eds., *Social Theory for a Changing Society*. Boulder: Westview, pp. 373–387.

Camic, Charles. 1997. "Uneven Development in the History of Sociology." *Schweizerische Zeitschrift für Soziologie/Revue Suisse de sociologie* 23:227–233.

Diop, Abdoulaye. 1965. *Société toucouleur et migration, l'immigration toucouleur à Dakar*. Dakar, I. F. A. Thèse, 3eme cycle, University of Dakar.

Diop, Abdoulaye. 1978. *La société Wolof tradition et changement*. Thèse d'état, Paris 5.

Du Bois, W. E. B. 1915. "The African Roots of War." *Atlantic Monthly* 115 (May): 707–714.

Elder-Vass, Dave. 2012. *The Reality of Social Construction*. Cambridge: Cambridge University Press.

Freyre, Giberto. 1946 [1933]. *The Masters and the Slaves. A Study in the Development of Brazilian Civilization*. New York: Knopf.

Ghurye, G. S. 1932. *Caste and Race in India*. London: Kegan Paul.

James, C. L. R. 1938. *The Black Jacobins: Toussaint L'Ouverture and the San Domingo Revolution*. London: Secker & Warburg.

Knöbl, Wolfgang. 2003. "Theories That Won't Pass Away: The Never-Ending Story of Modernization Theory. In Gerard Delanty and Engin F. Isin, eds., *Handbook of Historical Sociology*. London: Sage, pp. 96–107.

Knöbl, Wolfgang. 2022. *Die Soziologie vor der Geschichte*. Berlin: Suhrkamp.

Lachmann, Richard. 2013. *What is Historical Sociology?* Cambridge: Polity Press.

Mannheim, Karl. 1928. "Das Problem der Generationen." *Kölner Vierteljahrshefte für Soziologie* 7 (n.s.): 157–185, 309–330.

Mukerjee, Radhakamal. 1923. *Democracies of the East; a Study in Comparative Politics.* London: P. S. King. Mukerjee 1945.

Mukerji, Dhurjati Prasad. 1945. *On Indian History. A Study in Method.* Bombay: Hind Kitabs.

Nguyễn, Văn Huyên. 1944. *La civilisation annamite.* Hanoi: Direction de l'Instruction Publique de l'Indochine.

Patterson, Orlando. 1965/1967. *The Sociology of Slavery: Jamaica, 1655–1838.* London: MacGibbon & Kee.

Sarkar, Benoy Kumar 1932. *The Pressure of Labour upon Constitution and Law, 1776–1928: A Chronology of Ideals and Achievements in Societal Reconstruction.* Benares: Jnanmandal.

Skocpol, Theda. 1984. *Vision and Method in Historical Sociology.* Cambridge: Cambridge University Press.

Smith, Dennis. 1991. *The Rise of Historical Sociology.* Cambridge: Polity.

Steinmetz, George. 1993. Review of Dennis Smith, *The Rise of Historical Sociology,* in *American Journal of Sociology* 98(5): 1191–1192.

Steinmetz, George. 2005. "American Sociology's Epistemological Unconscious and the Transition to Post-Fordism: the case of Historical Sociology." In Adams, Clemens, and Orloff, (2005), pp. 109–157.

Steinmetz, George. 2008. "Présentation de W.E.B. Du Bois." *Actes de la recherche en sciences sociales,* nos. 171–172 (March): 75–77.

Steinmetz, George. 2017. "Field Theory and Interdisciplinary: Relations between History and Sociology in Germany and France during the Twentieth Century." *Comparative Studies* in Society and History 59(2): 477–514.

Steinmetz, George. 2018. "Bourdieusian Field Theory and the Reorientation of Historical Sociology." In Jeff Sallaz and Tom Medvetz, eds., *Oxford Handbook of Pierre Bourdieu.* Oxford: Oxford University Press, pp. 601–628.

Steinmetz, George. 2019. "American Sociology and Colonialism, 1890s-1960s." In *Reconsidering American Power: Pax Americana and Social Science,* edited by John Kelly, J. K. Jacobsen, and Marston H. Morgan. Oxford University Press, 2019, pp. 273–293.

Steinmetz, George. 2020. "Historicism and Positivism in Sociology: From Weimar Germany to the Contemporary United States." In Herman Paul, Adriaan van Veldhuizen, eds. *Historicism: A Travelling Concept.* London: Bloomsbury, pp. 57–95.

Steinmetz, George. 2022. "The History of Sociology as Scientific Reflexivity." In *The Palgrave Handbook of the History of Human Sciences.* D. McCallum, editor. London: Palgrave Macmillan, pp. 833–864.

Steinmetz, George. 2023. *The Colonial Origins of Modern Social Thought: French Sociology and the Overseas Empire.* Princeton: Princeton University Press.

Touma, Toufic. 1971–1972. *Paysans et Institutions Féodales chez les Druzes et les Maronites du Liban du XVIIe siècle à 1914.* Beyrouth: Université Libanaise.

Williams, Chad. 2023. *The Wounded World: W. E. B. Du Bois and the First World War.* New York: Farrar, Straus and Giroux.

Acknowledgments

The volume we are publishing here grew out of a congressional occasion, specifically a session devoted to "Critical Insights into Historical Sociology" coordinated by the undersigned and Prof. Ricardo A. Dello Buono (Manhattan College, USA), during the 13th Annual International Conference on Sociology, Athens, May 2019, and has since been enriched by additional contributions, thus highlighting the growing interest in Historical Sociology in our country as well.

I would like to thank all the authors both for their fundamental contribution to the construction of the volume and for their patience in waiting for its publication.

Finally, let me thank Enrico Campo for his precious editorial work and for the stimulating discussions about Historical Sociology we shared walking through the 'historical' Pisa.

The hope is that this book will be able to fit fully into the international debate and help defend and at the same time advance a perspective whose centrality, in the debate of the social sciences, cannot be doubted.

Notes on Contributors

Cory Blad
is Professor of Sociology and Dean of the School of Liberal Arts at Manhattan College. His work focuses on the effects of market liberalization on inequalities and political legitimation. His previous work has focused on the role of nationalism in political legitimation strategies as well as the impacts of economic liberalization on social inequalities and political change.

Andrea Borghini
is Professor of Sociology and Deputy Director at the Department of Political Sciences, University of Pisa (Italy). He mainly investigates topics related to the political transformations of the nation state, the sociology of Pierre Bourdieu, public sociology, historical sociology and the transformation of social control. He is editor of the scientific journal "The Lab's Quarterly". Among his recent works are "Science and Society in Karl Raimund Popper: some reflections starting from Positivismusstreit", (*Journal of Classical Sociology*, 2, 2015); *Exploring the Crisis. Theoretical Perspectives and Empirical Investigations* (with Enrico Campo, Pisa, 2015), *The Role of the Nation State in the Global Age* (Brill, 2016), "Public sociology and southern European societies: a critical view" (Revista espanola de sociologia, 1, 2020).

Enrico Campo
is a Research fellow of Sociology at the Department of Philosophy, University of Milan (Italy). His research interests include the sociological theory, the sociology of knowledge and the study of the relation between culture, technology, and cognition. He is the author of *Attention and its Crisis in Digital Society* (Routledge 2022; Italian edition Donzelli 2020) and co-editor of *Politics of Curiosities. Alternatives to the Attention Economy* (with Yves Citton, Routledge expected 2023) and *Exploring the Crisis. Theoretical Perspectives and Empirical Investigations* (with Andrea Borghini, Pisa University Press 2015).

Ricardo A. Dello Buono
is Professor of Sociology at Manhattan College in New York City. His books and articles have revolved around theorizing social problems and exploring lacunae in the sociology of development, with a regional emphasis on Latin America. He is the Latin American and Caribbean editor for the Sage journal *Critical Sociology* and is active in the Association for Humanist Sociology (AHS), the

Society for the Study of Social Problems (SSSP), the International Sociological Association (ISA) and the Latin American Studies Association (LASA).

Alfredo Ferrara

is Researcher in Political philosophy at the Department of Political science of the University of Bari "Aldo Moro". He has worked on the transformations of work and related forms of subjectivation starting from the crisis of the Fordist model, on neoliberalism, and on the thought of Antonio Gramsci. He published *L'ascesa politica del neoliberalismo. Accumulazioni molecolari, rivoluzione passiva ed egemonia* (Cacucci, Bari 2021) (*The Political Rise of Neoliberalism. Molecular Accumulations, Passive Revolution and Hegemony*), in which he analyses the political rise of Thatcherism and Reaganism in a long-term perspective by adopting a Gramscian approach. He is currently investigating the political implications of cybersecurity.

Elena Gremigni

is a PhD in History of Art and History and Sociology of Modernity. In 2020 she got the National Scientific Qualification for the position of Associate Professor. She is currently an adjunct Professor of Sociology of groups and Sociology of cultural and communicative processes at the University of Pisa and leads, with other scholars, the research group "Officina Bourdieu". Her main research interests concern the consumption practices of the products of the culture industry and the reproduction of social inequality within school systems.

Roberta Iannone

PhD., is Full Professor of General Sociology at the Department of Political Sciences of Sapienza University of Rome. She is the Delegate of the Rector Sapienza University for Merchandising and she is Scientific Co-Director of the "Rivista trimestrale di Scienza dell'Amministrazione. Studi di teoria e ricerca sociale". Her main research topics are the history of sociological thought, capitalism and social organizations.

Carmelo Lombardo

PhD, is Full Professor of Sociology at the Department of Communication and Social Research, Sapienza-University of Rome. His research interests include classical and contemporary social theory and methodology of social sciences. Among his recent publication, "Subjects of Objectivation. Exercises in Reflexive Socioanalysis", special issue of *Sociologia e Ricerca Sociale* (2022, with G. Ienna, L. Sabetta, and M. Santoro); *Against the Background of Social Reality. Defaults, Commonplaces, and the Sociology of the Unmarked* (Routledge,

NOTES ON CONTRIBUTORS

2022 forthcoming, with L. Sabetta); *Appearance of Nothingness. An Analysis of Concealed Strategic Actions* (in W. Brekhus, T. DeGloma, and W.R. Force, eds., *The Oxford Handbook of Symbolic Interaction*, 2021, with L. Sabetta).

Domenico Maddaloni

is Professor of Sociology at the University of Salerno, Department of Political and Communication Sciences. He is Head of the Sociology Unit of the Athens Institute for Education and Research (ATINER) and is co-editor of the *Athens Journal of Social Sciences* (https://www.athensjournals.gr/ajss/eb). His research interests concern sociological theory, social change, globalization, and migration. Among his publications: *La ilusiòn del progreso. La sociologìa y las teorias de la evoluciòn*, Planeta, Barcelona-Bogotà, 2013; "Between warfare and welfare. An ecological-evolutionary perspective on the rise and decline of national public social protection systems", *Sociologia e ricerca sociale*, 113: 120–142, 2017.

Alfonso Maurizio Iacono

holds a chair in History of Philosophy at the University of Pisa, Italy. He also taught at the Université de Paris 1 (Sorbonne-Panthéon), France. Formerly Dean of the Faculty of Letters, he is currently Director of the Pisa University Museum Network. His research areas of interest are the relationship between philosophy, politics and anthropology, with an emphasis on the eighteenth, nineteenth, and twentieth-century debates.

Gerardo Pastore

a PhD in History and Sociology of Modernity, is Associate Professor in Sociology at the Department of Political Science, University of Pisa (Italy). He teaches sociology of globalization; sociology of social control and deviance; sociology of health. He has conducted research on the knowledge society as part of a critical analysis of the processes of transformation of contemporary societies, focusing on inequalities and social inclusion processes, paradoxes of the knowledge society, highly skilled migration, university education in prison. He also studies the application of the Gramscian perspective to the above research areas. He has published about seventy scholarly works, including books, articles, and book chapters.

Eleonora Piromalli

is Researcher in Political Philosophy at the Department of Philosophy of the University of Rome "Sapienza". She has published a book on Michael Mann's theory of social power, a monography on Axel Honneth's paradigm of recognition, and one on Iris Marion Young's deliberative democracy, as well as many articles in international and Italian journals, such as *Philosophy and Social Criticism, European Journal of Political Theory* and *Quaderni di Teoria Sociale*. Her main focus of research is critical theory, with particular interest in the topics of social domination and social power, recognition, ideology, and alienation.

Lorenzo Sabetta

a PhD, is tenure-track Assistant Professor of Sociology at the Department of Communication and Social Research, Sapienza-University of Rome, and Adjunct Professor of Sociology at Luiss University. He works at the intersection of sociological theory, cultural-cognitive sociology, and sociology of knowledge. His recent publications include: *The Anthem Companion to Robert K. Merton* (Anthem Press, 2022, with C. Crothers); *Against the Background of Social Reality. Defaults, Commonplaces, and the Sociology of the Unmarked* (Routledge, 2022 forthcoming, with C. Lombardo); *Appearance of Nothingness. An Analysis of Concealed Strategic Actions* (in W. Brekhus, T. DeGloma, and W.R. Force, eds., *The Oxford Handbook of Symbolic Interaction*, 2021, with C. Lombardo).

George Steinmetz

is the Charles Tilly Professor of Sociology at the University of Michigan. His interests include the sociology of empires, states, and cities; social theory; and the history and philosophy of the social sciences. His publications include *The Devil's Handwriting: Precoloniality and the German Colonial State in Qingdao, Samoa and Southwest Africa* (2007), *Sociology and Empire* (2013), *The Social Sciences in the Looking-Glass* (2003). In April 2023 he published *The Colonial Origins of Modern Social Thought: French Sociology and the Overseas Empire*, and he is currently completing the second volume focused on 20th century British sociology.

Introduction

Andrea Borghini

When introducing the substantial volume dedicated to the topics of Historical Sociology, Adams *et al.* state that "historical sociologists are enthusiastically interdisciplinary" (2005, 10).

The interdisciplinarity evoked by the US authors is a double-edged sword. It may be theoretically professed, feeding the legitimate expectations of scholars intolerant to disciplinary barriers and to disputes between disciplines, but it is not always practicable, as it implies the abandonment of what Popper (1994) called the *myth of the framework*, i.e. the belief that discussion and dialogue are possible only if the participants share the same framework of basic assumptions.

It is therefore a question of fully understanding the reasons for affirming this, of placing it in the wake of the debate on Historical Sociology, of its criticalities and potentialities on one hand and of the meaning of this volume on the other, to then conclude about the possibility of concretely pursuing this path.

1 The Debate between Sociology and History

Obviously, we cannot delude ourselves into presenting, even in a concise form, a debate which in essence runs through the entire history of sociology and which risks making us lose ourselves in a *darksome wood* of definitions, labels, formulas that combine the terms of sociology and history in various ways, depending on the weight that the author and the authors have given and give to the two disciplines.

We limit ourselves, in any case referring to some of the contributions found in the text for additional information, to developing a brief reasoning by key themes, able to shed a light on the reasons why, as Abbott (1991) pointed out, the meeting between Sociology and History was a lost synthesis, and, at the same time, to bringing out the value of an approach that should be cultivated and relaunched in a firmer manner because of the contribution it can provide towards understanding the social world and its transformations.

When developing this brief reasoning, we will resort to a term – used by Thomas Kuhn in *The Structure of Scientific Revolutions* (1962) – *puzzle-solving*, used here with a double meaning, that is, of a problem that engages the scientific community in periods of normal science but also of a problem that can lead to abandoning the paradigm, in the belief that the usefulness and effectiveness of the term are further clarified over the course of these pages.

We have identified four puzzles, capable, in our opinion, both of providing a conceptual and historical map of the approach, and of highlighting its potential and criticality.

1.1   First Puzzle: the Unconscious Methodological Nationalism of Historical Sociology (Provincializing America?)

A first element that emerges from the analysis of the literature is the national nature of the approach.

In a recent contribution, which reviews the main contributions to 21st century sociology, Simon Susen (2020) refers to the unhappy fate of Historical Sociology in England, where it has gradually dissolved or has been marginalized following the pressures that sociology as an academic discipline has endured. The latter in fact was forced to submit itself to the tribunal of quantitative methods, to accept presentism as a temporal horizon, and was mortified by the managerialism and commodification of knowledge taught by universities and therefore deprived of those critical elements and of a historical complexity which constitute the lifeblood of the discipline, right from its origins.

This, the author explains, was due to the sense of inadequacy with respect to the methodological rigor attributed to the discipline but also to sociological currents (and methodological fashions) that rise impetuously from time to time and condition, in one direction or another, the international sociological community.

In our opinion, the fate of Historical Sociology in England allows us to grasp a first typical aspect attributable to the notion of *puzzle*: Historical Sociology has been strongly affected by the national matrix of sociology, further strengthened by privileging the State as a topic of research and of the "national path" as an autonomous matrix of the development of the various States, towards, for example, specific forms of political regimes.[1]

This focus on the national-methodological aspect, justified by the need to counterpose historical finalism, modernization theories and every other form of historical planning, in the name of the autonomy, peculiarities and originality of the historical routes of the individual countries, then led to producing a perverse effect which limited the systemic capabilities of the approach

---

1   Consider, among all, the famous volume by Barrington Moore emblematically entitled *Social Origins of Dictatorship and Democracy* (1966).

and undermined its original moral fiber. In other words, Historical Sociology has been the victim of a double forgetfulness, at least according to what some authoritative contemporary historical sociologists suggest: firstly that the fate of a discipline is played out by taking into account precisely the supranational atmospheres, what happens outside the state borders; and secondly, that these fates are often conditioned by the strength of the players from the point of view of the cultural capital and the cultural resources put into the game. And that there are interrelations between the supranational level and the national level which end up steering certain local historical and cultural developments.

We can explain ourselves better by turning to the two authors we have mentioned.

George Steinmetz states that "to understand the ebb and flow of historical interest among sociologists it is necessary to pay attention to *extra-scientific* changes such as macrosocial crisis and stabilization, as well as *intra-scientific* processes such as the varying relations between history and sociology in different periods and countries" (2007, 2) and in fact he uses this explanatory matrix to describe the different destinies and the alternating fortunes of Historical Sociology, for example, in the US and Germany.

Craig Calhoun is even clearer: he does not hesitate to speak of a *domestication* of Historical Sociology, which has essentially ended up being submissive to sociological events in the US establishing itself more as a method than as a theoretical project and thus forgetting its origins, its meaning, its aims: "Framing the project of historical sociology in methodological rather than substantive terms, however, has had the unfortunate effects of weakening ties to social theory and reducing much historical sociology to conventional mainstream sociological research using data from the past. The thematic importance of historicity as such is too often lost" (1996, 328).

Moreover, the same authors to whom we referred at the beginning (Adams et al. 2005) underline how Historical Sociology has a different history depending on the countries, but a version that ended up imposing itself over the others is the one that flourished in the US where the term itself was adopted and legitimized.

These dynamics have ended up subjugating Historical Sociology, including for example as regards periodization (Adams et al. 2005), to the strongest country, which in some ways justifies the need, which we mentioned earlier, to *provincialize America*.

A perspective that we feel may be capable of overcoming this methodological nationalism is that represented by the Global Historical Sociology. It "connotes the broad research program aimed at making sociology not only an intellectual endeavor inevitably engaged with long-term and large-scale processes of social change, but also a critical perspective constantly concerned with the geopolitics of knowledge and the multiplex configurations of power behind the regimes of theoretical and empirical legitimation wherein sociological thinking takes place" (Ascione and Chambers 2016, 303).

1.2   Second Puzzle: Institutionalization as Legitimation

A second element, closely related to the first, which is worth reflecting on, is the institutionalization of the discipline as a subfield, in an attempt to establish a perimeter and some boundaries to oppose the winds of insignificance and indifference. To survive in a "hostile" environment, says Susen "it had to be institutionalized [...], through means like postgraduate programs, dedicated journals and book series, specialist conferences, slots at mainstream conferences, and so on. Insofar as a particular genre or sub-discipline is relegated to the margins of an academic field, the only way in which it stands a realistic chance of escaping further peripheralization, if not extinction, is for its representatives and advocates to ensure that it retains a minimal degree of institutional stability, continuity, and presence at the scholarly levels of teaching, research, and divulgation" (2020, 161).

Susen attributes this tendency to the positivization processes of knowledge that would have interrupted the nascent dialogue between history and sociology: "in the US-American context, the strong presence of positivist frameworks was reflected – perhaps, most importantly – in both the *American Sociological Review* and the *American Journal of Sociology*, in which a large amount of quantitatively oriented research papers found a home" (161).

As was pointed out by another great exponent of this approach, Charles Tilly, institutionalization puts Historical Sociology at risk: "first, because the 'field' lacks intellectual unity and, by its very nature, will forever lack it; second, because institutionalization may well impede the spread of historical thinking to other parts of sociology. The other parts need that thinking badly" (Tilly quoted in Smith 1991, 3).

Once again. we will try to better explain this second puzzle: institutionalization is necessary, according to Susen, in order to avoid the risk of a further marginalization of the approach and therefore it is pursued and essentially achieved, but, at the same time, it ends up mortifying the transdisciplinary nature of its historical dimension, as the inclination and distinctive feature of sociology.

Steinmetz again: "the creation of a coherent subfield seems to have protected historical sociology and transformed its internal dynamics, while at the same time inoculating the rest of the discipline against any criticism of "mainstream" sociology that it might have to offer" (2007, 5).

And Calhoun: "the leading American historical sociologists, Charles Tilly and Theda Skocpol-elected to play on the turf of their mainstream colleagues, not just in placing an emphasis on empirical research ahead of theory and epistemological critique but in putting forward a methodological argument for the nature and conduct of historical sociology. This was a crucial step in domesticating the once radical and challenging movement for historical sociology and rendering it merely a disciplinary subfield distinguished by methodology" (1996, 309).

This second puzzle is further characterized by a corollary: the institutionalization of an approach that also struggles to be defined and self-define itself as such, can be read in an inspiring manner in a field key and with field effects recalling a Bourdieu-style. Given that for the French sociologist those who act in the field "make any efforts to impose this or that criterion of competency, of membership, that may be more or less successful in various conjunctures" (1992, 100), it appears evident (once again also from periodization) how in the field of Historical Sociology a dominant approach represented by the hegemonic attempt of Comparative Historical Sociology, strongly based on a methodology close to that of the exact sciences (the positivist unconscious to which Steinmetz refers), has long reigned, against which, in terms of opposition and reconfiguration of the field, the narrative turn of the third wave took position.

1.3   *Third Puzzle: Criticism as the Only Direction of the Discipline*

It is evident that Historical Sociology contains a strong critical connotation, as it contraposes stagism ("the simplistic periodization of society into these three key historical stages, that is, (a) 'premodern', (b) 'modern', and (c) 'late modern'/ 'postmodern'", Susen 2020, 157) and presentism (how can we forget Elias' lesson in *The retreat of sociologists into the present*? 1987), with the conviction that "seeing the present in relation to the past is an important way of recognizing its contingency" (Susen 2020, 150) and contextualizing human actions.

This penchant towards criticism, towards juxtaposition, is in some ways a constant of the approach, and helps both to position it in relation to other approaches, and to define it better. And to provide value to its tasks with respect to being a sociologist today but at the same time it reduces its impact and limits its action at a time when it is necessary to call on Historical Sociology for a unitary position. In other words, unsystematicity and fragmentation constitute at the same time the substance of the approach but also its limit.

1.4   *Fourth Puzzle: In Search of a Definition*

A final aspect that deserves to be underlined concerns the definition. In light of what has just been said and retracing the historical story of the approach, we note how there has always been a great emphasis on the need to bring together history and sociology, from Mills, historical sociologist – "all sociology worthy of the name is 'historical sociology' (Mills 1959, 146) – to Carr (historicist) – 'the more sociological history becomes, and the more historical sociology becomes, the better for both' (Carr 1964, 66)" (Kumar 2009, 392) as well as how it was initially assumed that sociology was historical (Abrams 1982). The problem, however, is that if we look for an exhaustive and complete definition, we find it hard to identify one.

We will not review, for reasons of brevity, all the definitions that have been formulated over time, we will instead limit ourselves to pointing out how, following and developing the outline provided by Susen, in the end there is a need to distinguish two areas, between a *historically oriented sociology* and a *historical sociology*, a way through which sensitivity towards historicity is preserved: "on the one hand, there is '*historically oriented sociology*,' 'which can hold out the promise of informing and transforming other wings of sociology, most notably through its revision of existing theoretical positions.' On the other hand, there is '*historical sociology*,' which can be conceived of as 'a named and legitimated sub-field with its own codified corpus of reference points, texts, and modes of reproduction such as PhD training and tenure-track jobs.' The former reflects a *general program*, in the sense that it is *historically conscious*, seeking to ensure that all branches of sociology generate knowledge capable of accounting not only for the historicity of society, but also for the historicity of the terminologies and methodologies employed to collect and to examine data within disciplinary boundaries. The latter constitutes a *specific program*, in the sense that it is *historically focused*, aiming to guarantee that it converts itself into a major sub-discipline with its own paradigmatic identity and presuppositional horizon of scientific tools, permitting its supporters to carve a niche for themselves in the discursive and institutional landscape known as sociology" (2020, 161–2).

Both definitions give an account of the complexity of historical-social phenomena, but the *puzzle* re-emerges here too to the extent that the absence of an agreed-upon definition, even the tendency to identify two sides of the approach, albeit connected, leads to a field that is not very homogeneous and is at risk of marginality, inconsistency, oblivion.

Of course, its interdisciplinary position also contributes to this result (as we deduce from the phrase by Adams *et al.* cited at the beginning) as do the relations with History on which we have not lingered.

2   This Book

In light of what has been discussed up to now, and having underlined the inter-disciplinary, open, anti-dogmatic and unsystematic nature of the approach, the contributions present in the text, which recall a variety of classical and contemporary authors – from Mann to Bourdieu, from Gramsci to Lukacs etc. –, and the topics – from the history of concepts to habitus, from historical process to emancipatory social science, etc. – reflect the features of the approach as well as enhance its relevance in the international sociological landscape.

Let's try to present them, albeit briefly, by following a thematic path.

Ricardo A. Dello Buono, in the essay of the volume entitled Elements for an Emancipatory Historical Sociology: Revisiting Lukács via Mészáros, provides tools to understand the interpretative sequence of the present through the past, resorting to a reinterpretation of the Marx-Weber fissure through the legacy of the Hungarian Marxist philosopher György Lukács.

According to Dello Buono, Lukács developed key theoretical elements that accommodated many of Weber's central concerns. These elements form the basis upon which a paradigm of emancipatory Historical Sociology can be erected. In his work, Dello Buono argues that Lukacs theoretical contributions taken as a whole provide foundational elements for a critical framework of critical sociology that was better drawn out in the voluminous work of his student, the late István Mészáros (1930–2017). In short, Dello Buono proposes that the emancipatory presuppositions of an enhanced dialectical approach rooted in the foundation of Lukács and Mészáros offers strategic elements for building a praxis-oriented paradigm of Historical Sociology; one that can better speak to the unfolding crises of the present day and the urgency to transform it.

In line with the critical approach of the previous essay, Gerardo Pastore works on Antonio Gramsci's contribution to a critical and Historical Sociology through the analysis of his main writings and the most acclaimed reference literature, in order to reconstruct the relationship of this scholar with sociology, and then go on to examine the main social and sociological issues recurring in his texts. Following this line of reflection, some themes and major Gramscian categories – historical block, hegemony, subordinate social groups, passive revolution, civil society, intellectual and moral reform etc. – become a sociological conceptualization in the context of a description-interpretation of the complex mechanisms that work in becoming social processes. The critical social theory of Antonio Gramsci does not stop here, but goes further: the analysis and criticism of social reality are followed by a political project for the realization of a possible, possible alternative society. A project that still deserves proper consideration in an era of great transformations, but still dense with profound contradictions.

Domenico Maddaloni, in his contribution The Historical Sociology of Long-Term Social Change: Notes on the Contribution of Christopher Chase-Dunn to World-System Analysis, tries to discuss the evolutionary, comparative-historical approach on world-systems analysis developed by the American sociologist Chris Chase-Dunn. The chapter outlines the approach developed by Chase-Dunn and collaborators, in order to highlight its main features and its usefulness for the analysis of social changes in the world of today.

The three authors cited use scholars of the past to shed light on the traces of a highly problematic present, thus trying to enhance the link between different historical times.

Even more explicit terms are used by Cory Blad, on the one hand, and Alfonso Maurizio Iacono and Enrico Campo on the other, engaged in a cogent criticism of Capitalism. Cory Blad in The Great Oscillation: Historicism, Polanyi's Double Movement, and Embedded Dynamics of Capitalism, claims that *Double movement* provides a distinct path toward understanding Polanyi's contributions to not only historical political economy, but also the ways in which specific global political economic developments, such as the ideology of neoliberalism, can be understood in both contemporary and historical contexts. Interestingly, the concept demonstrates remarkable flexibility in historical context, particularly when we are able to examine both the direct application (i.e., presence) and indirect circumvention (i.e., presumed absence) of the double movement dynamics. The chapter chronicles the historical and theoretical impact of the double movement and highlights the ways in which a limited historical prognostication has surged in theoretical value as a result of broad global neoliberalization initiatives.

Alfonso Maurizio Iacono and Enrico Campo in Depth in the inexhaustible surface of things: postmodernism and the fetishism of commodities, wonder about the meaning of the debate between the modern and postmodern now that the debate seems to have lost vitality even for proponents of postmodernism. The Authors believe it necessary because the debate carries with it traces of unresolved issues that have tormented modernity and that are still of political relevance today, such as the ecological crisis and, more generally, to the difficulty of finding an adequate narrative for our times that permits us to understand the challenges and is, at the same time, open to otherness and does not claim to be a universal or totalizing discourse.

Looking at essays that focus on the contribution of individual authors, without losing sight of the analysis of medium-long term processes, we first encounter the contribution of Roberta Iannone who in Method, history, and society. The main road by Werner Sombart analyses the position of Sombart and his idea of Historical sociology as science of critical soul.

Starting from the division between the sciences of nature and the sciences of spirit, Sombart focuses himself on the science of the soul, that is, a type of science that, in relation to the objectives and proceedings, and in line with the whole previous epistemological tradition, is considered by Sombart as irreconcilably opposed to the natural sciences. On the other hand, Sombart remarks that it is the subject of the treatise, the totality of the human being, which makes the mark of the science of the spirit obvious. Indeed, for the author, only the sciences of the soul can aspire to approximate the complexity of man. A science of the soul is a critical way: this is the definitive sense that, at the end of this itinerary, the author assigns to the work, rhetorically asking whether we should consider it a new science, a propaedeutic science, a universal science, or – the hypothesis he would go for – a fundamental science

Elena Gremigni, with her essay on Habitus, historical processes and art experience. Some remarks on Pierre Bourdieu's early reflections on the genealogy of the judgment of taste, intends to make a contribution to the analysis of Bourdieu's early reflections on the genealogy of the judgment of taste and their connection with the construct of *habitus*. Starting from a synthetic history of *habitus* the author highlights its historical dimension, while in the final part attempts to demonstrate how Bourdieu's research on art fruition contributed to and permitted his focus on the key role played by this concept in understanding the genesis of human behavior. In this sense, these reflections on the historical significance of *habitus* as a concept raise further questions, to be discussed in the conclusions, regarding the limits of freedom of social agents.

In his contribution, Andrea Borghini compares Bourdieu and Elias on one hand, and Historical Sociology on the other, to emphasize how the two authors and this approach can be read by juxtaposing them.

In the first part of the work, Borghini develops the contribution of Bourdieu and Elias to Historical Sociology, while in the second he focuses his attention on and uses the two authors to discuss the topic of the State, its genesis, its historical trajectory, its purpose, in order to understand the profound reasons for its revival that has been going on for some time now.

According to Borghini, Bourdieu and Elias, by vocation and conviction, are historical sociologists who shy away from crystallized categorization and, through their own thought, provide value to an approach that is not in itself very systematic such as that of Historical Sociology. Then again, the approach is an approach which is already not very inclined towards dogmatism and disciplinary orthodoxy and cannot but welcome two outsiders like Bourdieu and Elias.

Indeed, as the title of the volume *Beyond Dogmatism* that we are introducing states, Bourdieu and Elias have also made anti-dogmatism their banner. Furthermore, the intolerance towards ascribed sociological categories is the result, in turn, of an attitude towards History and its relationship with Sociology that fits perfectly within a 'non-paradigm' such as that represented by Historical Sociology, which even today, after decades of debates and publications, it is difficult to define once and for all.

Finally, Eleonora Piromalli in Michael Mann's History of Social Power, examines the author of one of the most innovative models in contemporary power research and Historical Sociology, the IEMP model (4 ideal-types: ideological, economic, military and political power). This approach finds its closest inspiration in Max Weber: through an analysis adopting the ideal-type as its fundamental paradigm, it combines history, theoretical sociology and the reference to empirical data. These ideal-types are always intertwined in social reality and constitute the "organizational tools" that human beings, in forming networks of collective action to fulfill their purposes, have adopted since the dawn of civilization. The four sources of social power interrelate through the individual and collective action of subjects and they produce the concrete relations of power, social stratifications, institutions and "crystallizations" recognizable in the different phases of human history.

We conclude this brief presentation with the last two essays which in some ways broaden the horizon of the matters and offer suggestions for future research.

Carmelo Lombardo and Lorenzo Sabetta highlight in the Sociology of Concepts or the Sociology of Judgments? Schmitt, Benjamin, Weber, what is the sociology of concepts. Primarily conceived as a tool for thwarting the narrative of modernity, this mode of investigation echoed in the work of an otherwise antithetical interpreter of political theology, Walter Benjamin.

Aimed at occupying, weaponizing, imposing, and mobilizing concepts, this approach does not (nor, indeed, intend to) provide a logical model or a pragmatic toolbox for articulating political judgments. In this view, we attempt to expand on the nexus between the history of concepts (their diachronic mutations occurring over different timescales) and their usage (the contingency of their concrete displacements into certain fields). By turning to the Weberian judgment model, we thus analyze an alternative framework for interpreting how meaningful historical-cultural phenomena are interrelated – a framework that points to the possibility of developing a still-relevant sociology of judgments, viable for evaluating political actions without falling either into teleological and contextual justificationism or into universalistic and abstract normativism.

Finally, Alfredo Ferrara, in his In search of dialogue with history. A political science research perspective claims that Political science, has progressively abandoned its dialogue with the discipline of history. Nevertheless, a closer examination of the dialogue between these two disciplines reveals that it is much more pronounced than it might seem. In this article he offers a preliminary map of this dialogue in three different stages: the birth of political science in the Anglo-Saxon world, the distancing between political science and history, the renewal of this dialogue that has occurred in the last thirty years, especially through the rise of new institutionalism and historical institutionalism.

Clearly these are broad-spectrum reflections, which hold authors and processes together, in a continuous conceptual cross-reference between them, which Norbert Elias would have greatly appreciated.

3   Open Matters

In our opinion, among the many elements that have emerged from the discussion held so far, there are some that deserve a further, brief, emphasis.

– Historical Sociology, given the lengthy debate that accompanied its genesis and development, is better defined *ex negativo*, by falsification rather than by verification, more by saying what it *is not* rather than by saying *what it is*.

 This does not solve the problem of finding a definition, but somehow places and positions the approach with respect to its supporters and to other approaches and explains its intrinsic anti-dogmatic and open nature.

– Historical Sociology, due to the risk it runs by institutionalizing itself, is a sociological style which remains open. Kumar too, whom we referred to in our contribution in the work, expressed himself in a similar manner some time ago and concluded by saying that it is simply an *approach, a way of studying sociology* (2009, 392).

References

Abbott, Andrew. 1991. "History and Sociology: The Lost Synthesis." *Social Science History* 15 (2): 201–38.

Abrams, Philip A. 1982. *Historical Sociology*. Ithaca: Cornell University Press.

Adams, Julia, Elisabeth S. Clemens, and Ann S. Orloff. 2005. *Remaking Modernity: Politics, History and Sociology*. Durham, NC: Duke University Press.

Ascione, Gennaro, and Ian Chambers. 2016. "Global Historical Sociology: Theoretical and Methodological Issues. An Introduction." *Cultural Sociology* 10 (3): 301–16.

Bourdieu, Pierre, and Loïc J.D. Wacquant. 1992. *An Invitation to Reflexive Sociology.* Cambridge, UK: Polity Press.

Calhoun, Craig. 1996. "The rise and domestication of historical sociology." In *The Historic Turn in the Human Sciences,* edited by T.J. McDonald, 305–38. Ann Arbor: The University of Michigan Press.

Carr, Edward. H. 1964. *What Is History?* Harmondsworth: Penguin.

Elias, Norbert. 1987. "The Retreat of Sociologists into the Present." *Theory, Culture & Society* 4(2–3): 223–47.

Kuhn, Thomas S. 1962. *The Structure of Scientific Revolutions.* Chicago: The University of Chicago Press.

Kumar, Krishan. 2009. "Historical Sociology." In *The New Blackwell Companion to Social Theory,* edited by Bryan S. Turner, 391–408. New York: John Wiley & Sons.

Mills, Charles. W. 1959. *The Sociological Imagination.* New York: Oxford University Press.

Moore, Barrington. 1966. *Social Origins of Dictatorship and Democracy.* Boston: Beacon Press.

Popper, Karl. 1994. *The Myth of the Framework: In Defence of Science and Rationality.* London and New York: Routledge.

Smith, Dennis. 1991. *The Rise of Historical Sociology.* Cambridge: Polity Press.

Steinmetz, George. 2007. "The Historical Sociology of Historical Sociology. Germany and the United States in the twentieth." *Sociologica, Italian journal of sociology on line,* no. 3: 1–28.

Susen, Simon. 2020. *Sociology in the Twenty-First Century. Key Trends, Debates, and Challenges.* Basingstoke: Palgrave Macmillan.

CHAPTER 1

Elements for an Emancipatory Historical Sociology

Revisiting Lukács via Mészáros

Ricardo A. Dello Buono

Historical sociology has been the site of great theoretical disputes and wherever polemics are found, dogma is never far behind. While the ebbs and flows of historical sociology track the intra-disciplinary vagaries of sociologists and historians alike, its recurrent surges in academic importance seem to reflect periods of broader social crisis (Steinmetz 2007). Historical sociology *qua* subfield of sociology has largely assumed that its task is to aptly apply social theory in order to construct a more nuanced, causal explanation of the past, rather than to demonstrate the pressing relevance of history to the concerns of the present (Kumar 2008). Yet, never has a focus on the present been more necessary in view of the deepening and political-economic-ecological-epidemiological crisis of recent years, an enveloping systemic crisis which some have dubbed "catastrophe capitalism" (Foster 2020).

In the forking paths of the discipline's development, one foundational point of contention towers over all others. I refer here to the epistemological, methodological and theoretical divide that separates the formative historical sociologies inherited from Karl Marx and Max Weber. The paradigmatic confrontation between historical materialism and the *Verstehende* Weberian framework has more than any other factor acted to thwart the consolidation of the discipline, resulting in an enduring *methodenstreit* that has carried over into the 21st Century.

The present work revisits the Marx-Weber fissure through the legacy of the Hungarian Marxist philosopher György Lukács. Lukács, intimately familiar with the formative period of Weber's sociology, stands out in the Marxist tradition as a critic of the prevailing dogmas of his day. Seeking to nurture and further develop the full critical potential of Marxist dialectical analysis while acutely perceiving its vulnerability to doctrinaire ossification, Lukács developed key theoretical elements that accommodated many of Weber's central concerns. These elements form the basis upon which a paradigm of emancipatory historical sociology can be erected, one that prioritizes the creation of a stock of knowledge oriented towards emancipation via revolutionary transformation.

It is evident that the pivotal yet incompletely digested opus of Lukács continues to inspire theoretical debate and periodic re-examinations of his work (e.g.,
Thompson 2020; Smulewicz-Zucker 2020; Westerman 2019; Kavoulakos 2020;
Feenberg 2014). Lukács' most famous work *History and Class Consciousness*
(1923) was severely disparaged in the Soviet-dominated Marxist camp while
largely ignored by Western Marxists until its English language edition appeared
in 1967, complete with a self-critical preface by the author. As Lukács later
work has become increasingly available to an English-speaking readership,
appreciation continues to grow of his theoretical achievements that spanned
a lengthy lifespan of evolving sophistication, often stunted by self-censorship
during his time living in Soviet-era socialism and later reconditioned by the
contradictions of Cold War-era Western-European societies.

The bulk of academic consideration accorded to Lukács focuses on his
Hegelianizing influence that unfolded rather unevenly into the Frankfurt
School tradition of critical theory. In this work, I argue that his theoretical
contributions taken as a whole provide foundational elements for a critical
framework of historical sociology that was subsequently drawn out in the
voluminous work of his student, the late István Mészáros (1930–2017). In short,
I propose that the emancipatory presuppositions of an enhanced dialectical
approach rooted in the foundation of Lukács and Mészáros offers strategic elements for building a praxis-oriented paradigm of historical sociology; one that
can better speak to the unfolding crises of the present day and the urgency to
transform it.

1   The Legacy of György Lukács

György Lukács grew up in his native Hungary as a close childhood friend of
Karl Polanyi, the influential, Vienna-born thinker whose family relocated to
Budapest (Dale 2009). Indeed, Lukács lived on the same street as the Polanyi
family whose home was a prominent meeting place in radical intellectual circles. Polanyi's mother hosted many social encounters of restless intellectuals in
which Lukács participated. Polanyi and Lukács engaged intellectually, beginning in the Galilei Circle, a student organization co-founded and led by Polanyi
in 1908 (Csunderlik 2016). Revolutionary anarcho-syndicalist Ervin Szabo, one
of Polanyi's cousins, was an ideological mentor of the organization that helped
politicize it, transforming it from a club aimed at free-spirited intellectual
exploration to a revolutionary organization. This collective would eventually
help produce some of the key revolutionary actors who spearheaded the short
lived Hungarian Soviet Republic of 1919 (Perecz 2008).

When Lukács left for Germany in 1906 to continue his studies, he was introduced to Georg Simmel at the University of Berlin and became a regular participant in the informal, private seminars held at the Simmel residence. While in Berlin, Lukács also engaged the work of Wilhelm Dilthey, the neo-idealist who occupied the Chair of Philosophy once held by Hegel. This early, formative opportunity for reflection served to cement into place a rejection of mechanistic positivist approaches, pushing Lukács into serious contemplation of the dynamic cultural-historical connections shaping historical actors.

In his visits to Heidelberg, Lukács also became a prominent member of Max Weber's circle of intellectuals (Tarr 1989) and their mutual interests initially revolved around common concerns regarding ethics and the importance of aesthetics. Weber organized frequent encounters with international intellectuals and Lukács and Ernst Bloch became regular participants. By 1913, Lukács had settled in to Heidelberg and developed a more sustained, intimate friendship with Weber and his wife. While there is much that could still be drawn out of this intellectual relationship, Weber and Lukács clearly shared in common a rejection of dogmatic economic determinism. Their views were of course later destined to part ways. Weber's attempt to bridge the Methodenstreit led him to assimilate the Austrian Marginalist view on the separation of values and research, extoling a value-neutral approach as a virtuous methodological posture. This would help set him apart from the "socialists of the Chair" that surrounded Weber's intellectual godfather, Gustav von Schmoller of the German Historical School, a position that led Weber to abandon the *Verein Fur Sozialpolitik* in 1909. Lukács came to know a Weber busily involved with developing his verstehende approach to sociology alongside of a nationalistic pursuit of social democratic politics.

For his part, Lukács found the nationalist support among intellectuals for the German war effort during World War I to be highly disagreeable. In 1917, he concluded his studies in Heidelberg and returned to Budapest where he founded a venue for theoretical discussion known as the Sunday Circles (more often now referred to as the Lukács Circles) (Dale 2009, 16). These informal discussions were modelled after the private meetings reminiscent of those organized by Simmel in Germany for which Lukács still had fond memories. But Lukács was being rapidly radicalized by events in Hungary and by the end of 1918, he joined the Hungarian Communist Party. By 1919, Lukács was already the editor of the communist party newspaper and would be swept up into the Hungarian Revolution in which he was appointed Deputy Ministry of Culture and Education.

The Hungarian communist revolution of 1919 was short-lived as the Soviet Republic it established became encircled and overrun. Lukács joined the underground resistance but was soon forced into exile to Vienna while many communists were summarily executed. During this period of exile from 1919 to 1923, he would write the essays that make up his most famous early work, *History and Class Consciousness* published in 1923. He met with various revolutionaries in exile during this period, including Antonio Gramsci who was also in Vienna at the time. Lukács edited the Marxist journal *Communism* that was so highly regarded by Lenin that it earned him an invitation to Moscow in representation of the Hungarian Communist Party for the 1921 Third Congress of the Cominterm.

The real-life experience that Lukács eventually had with "actually existing socialism" shaped his concerted dialogue with an increasingly dogmatic Soviet Marxism in power and a lifelong commitment to socialist emancipation. After moving in and out of Austria, Germany and Hungary, he relocated to Russia in 1930. Even though his work *History and Class Consciousness* left him in disfavor with Stalinist orthodoxy, his time in Russia served to put him in touch with the early, unpublished works of Marx. As the ideological and political crackdown intensified under Stalin, Lukács was eventually incarcerated for two months in mid-1941 during a series of purges of intellectuals which nearly cost him his life. An execution order for Lukács was personally lifted by an allegedly inebriated Stalin thanks to the well-timed intervention of a high-ranking supporter of Lukács. Spared from the violent purges, Lukács relocated to Hungary in 1944 where he attained an academic appointment. As a radical at odds with the status quo as well as with the post-war Communist parties of the era, he became re-immersed in the study of Hegel.

The Hungarian Communist Party revolt of 1956 gave his political activism another lease on life. The rebellious Nagy government with which he aligned offered a historic opportunity to move towards a renovated path to socialism. Lukács was briefly named Minister of Culture and Public Education but the regime proved to be extremely short-lived. Following the Soviet intervention and the detention of Hungary's rebellious leadership, Lukács was arrested and held in Romania, having now been expelled from the Communist Party. He was later allowed to return to Hungary in the 1960's but remained excluded from academic posts. Following the subsequent Soviet reforms under Khrushchev, Lukács rejoined the Communist Party in 1969 and managed to produce a massive manuscript on social ontology. Despite being unfinished at the time of his death in 1971, his two-volume work *Toward an Ontology of Social Being* continues to inspire theorists to unpack his insights.

In the end, the contrast between Weber and Lukács could not be greater. Despite their loyal friendship right up to former's death in mid-1920 from an otherwise ebbing Spanish Flu pandemic, Weber was dedicated to building a "respectable" German school of social scientific understanding. For his part, Lukács would defy Weber's insistent rejection of Bolshevik "experiments" through a lifetime of work on building an emancipatory framework dedicated to overthrowing capitalist domination.

While Lukács had gradually eked out his opposition to the neo-Kantian platform of Weberian analysis, beginning in 1918 with his participation in the Hungarian Communist Party, his ultimate achievement was to defend the dialectical method against mechanistic, dogmatic interpretations of Marxism and critically evaluating the social, organizational and political applications made in its name. Complicating a full appreciation of the intellectual achievements of Lukács were the endless, ongoing contradictions, political pressures, and ideological concessions exerted upon his theorizing under the twists and turns of the Soviet Bloc era.

2   Hegelian Marxism vs Neo-Kantian Sociology

For over a century, various thinkers have directly or indirectly labored to reconcile the Weberian critique of the rationalization of modern life to the Marxian critique of capitalism. Lukács saw this as a need to "complete" Marx and would become fully immersed in a critical dialogue with the Hegelian dialectical approach so firmly rejected by Weber. The intimate friendship that Lukács shared with Weber clearly afforded the possibility of an infiltration of Weber's reasoning into his work. Clearly, the general thrust in reasserting the importance of human subjectivity in historical reasoning was a shared concern of the two that flourished with the intellectual circles they occupied in common. But while Weber would opt for a neo-Kantian resolution to the raging paradigmatic polemics within German and Austrian non-Marxist political economy during the final decades of the 19th Century, Lukács endeavored to re-fortify the critical thrust of Hegelian dialectics within the Marxist framework that could inform revolutionary praxis.

In that sense, the greatest influence of Weber upon Lukács was to set theoretical markers of concern, most decisively regarding the role of human subjectivity in social change. This served to awaken in Lukács a re-examination of human consciousness in history and in working through this enigma, he returned to Marx for his theoretical answers and to Lenin for validation or refutation in actual historical practice. Unlike Weber, Lukács sought this resolution as a guide to revolutionary praxis, rather than solving an intellectual puzzle aimed at academic discipline building. Lukács was already placing his ideas at work in 1919 through his active participation in the short-lived Hungarian Soviet Republic.

The methodological seepage of Weber's neo-Kantian categories into Lukács *History and Class Consciousness* in 1923 would be critically engaged and revised in his later work. Many Cold War theorists tried to dismiss this fact by attributing it exclusively to the accommodation to ideological pressures being exerted from Stalinist authorities. In the larger context of the opus of Lukács, *History and Class Consciousness* represents the author's initial transition from a neo-Kantian fog into the reconstitution of his paradigmatic elements for an emancipatory historical sociology. But for the vast majority of neo-Marxist observers, including those who founded the Frankfurt School of Critical Theory, these early formulations represented the crowning achievement of Lukács, paving the way for one of the various lanes of Weberian-Marxist thought.

At the crux of Weber's influence upon the early Marxist work of Lukács in *History and Class Consciousness* is the former's ideal typical social development of increasing rationalization. Tarr (1989) goes so far as to characterize Lukács as a "Weberian Marxist." He based this simplistic view based on a selection of their reflections on socialism, power, the role and social basis of leadership. While Lukács struggled to employ Weber's notion of rationality in capitalist social relations as a lucrative insight, Weber saw it as a main focus of historical sociological analysis.

As Tosel (2008) points out, Lukács in his later work strongly critiques the Weberian approach to capitalist rationalization and abandoned his earlier, equally idealistic notion of a proletariat capable of resolving its historical alienation of subject and object. Rather, he sought to reconstruct a materialist ontology in pursuit of an emancipatory path in view of the failures of Stalinist formations to realize a radical democratization of post-capitalist social relations. Human labor *qua* social being is the cornerstone of his reconstructed ontology where revolutionary praxis signifies a realization of the maximum, conscious expression of the human potential residing in the oppressed, acting for itself in struggle against the limits established by existing social conditions of a given historical moment. In this mode of dialectical logic, Lukács would continue to express optimism that the existing socialist formations of the 1960's could achieve a radical democratization through praxis.

In his *Destruction of Reason*, Lukács (1978, 6) made reference to a "double transformation" of social relations and the metabolic relations between humanity and nature, arguing for the need of a "rational coordination and reconciliation of both realms." The fundamental epistemological break between Marx and Weber, one that precludes any coherent synthesis, is the competing conceptions of neo-Kantianism and Hegelian Dialectics. As Lukács so eloquently put it: "it was Hegel who first pointed the way forward in assert-ing the necessity of attaching greater ontological weight to 'becoming' rather than 'being'" (64). Indeed, Lukács devoted considerable attention to Marx's philosophic encounter with Hegel. Hegel's methodological critique of Kant effectively historicized the latter's doctrinaire critique of Reason, thereby overcoming the pessimism embedded in the "Kantian dilemma." According to Lukács, the principle defect of the Hegelian mindset was Hegel's own insistence on the methodological priority of logic in his system, something that sealed the fate of the "System" that would be so recklessly posed ideologically as an "End of Philosophy." From Lukács' point of view, Hegel's dialectical method only reached its sociological potential after it was reformulated by Marx.

As Lukács developed his theoretical legacy, the challenge was to steer clear of two brands of flawed historical thought. The first was any lapse into episte-mological neo-Kantianism of the sort championed by Max Weber. It was that reasoning which would take an even more reactionary turn in the phenome-nological sociology of Alfred Schutz and the various theoretical lineages that followed, including Berger and Luckmann's (1966) *The Social Construction of Reality* along with some apolitical strains of what would later became dubbed social constructionism (Dello Buono 2015).

For Lukács, the other brand of flawed historical approaches was associated with the social sciences groomed under Stalinism in which a clumsy and stag-nant version of dialectical materialism or DIAMAT was imposed across gen-erations of official USSR-sanctioned pseudo-theorizing, leading to a major collapse of the critical and dialectical thrust of Marxism. For Lukács, recover-ing the critical power of dialectical analysis was the only path forward.

The ontology of contradictory social processes developed by Lukács is the salient form of a unified social whole, offering a complexity that lends itself towards critique and social transformation. Social ontology implies an analysis of the real elements with causal powers that interact to produce social events (Elder-Vass 2012, 19). A materialist approach roots social ontology entirely in the collective intentional behavior of human beings. The difficult challenge that remained was how to most adequately characterize human agency as it unfolds within the causal influences of social structural constraints. The reac-tionary element of neo-Kantianism precisely revolves around an assertion that things that reside inaccessibly outside of us dynamically influence us (261). The totality of human praxis is constituted by the dynamic interconnections of historically particular, elemental moments. In this case, the epistemological necessity that emerges is clear. If social reality itself is invariably a result of dynamic process, this reality can only be gasped through an equally dynamic, processual approach.

As Lukács pointed out, Lenin notably grasped the theoretical and political importance of all this in the epistemological reflections articulated in his *Philosophical Notebooks,* viewing the Hegelian dialectical method as a critical approach carrying a "theory of knowledge" (Lukács 1978, 78). Anderson (1995) recognized the influence of Hegel in Lenin's *Philosophical Notebooks* as an important factor in the Soviet leader's evolving thinking with respect to the Second International that Lukács would be among the first to adequately assess. Prior scholarship on Lenin's theoretical views tended to downplay the importance of the *Philosophical Notebooks*, while for Lukács, it served as a platform for germinating emancipatory insights. Lenin built upon this re-thinking of dialectics to fully explicate his analysis on the state and imperialism. The downplay of Lenin's reconsideration of Hegel became officialized in the Soviet Union with the republication of the vastly inferior work, *Materialism and Empirio-Criticism,* where Lenin espoused a Second International-style rejection of all things "idealist," setting the standard for qualifying all future "idealist deviations" throughout the Stalinist era of Diamat. Glossed over was Lenin's own call for Marxist theorists to contemplate and consolidate a materialist rethinking of Hegel's dialectics (151). Indeed, it was Lukács who would ultimately pick up this thread as he laid the foundations for an emancipatory, neo-Marxist historical paradigm.

3   Reconciling Lukács with Objective History via Mészáros

Lukács recognized in Lenin's work a dialectical approach that both captures the objective dynamic of the social reality as well as one which elucidates the academic path to grasping it, all in a way that promotes progressive social transformation. The central unifying category that Lukács works through is that of praxis. A sociology rooted in praxis is not a theory of how to manage irresolvable contradictions, but rather one based in an analysis of the way in which irresolvable contradictions can be seen to unfold in history, generating an emancipatory dynamic of social change constantly aimed at their resolution. The political and strategic significance of this approach derives from how human participants can step back, analyze, and re-insert themselves in their history in more conscious fashion capable of favorably altering its course. This greatly resembles the dialectical approach of Gramsci to praxis where understanding is inextricably integrated with activism, with politics, and with making history.

Reconsidering the legacy of Lukács amounts to a useful endeavor in explicating a conceptual baseline for an emancipatory historical sociology. In the tradition of historical materialism, he is most widely known as an early critic of dogmatic versions, the kernel of which was first found in his *History and Class Consciousness* (1923). In that work, Lukács explicated a theoretical vision of "totality" as a pivotal bedrock for understanding history from a Marxist view where contradictory forms of class-based subjectivity could become the basis of a restructuring crisis. Its significance was two-fold. On the one hand, he challenged the traditional dogmatism of static counter-positioning of what "is" and what "ought to be" as a critical basis of apprehending history. At the same time, his dialectical conception of "totality" was a rejection of mechanical, evolutionary portrayals of history that in radical circles hardened in the Second International. It usefully provided a Marxist framework for understanding anti-bureaucratic, revolutionary upsurges of worker's councils when they arose to challenge ossified bureaucratic statism that veered back to capitalist forms of administration. The kernel of this dialectical unfolding of class consciousness reflected Lukács' representation of history in an unfolding social process of the working class as both subject and object of human development.

The practical impact of *History and Class Consciousness* was to flip dogmatic economic determinism back to a more dialectical yet still inflated subjectivistic conception that unacceptably minimized the capacity of capital to impose its structural logic over all forms of social activity. This fuelled an initially excessive optimism that class domination could be overthrown by exploding the alienated repositories of workers' consciousness. It was in this spirit that Lukács developed his notion of reification. The active expression of revolutionary class conscious was tantamount to achieving a global positioning to confront the structural weaknesses of capital.

Another trademark insight of Lukács was his emphasis on understanding history as a guide to political action in the present. In his era, this prioritized an appreciation of the role of the vanguard proletarian party and that of the workers' Soviets in order to formulate, articulate, and propagate class consciousness that was seen as the subjective mobilizing force of the working class as a historical actor. Lukács insisted that historical actors are by definition human collectives and his emphasis on developing a materialist theory of collective class consciousness is what propelled him to grapple with an analysis of social ontology that would characterize his later works.

Lukács was aware of the necessity to confront the question of ontology in any coherent theorizing of emancipation and so he effectively dedicated the final decades to elaborating an ontology of social being (Duayer and Medeiros, 2005). His lifelong concern right up to his death in 1971 was to keep intact the Marxian dialectical formulation in which human praxis is the sole source of emancipatory social change.

The principal torchbearer of the Lukácsian emancipatory project who emerged in the 1970s was the Hungarian theorist István Mészáros. A former student of Lukács, Mészáros would later emerge as a leading Marxist theoretician of social transformation in exploring the contours of social change while remaining acutely sensitive to the structural limits imposed by global capital. Mészáros, like Lukács, sought to pull back onto the playing field those principles that are generally kept hidden by the capitalist system, whether attributable to inherent qualities of the human condition or functional prerequisites of modern, industrial production. In political terms, the empowerment of unwilling systemic participants in their collective self-exploitation requires exposing the nerves of that system's ongoing reproductive mechanisms.

In the view of Mészáros, capital is a historically specific system of "social metabolic reproduction." Ecological concerns in this conception of history are intimately connected to the social metabolic order whose contradictory character amounts to an incessant expropriation of surplus value that is fundamentally out of control. Following Lukács, capital's drive for profits creates a historically situated type of rationalization that shapes both human social relations and the relations between humanity and nature. This logic derived from capital's particular social metabolic order shapes all institutional orders, resulting in its totalizing imposition on social organization. The limitation of capital is its inability to plateau in a stable manner, instead driving uncontrollably towards a globally expanding accumulation until it reaches its absolute limits (Clark and Foster 2010, 16–7).

In his voluminous work, Mészáros sets forth a more nuanced analysis of the historically constructed mediations that allow for the systemic reproduction of global capital. He strategically distinguishes between first and second order mediations. Second order mediations under capitalism essentially consist of alienated practices in the Marxian sense, involving an inevitably hierarchical practice of appropriation of the product of producers under conditions of structured relations of production in which some dynamic degree of control over the laborers is exerted. First order mediations, in contrast, consist of all those principles of coordination that indispensably provide for reproduction of production relations in a systemic configuration.

It is here that the Mészáros critique of Lukács is instructive. Lukács struggled to reunite the subjective and objective aspects of capitalist crisis and this meant transcending the subjective alienation of the worker from his objectified conditions in wage-labor. He for too long sought out a reconciliation of the subject and object that has never existed in history and in this sense, disconnected from a viable historical materialism for what seemed more akin to the search for a fabled "fountain of youth." Grappling with this weakness in Lukács,

Mészáros benefited from a critical reading of thinkers like Sartre in abandoning the idealistic quest. In its place, he aims for both the possible and necessary re-constitution of the creative human laborer in unity with the objective relations that require the continual exercise of that creativity in production, rather than with relations that must suppress it in order to achieve their reproduction (Mészáros 2012, 312). The weakness in Lukács is attributed to his inability to fully disengage from the influence of Weber's dualist, neo-Kantian conception of human subjectivity that even today remains predominant in much of historical sociology.

The framework created by Mészáros identifies the interstitial spaces of structural dilemmas that cannot be resolved within capitalist practice. Radical solutions to these contradictory practices can only grow out of an empowered praxis that actively engages and defies the structurally limited regimes in power with a strategic and decidedly emancipatory agenda. Following Lukács, Mészáros advocates the active pursuit of self-critique via a praxis-centered approach. The ongoing emphasis to unite theory and practice requires continual confrontation with envisioned goals and concrete results, theoretically informed strategies and practical results. This amounts to an important value-engaged element for re-imagining an emancipatory historical sociology. Under an imperative of consciously intended social transformation, the creative dedication to emancipatory struggle must be continually re-examined, assessed and re-formulated in accordance with the enabling possibility presented by a larger social movement scenario.

Hence, the insistence of Mészáros for retaining a radically different imaginary of human social relations present in a dialectical analysis constitutes the practical alternative to a terminal Weberian cynicism. It informs an emancipatory historical sociology that views social processes as part of larger, really existing structural totalities. It requires an ongoing, self-critical study of structurally defined moments, emphasizing the need for a radical re-examination of the historically situated systemic requirements of global capitalism. This is done through an analysis of the existing set of mediations that allow for the systemic reproduction of global capital. Any construction of a counter-hegemonic set of mediations must by real necessity emerge out of ongoing practices of resistance and struggle.

As Mészáros concretely argued in 2010: "In view of the structural crisis of the capital system in its entirety, the conflict in question is structural and not conjunctural ... and the magnitude of the stakes involved could not be greater .... Only the historically viable institution and consolidation of the hegemonic alternative to capital's ever more destructive social reproductive order can offer a way out from the deepening structural crisis" (Mészáros 2010b, 270).

4   Conclusion

When Mészáros died in 2017, the 21st Century was already falling into the throes of sequential regional, viral epidemics that just two years later would explode into a global pandemic of unprecedented proportions. Mészáros provides a historical framework to guide a transformative critical analysis of this deepening epidemiological, ecological, economic and political crisis. In *The Structural Crisis of Capital*, he considers that every set of historical social relations establishes certain structural limits by which it is impossible to go beyond without disrupting the ongoing reproduction of those social relations in a social metabolic, self-expanding process (Mészáros 2010a). This observation foretells a pending future of organized, transformative praxis as capital bumps up against its limits, including its absolute ecological limits.

An emancipatory historical sociology should identify and explain how irresolvable systemic contradictions unfold in history with the ultimate aim of generating insights into how an emancipatory dynamic of praxis can achieve systemic change. The contribution of Meszaros is to emphasize the need for a radical and self-critical re-examination of the historically situated systemic requirements of global capitalism. This is done through an analysis of the existing set of mediations that allow for the systemic reproduction of global capital. Any construction of a counter-hegemonic set of mediations must by real necessity emerge out of ongoing practices of resistance and struggle.

The unsustainability of capital's metabolism historically unfolds with successive forms of antagonistic mediation confronting waves of popular resistance that seize on strategic opportunities to act historically for itself. Lukács saw the possibility of explosive class consciousness in the face of class oppression. Mészáros qualifies this framework with a structural analysis of global capital that perpetually seeks to recalibrate its mediations to achieve an adequate "mediatory adjustment." This underlines the importance for revolutionary praxis to discover and employ the concrete structures that can lead to a genuine consolidation of workers self-management in a superior system of social metabolism, the transition to which is necessarily and inevitably fraught with limitations and contradictions (Mészáros 1995, 383–4). The ongoing self-critique of strategic collective resistance is the dialectical antidote for defeating the entrapment of systemically-generated and pseudo-emancipatory dogmas alike.

As Mészáros argues in *Beyond Capital* (1995, 320), Lukács consistently minimized the importance of objective factors in his analysis in favor of idealizing the party, reflecting the urgency of consolidation of a revolutionary vanguard at particular historical moments of his militancy. Lukács estimated that the objective conditions for revolution were already present at several historical moments, but lacked the crucial factor of a potent working-class consciousness. Mészáros accorded a more concerted consideration of the objective capacity of capital to restore profitability and maintain its long-term expansion even while intensifying the magnitude of its eventual encounter with structural crises.

For Mészáros, Lukács was the seminal thinker that challenged dogma in the Marxist tradition by on the one hand critiquing reformists of various stripes in his times while at the same time insisting that any one of Marx's substantive conclusions could be questioned in the light of new evidence and discoveries, without undermining the underlying logic and revolutionary potency of the Marxist dialectical approach. It is this methodological assertion that establishes Lukácsian thought as a useful paradigm of emancipatory historical sociology.

In *Beyond Capital* (1995), Mészáros analyses the emancipatory struggles in a post Stalinist era where globalized capitalism has become fully consolidated and immersed in a structural crisis that revealed its final limits. Given the failure of Stalinist formations to transcend the capital form by relying upon a state-led strategy of surplus-value extraction designed to "out-compete" the capitalist West, it stagnated and collapsed under the weight of its own objective and subjective contradictions. For Mészáros, the challenge is to identify a radically different mode of social metabolism since he sees no emancipatory "halfway house" with capitalism.

As Tosel (2008, 172) aptly summarized, Mészáros employed the Lukácsian ontology as his system of logic to anticipate the novel forms of crisis unfolding in capital's accelerating crisis. This requires a radical critique of earlier attempts at socialist breakout along with strategic insights for revitalized mass movements and emancipatory social formations that can transcend outmoded capitalist social relations with new forms of social metabolism.

The value of the analysis put forth by Mészáros is to recognize the historical potential as well as the structural limits of capital to overcome its contradictions and maintain its "social metabolic control." The various phases of welfare-state development, mixed-economy and neoliberalization reflect capital's agility while critical analysis of the same can expose its gradual exhaustion of concrete alternatives in achieving reproduction. The range of options within the structural limits of capital begin to close in and constrain its historic capacity for expansion, just as Marx himself imagined, albeit only partially visualized through a 19th century lens.

While it is tempting to view the crisis of the first quarter of the 21st Century as a conjuctural one, Mészáros (2010a) insists that we are in the very same structural crisis that began in the early 1970s. As early as the 1960s, Mészáros vigorously disputed the Frankfurt School's notion that capitalism had somehow outrun its historical contradictions and instead predicted that the incipient global downturn of that period differed from the recurrent fluctuations of the business cycle and its conjunctural mini-crises. The Lukácsian legacy carried forth by Mészáros contemplates a structural crisis of capital where the system no longer permits its own social metabolic reproduction. In his words, "Capital's mode of social metabolic reproduction is structurally incapable of establishing and maintaining a historically sustainable relationship of human beings to nature just as it is incapable of overcoming alienation active in its secondary order of mediations" (Mészáros 2010b, 417). The epidemiological layer of the current century's systemic crisis, with its profound objective and subjective layers, has unleashed new forms of popular resistance that begs for analysis that can inform organized, transformative praxis within the structural spaces that constrain and shape their mobilizing efforts. Pursuing an emancipatory historical sociology amounts to the employment of such an analysis.

References

Anderson, Kevin. 1995. *Lenin, Hegel, and Western Marxism: A Critical Study*. Urbana, IL: University of Illinois Press.

Clark, Brett, and John Bellamy Foster. 2010. "The Dialectic of Social and Ecological Metabolism: Marx, Mészáros, and the Absolute Limits of Capital." *Socialism and Democracy* 24 (2): 124–38.

Csunderlik, Péter Tibor. "The history and reception history of the Galilei Circle (1908–1919)." Phd diss., Budapest: Eötvös Loránd University, 2016.

Dale, Gareth. 2009. "Karl Polanyi in Budapest: On his Political and Intellectual Formation." *European Journal of Sociology* 50 (1): 97–130.

Dello Buono, Ricardo A. 2015. "Reimagining Social Problems: Moving Beyond Social Constructionism." *Social Problems* 62 (3): 331–42.

Duayer, Mário, and João Leonardo Medeiros. 2005. "Lukács critical ontology and critical realism." *Journal of Critical Realism* 4 (2): 395–425.

Elder-Vass, Dave. 2012. *The Reality of Social Construction*. Cambridge: Cambridge University Press.

Feenberg, Andrew. 2014. *The Philosophy of Praxis: Marx, Lukács, and the Frankfurt School*. New York: Verso Books.

Foster, John Bellamy, and Intan Suwandi. 2020. "COVID-19 and Catastrophe Capitalism Commodity Chains and Ecological-Epidemiological-Economic Crises." *Monthly Review* 72 (2): 1–20.

Kavoulakos, Konstantinos. 2020. *Georg Lukács's Philosophy of Praxis: From Neo-Kantianism to Marxism*. London: Bloomsbury Academic.

Kumar, Krishan. 2008. "Historical sociology." In *The New Blackwell Companion to Social Theory*, edited by Bryan S. Turner, 391–408. Oxford: Wiley-Blackwell.

Lukács, Georg. 1978. *The Ontology of Social Being*. Vol. 2. London: Merlin Press.

Mészáros, Istvan. 1995. *Beyond Capital*. London: Merlin Press.

Mészáros, Istvan. 2010a. *The Structural Crisis of Capital*. New York: NYU Press.

Mészáros, Istvan. 2010b. *Social Structure and Forms of Consciousness – Volume I: The Social Determination of Method*. New York: Monthly Review Press.

Mészáros, Istvan. 2012. *The Work of Sartre: Search for Freedom and the Challenge of History*. New York: Monthly Review Press.

Perecz, László. 2008. "The background scenery: 'Official' Hungarian philosophy and the Lukács Circle at the turn of the century." *Studies in East European Thought* 60 (1–2): 31–43.

Smulewicz-Zucker, Gregory R. 2020. *Confronting Reification: Revitalizing Georg Lukács Thought in Late Capitalism*. Leiden: Brill.

Steinmetz, George. 2007. "The Historical Sociology of Historical Sociology: Germany and the United States in the twentieth century." *Sociologica*, no. 3 (Nov-Dec): 1–28.

Tarr, Zoltan. 1989. "A note on Weber and Lukács." *International Journal of Politics, Culture, and Society* 3 (1): 131–139.

Thompson, Michael J. ed. 2020. *Georg Lukacs and the Possibility of Critical Social Ontology*. Leiden: Brill.

Tosel, André. 2008. "The Late Lukács and the Budapest School." in *Critical Companion to Contemporary Marxism*, edited by Jacques Bidet and Stathis Kouvelakis. Leiden: Brill.

Westerman, Richard. 2019. *Lukács Phenomenology of Capitalism: Reification Revalued*. Cham, CH: Palgrave Macmillan.

CHAPTER 2

Antonio Gramsci's Contribution to a Critical and Historical Sociology

Gerardo Pastore

1   Theoretical Premises

The work of Antonio Gramsci distinguishes itself through its interdisciplinary nature, and it addresses issues and problems that are typical of human and social sciences (D'Orsi 2014; Filippini and Rosati 2013; Gallino 1975; Paci 2013; Vacca 2017). Despite his intellectual output being intermittent, it shows an internal ideal and theoretical consistency: the permanent yardstick for this is the struggle for the emancipation of the subordinate classes and a more fair society (Santucci 2010). Nevertheless, the sociological studies give little space to the significant theoretical and methodological contribution of Antonio Gramsci (Gallino 1975; Filippini and Rosati 2013; Pastore 2011). Certainly, Gramsci cannot be considered strictly a sociologist, and it can be added that he did not have this aspiration. In the Prison Notebooks a critique of positivist sociology is primarily expressed (Paci 1992, 2013). But a "sociological imagination" in the Prison Notebooks can be seen in the main addressed issues and the elaborated categories (Ferrara 2015; Filippini 2015, 2017; Pastore 2011, 2018).

This is an unusual author. His intellectual production – and above all because of the real difficulties associated with the detention – is discontinuous, consisting mainly of short writings, notes, a set of scattered fragments that make unitary reading or monographs more complicated. Gramsci himself regarding the temporary nature of his work emphasizes that "unconstitutional affirmations may often be called 'first approximation': some of them in further research could be abandoned and perhaps the opposite declaration could prove that exact" (Q 8, 935).

In the same direction there is the clarification with which Notebook Eleven opens:

> The notes contained in this notebook, as in the others, have been dashed off, almost without pausing for the ink to dry, as a rapid aide-mémoire. They are all to be revised since they certainly contain inexact formulations, false juxtapositions and anachronisms. Written without having at

hand the books that are mentioned it is possible that, on checking, they might have to be corrected radically because just the opposite of what is written turns out to be true.

Q 11, 1365

The risk, therefore, is to "betray" Gramsci. But this is an inevitable betrayal to the extent that, as Prestipino remembers, we approach Gramsci's writings as "an extraordinary corpus, which can also be interpreted with another spirit and with other criteria" (Prestipino 2000, 6).

With this aim – through the analysis of Gramsci's main writings and the most acclaimed reference literature – this essay intends to reconstruct the relationship of this scholar with sociology, and then go on to examine the main social and sociological issues recurring in his texts. In the first part, it examines the views Gramsci explicitly formulates on social sciences and on sociology. The critique against sociology is powerful. It should not, however, escape that the annotations concern the sociological production he had been able to attend and, therefore, predominantly the dominant positivist sociology in those years in Italy, regarded as a press-technical attempt to overcome the philosophy of practice. But it is in the philosophy of praxis, as shown in the second part of this work, that it is possible to perceive a Gramscian science of society, for which the historical subject recognizes a decisive role in the process of transformation of society and, beyond this any law of balance or social evolution.

Following this line of reflection, some themes and major Gramscian categories – historical block, hegemony, subordinate social groups, passive revolution, civil society, intellectual and moral reform etc. – become a sociological conceptualization in the context of a description-interpretation of the complex mechanisms that work in becoming social processes. The critical social theory of Antonio Gramsci does not stop here, but goes further: the analysis and criticism of social reality are followed by a political project for the realization of a possible alternative society. A project that still deserves proper consideration in an era of great transformations, but still dense with profound contradictions.

2   Sociology Rejected

Reflections on the "sociological questions" in the work of Antonio Gramsci would make no sense if we let ourselves be guided by the judgements this author expressed on the discipline. Above all in the *Prison Notebooks*[1] there is a critique of sociology, understood as a way to go beyond the philosophy of praxis and, more precisely, as a reduction of a "concept of the world to a mechanical form that gives the impression of having all of history in one's pocket."

For Gramsci:

> Sociology has been an attempt to create a method of historical and political science in a form dependent on a pre-elaborated philosophical system, that of evolutionist positivism, against which sociology reacted, but only partially. It therefore became a tendency on its own; it became the philosophy of non-philosophers, an attempt to provide a schematic description and classification of historical and political facts, according to criteria built up on the model of natural science. It is therefore an attempt to derive "experimentally" the laws of evolution of human society in such a way as to "predict" that the oak tree will develop out of the acorn. Vulgar evolutionism is at the root of sociology, and sociology cannot know the dialectical principle with its passage from quantity to quality. But this passage disturbs any form of evolution and any law of uniformity understood in a vulgar evolutionist sense.
>
> Q 11, 1432

And he is even more incisive in note 1 of the same Notebook:

> The so-called laws of sociology which are assumed as laws of causation (such-and-such a fact occurs because of such-and-such a law, etc.), have no causal value: they are almost always tautologies and paralogisms. Usually they are no more than a duplicate of the observed fact itself. A fact or a series of facts is described according to a mechanical process of abstract generalization, a relationship of similarity is derived from this and given the title of law and the law is then assumed to have causal value. But what novelty is there in that? The only novelty is the collective name given to a series of petty facts, but names are not an innovation.
>
> Q 11, 1433

---

1 For the quotations from Antonio Gramsci's *Prison Notebooks*, the letter Q, is used followed by the number of the notebook and the indication of the page. The reference edition is the following: Antonio Gramsci, *Prison Notebooks*. Gramsci Institute critical edition edited by Valentino Gerratana, 4 vols., Einaudi, Turin, 1975.

Understanding which sociology Gramsci refers to in these circumstances is not at all simple, but a delicate problem that requires some preliminary considerations.

Before anything else, we must remember that at first the Gramscian reflection revolved around the reduction of historical materialism to Marxist "sociology" (Q 7, 856). Subsequently – as the above-mentioned passages from the period 1932–33 show – his attention was no longer limited to Marxism but extended to the more general history of contemporary culture (Q 11, 1366–75). This means that "the critique of 'Marxist' sociology does not appear separate from the criticism of non-Marxist or 'bourgeois' sociologies [...] The different sociologies are traced back by Gramsci to a common cultural history, without therefore denying either of them its own specificity" (Razeto Migliaro and Misuraca 1978).

The subject of the controversy is predominantly the positive orientation of the various tendencies – both internal to Marxism and opposed to it – the academic examines in the context of a broad history-criticism of culture. The very idea that society can systematically operate forces – laws – capable of coercively determining individual destinies and placing constraints on human actions is therefore rejected.

As far as Gramsci's judgement on sociology is concerned, it should be noted that his gaze is focused in particular on the Italian situation. So not generically on sociological positivism, but "on the distorted and backward look that this had assumed in Italy" (Gallino 1975, 92), and which was the only one with which Gramsci was familiar.

We must not forget that in the first fifty years of Unity, sociological studies in Italy were almost totally preoccupied with the need to define the specific subject of the discipline (Toscano 2002). It was a "sociology of sociology," a circumstance that led to registering the lack of a direct relationship between social issues and sociological analysis. Theorizing in the mental perimeter of academia on the one hand and empiricism devoid of horizons on the other revealed the same problem: the absence of an idea and a "real" experience of society. Italian sociologists were extraneous both to the material events occurring before their eyes or near them, and to the "official" cognitive processes of those events. The eternal past of the *community* acted in them, although they spoke of *society* and did not distinguish one from the other, immersed in consideration of the indeterminate and omnipresent social sphere (Toscano 2010).

Gallino (1975, 92) notes that it is obvious "that the profound sense of historicity and the structure of every social condition possessed by Gramsci should repulse the crude attempts of the Niceforo and Sergi, Carli and Sighele to explain this or that occurrence by tracing it back to biological factors inherent in the individual, or to biological analogies applied to the 'social organism.'" The same considerations also apply to the positivists of the Lombrosian school, who Gramsci sees as excessively obsessed with the problem of crime, to the point of placing it at the center of sociological analyses and political activity (Q 3, 327; Q 25, 2293 -4).

On the basis of the elements which emerge from the *Notebooks*, it is possible to deduce that Gramsci only managed to capture reflections, often distorted, of sociology and its developments in Europe and overseas. Of course, there is no lack of direct or indirect references to the works of numerous masters of sociological thought, but it is possible to suppose that Gramsci's "sociology" cannot and should not be sought in his direct relationship with the discipline and with the main masters of sociological thought. The limits (and disinterest) in this sense are obvious and – it must be added – justified, if we take into account the conditions in which he was forced to work. The regime of detention, as we know, imposed (and imposes) strong restrictions and obligatory selections, made even more severe in this case by his poor state of health. If in the *Notebooks* there exists (and exists!) an operating sociological imagination, it should rather be grasped in the main questions raised and in the categories developed for their analysis. This is how we see the emergence of that "subjective virtue that favors understanding of the sociological spirit beyond any formalisation and reduction," which allows us to "gather from the background noise the voices and dialects of what comes into the world and still bears the minute and innumerable scraps of things caught in the Aristotelian passage from potency to act" (Toscano 2010).

But before providing any further development, another important theoretical-methodological step is needed to clarify the Gramscian perspective.

3   The Marxism of Gramsci

In interpreting social reality, Gramsci's starting point is clearly of Marxist origin. Gramsci's Marxism is attributable to the philosophy of *praxis*; a precise orientation, therefore, in the direction of the philosophical autonomy of Marxism against its reduction to a canon of historical interpretation done by Benedetto Croce (Frosini 2003). Gramsci does not hide the centrality of the lesson of Antonio Labriola, who, "affirming that the philosophy of Marxism is contained in Marxism itself, is the only one that has attempted to give historical materialism a scientific basis" (Q 3, 309).

Gramsci's particular vision of reality and original position are clearly introduced in the first notes of Q 11, where he writes:

In acquiring one's conception of the world one always belongs to a particular grouping which is that of all the social elements which share the same mode of thinking and acting. We are all conformists of some conformism or other, always man-in-the-mass or collective man. The question is this: of what historical type is the conformism, the mass humanity to which one belongs? When one's conception of the world is not critical and coherent but disjointed and episodic, one belongs simultaneously to a multiplicity of mass human groups. The personality is strangely composite [...] To criticize one's own conception of the world means therefore to make it a coherent unity and to raise it to the level reached by the most advanced thought in the world. It therefore also means criticism of all previous philosophy [...] The starting-point of critical elaboration is the consciousness of what one really is, and is "knowing thyself" as a product of the historical process to date which has deposited in you an infinity of traces, without leaving an inventory. The first thing to do is to make such an inventory.

Q 11, 1376

And, as continued in the second note of the same *Notebook*:

One's conception of the world is a response to certain specific problems posed by reality, which are quite specific and "original" in their immediate relevance. How is it possible to consider the present, and quite specific present, with a mode of thought elaborated for a past which is often remote and superseded? When someone does this, it means that he is a walking anachronism, a fossil, and not living in the modern world, or at the least that he is strangely composite. And it is in fact the case that social groups which in some ways express the most developed modernity, lag behind in other respects, given their social position, and are therefore incapable of complete historical autonomy.

Q 11, 1377

The above passages present an integral and general conception of reality. Meanwhile, further indications of method for analysing social processes – a real *modus operandi* – emerge from the particular interpretation of Marx's lesson (1859) discussed in *Notebook 11*:

The question of the 'objectivity' of knowledge, according to the philosophy of praxis, can be treated by starting from the proposition contained in the Preface to A Contribution to the Critique of Political Economy that "men become conscious (of the conflict between the material forces of production) on the ideological level" of juridical, political, religious, artistic and philosophical forms. But is this consciousness limited to the conflict between the material forces of production and the relations of production – according to the letter of the text – or does it refer to all conscious knowledge? This is the point to consider and which can be treated along with the whole ensemble of the philosophical doctrine of the value of the superstructures. In such a case, what will be the meaning of the term "monism"? It will certainly not be idealistic or materialistic monism, but rather the identity of contraries in the concrete historical act, that is in human activity (history-spirit) in concrete, indissolubly connected with a certain organised (historicised) "matter" and with the transformed nature of man. Philosophy of the act (praxis, development), but not of the "pure" act, but rather of the real "impure" act, in the most profane and worldly sense of the word.

Q 11, 1492

It should be noted, following the observations of Luporini, that "the methodical moment (referring both to knowledge and to practical action) and the 'concept of the world' moment condition and prove each other reciprocally, in Gramsci's thought, and cannot be separated without serious distortion. It is not only a question of the evidence that can be drawn from countless quotable passages, but of the profound, organic connection of his thought" (Luporini 1987, 70–1).

In this overall redefinition of Marxist theory, the "superstructures" are no longer a simple reflection of economic structure, but must be thought of as a sphere intimately and intrinsically linked to it (Frosini 2003). The metaphor used in *Notebook* 4 makes the idea clear:

If men become aware of their task in the terrain of superstructures, this means that between structure and superstructures there is a necessary and vital connection, as in the human body between the skin and the skeleton: it would be a mistake if it were said that man keeps himself erect in the skin and not in the skeleton, and yet this does not mean that the skin is an apparent and illusory thing, especially since the situation of the skinned man is not very pleasant.

Q 4, 437

Thus Labriola's theme of the change in Marxism from the theory of capitalist society to the theory of the "formation" of new instruments of human organization, capable of promoting and supporting the transition to a new social form, is brought to the fore (Badaloni 1975). It is no coincidence that in the Gramscian philosophy of *praxis* we do not see signs of the theory of alienation; ideologies do not appear as "false consciousness" but represent the forms in which individuals and social groups elaborate their awareness, or their unawareness, of the relations of production (Vacca 1999).

Holding together "theory" and "praxis," Gramsci develops a series of themes – such as "hegemony," "civil society," "historical bloc," "organic intellectual," "passive revolution," "popular culture," "new common sense," "history of subordinate groups" and many others – as many interpretative categories for interpreting the dynamics under way in contemporary society. A way of proceeding that leads to full awareness of the contradictions and conflicts present in society (Badaloni 1987). On this basis, the philosophy of praxis thus appears as "the full consciousness of contradictions, in which the same philosopher, understood individually or understood as a whole social group, not only understands the contradictions but places himself as an element of contradiction, elevates this element to the principle of knowledge and therefore of action" (Q 11, 1487). This is possible precisely because "the philosophy of praxis continues the philosophy of immanence, but purifies it of all its metaphysical apparatus and leads it to the concrete terrain of history" (1438).

Arguments that seem to make the philosophy of *praxis* a true science of society, a sociology *sui generis*, which finds its foundation in the intrinsic ability to free every intellectual inquiry from the forms of mere philosophical speculation (Pizzorno 1975), in a concrete work of relativization and historicization of the same idea of society (Cerroni 1992). Gramsci deals with the typical problems of history, sociology and political science "anticipating orientations that only later develop at institutional level. This anticipation was possible because in Gramsci, Marxism and the social sciences had been adequately historicized and critically recovered in order to analyse and theorise their own historical political phase."

Once the methodological perspective has been clarified, questions concerning the development of societies, social changes and, therefore, the processes of differentiation and integration remain to be addressed.

4   Towards an Interpretation of Social Change

In continuity with the previous elaborations, we can note that when Gramsci faces the crucial issue of Marxism – or the relationship between structure and superstructure, between theory and praxis, between material forces and ideologies – he rejects every deterministic and mechanistic view of the relations in question, and reiterates that only ultimately can economy be considered the determining factor in history (Q 4, 462; Q 13, 1592). In the *Prison Notebooks*, the distinction between social relations of production and all other superstructural forms such as ideas, customs, morals, human will, etc. is considered abstract. "Structures and superstructures form an "historical bloc." That is to say the complex, contradictory and discordant ensemble of the superstructures is the reflection of the ensemble of the social relations of production" (Q 8, 1051) and, therefore, a necessary reciprocity between structure and superstructures is to be configured as "the real dialectical process" (1052).

The question is better articulated in the considerations related to analyzing the forces and the different levels of "power relations" that operate in the history of a given period.

A first level is closely related to the structure and is independent of men's will:

> On the basis of the degree of development of the material production forces there are social groupings, each of which represents a function and has a given position in the production itself [...] This fundamental alignment allows us to study whether in society there are the necessary and sufficient conditions for its transformation, that is to say, it allows us to check the degree of realism and feasibility of the different ideologies that were born in its own terrain, in the terrain of the contradictions it generated during its development.
>
> Q 13, 1583

In the following passages Gramsci proceeds in his analysis, distinguishing different moments within a second political level:

> The first and most elementary of these is the economic-corporate level [...] A second moment is that in which consciousness is reached of the solidarity of interests among all the members of a social class – but still in the purely economic field [...] A third moment is that in which one becomes aware that one's own corporate interests, in their present and future development, transcend the corporate limits of the purely economic class, and can and must become the interests of other subordinate groups too. This is the most purely political phase, and marks the decisive passage from the structure to the sphere of the complex superstructures; it is the phase in which previously germinated ideologies become "party," come into confrontation and conflict, until only one of them, or at least

a single combination of them, tends to prevail, to gain the upper hand, to propagate itself throughout society – bringing about not only a unison of economic and political aims, but also intellectual and moral unity, posing all the questions around which the struggle rages not on a corporate but on a "universal" plane, and thus creating the hegemony of a fundamental social group over a series of subordinate groups. (1583–4)

Finally – dealing with the last level in the balance of power, the politico-military one – he considers it appropriate to add a concluding remark:

But the most important observation to be made about any concrete analysis of the relations of force is the following: that such analyses cannot and must not be ends in themselves (unless the intention is merely to write a chapter of past history), but acquire significance only if they serve to justify a particular practical activity, or initiative of will.

They reveal the points of least resistance, at which the force of will can be most fruitfully applied; they suggest immediate tactical operations; they indicate how a campaign of political agitation may best be launched, what language will best be understood by the masses, etc. The decisive element in every situation is the permanently organised and long-prepared force which can be put into the field when it is judged that a situation is favourable (and it can be favourable only in so far as such a force exists, and is full of fighting spirit). Therefore the essential task is that of systematically and patiently ensuring that this force is formed, developed, and rendered ever more homogeneous, compact, and self-aware. (1588)

Although, in continuity with Marxian theories, it is possible to find in Gramsci a reading of the differentiation of society into antagonistic groups, starting from the different economic and technical functions, a particular 'sociological sensitivity' must also be noted, which leads him to investigate the value of cultural and thought elements within a broader reflection on the issues of societal change and integration processes.

Indeed, discussing *progress* and *becoming*, in *Notebook* 10 Gramsci interrogates himself on a central question: what is man? What is human nature? And he develops it in the following terms:

If man is defined as an individual, psychologically and speculatively, these problems of progress and becoming are insoluble or remain purely verbal. But if man is conceived as the ensemble of social relations, it then appears that every comparison between men, over time, is impossible, because one is dealing with different, if not heterogeneous, objects. Moreover, since man is also the ensemble of his conditions of life, one can provide a quantitative measurement of the difference between past and present, since one can measure the extent to which man dominates nature and chance. Possibility is not reality: but it is in itself a reality. Whether a man can or cannot do a thing has its importance in evaluating what is done in reality. Possibility means "freedom" [...] But the existence of objective conditions, of possibilities or of freedom is not yet enough: it is necessary to "know" them, and know how to use them. And to want to use them. Man, in this sense, is concrete will, that is, the effective application of the abstract will or vital impulse to the concrete means which realise such a will [...] Man is to be conceived as an historical bloc of purely individual and subjective elements and of mass and objective or material elements with which the individual is in an active relationship. To transform the external world, the general system of relations, is to potentiate oneself and to develop oneself.

Q 11, 1337–8

In this analysis, it seems that Gramsci introduces a theme that is central to all 'mature' sociology and in some ways still present in the contemporary sociological debate: the relationship between subject and system, between individual and society or, expressed otherwise, between freedom and necessity of historical action. But from his point of view, "the question about being changes into one about becoming: what can man become? Ontology translates into morality, philosophy into politics, the noun into the verb" (Baratta 2007, 31). And, Baratta observes, "it is not a question of the Kantian primacy of practical reason – a competition entirely played out in the house of *pure* reason – but, on the path opened up by Marx since the *Theses on Feuerbach*, of philosophy's radical and definitive renunciation of the claim of the self-foundation of theoretical discourse under the umbrella-guarantee of God or of the *cogito*: a dialectic of theory and praxis, in short, which means relationality between 'interpretation' and 'transformation' of the world" (31).

Thus social change finds its raison d'être in a specific form of "collective action," which for Gramsci is the struggle (Q 16, 1878); or the conflict as a result of a process "which has as its actors men and the will and capacity of men."

5   Interpreting the Social Reality: Analysis and Processes

Italy and its history constitute a great social laboratory for Gramsci. Gramsci tries to explain the anomalies of this country which, however rapid in producing the fundamental aspects of the modern world, shows itself incapable of achieving authentic and coherent national unification. With reference to the Italian Risorgimento, Gramsci notes that the Italian bourgeoisie has shown all its political shortsightedness by acting without regard for the demands and needs of the working classes. Without resolving the contradictions of the old society. The persistence of elements of continuity between the old and the new government leads Gramsci to express himself in terms of "passive revolution," that is, of unfinished revolution (Q 19, 2010–78). What seems to emerge from Gramsci's reading of Italy's history is the lack of a meeting between nation and people. The highlighted aspects invite us to reflect on the poor national and state spirit in the modern sense (Q 3, 325), the cause and consequence of that "narrow and small" individualism (Q 15, 1754).

> Individualism is merely brutish apoliticism; sectarianism is apoliticism, and if one looks into it carefully is a form of personal following [clientele], lacking the party spirit which is the fundamental component of "State spirit." The demonstration that party spirit is the basic component of "State spirit" is one of the most critically important assertions to uphold. Individualism on the other hand is a brutish element, "admired by foreigners," like the behaviour of the inmates of a zoological garden. (1755)

However, these notes should not lead us to an error of assessment: criticism of the Risorgimento does not correspond to rejecting it. Recognizing the features of a "passive revolution" in this process does not mean denying the importance of national unity, an important step for a general modernization of the country (D'Orsi 2005), but reiterating the need for a "moral and intellectual reform" to rebuild the historic rift between state and nation.

The analysis of society and social problems conducted by Gramsci, as far as the focus is on the Italian reality, is global in all respects. The themes are often intertwined and give rise to original interpretations which, selectively revisited, show themselves to be actual and actualizable, making it possible to grasp and problematize the sedimentation of some social, economic and cultural processes. As Pizzorno (1975) notes, in the Prison Notebooks the correspondence between the generalized descriptions implicit in the notions of historical bloc, hegemony, political direction, ideology, function of the intellectuals and certain generalized descriptions of sociology is almost perfect.

A first example may be the concept of historical bloc. This should be considered as a useful tool for analyzing the ways in which a system of cultural values (which for Gramsci is ideology) "penetrates, transmits, socializes and integrates a social system" (Q 7, 868–9). The examples offered are numerous. Simply think of the issues related to the organization of culture and the function of intellectuals. In this case, starting from interstitial elements we consider "every day, minute phenomena, in some way 'structured' in collective life" (Pizzorno 1975, 117–8) which, if on the one hand restore the complex stratification of power systems, on the other allow detection of deep fractures in society and the weakness of social ties. A separation that Gramsci clearly reports in the following passage of his Prison Notebooks:

> The popular element "feels" but does not always know or understand; the intellectual element "knows" but does not always understand and in particular does not always feel [...] The intellectual's error consists in believing that one can know without understanding and even more without feeling and being impassioned (not only for knowledge in itself but also for the object of knowledge): in other words that the intellectual can be an intellectual (and not a pure pedant) if distinct and separate from the people-nation, that is, without feeling the elementary passions of the people, understanding them and therefore explaining and justifying them in the particular historical situation and connecting them dialectically to the laws of history and to a superior conception of the world, scientifically and coherently elaborated – i.e. knowledge. One cannot make politics-history without this passion, without this sentimental connection between intellectuals and people-nation.
>
> [...] If the relationship between intellectuals and people-nation, between the leaders and the led, the rulers and the ruled, is provided by an organic cohesion in which feeling-passion becomes understanding and thence knowledge (not mechanically but in a way that is alive), then and only then is the relationship one of representation. Only then can there take place an exchange of individual elements between the rulers and ruled, leaders [directors] and led, and can the shared life be realised which alone is a social force – with the creation of the "historical bloc".
>
> Q 11, 1505–6

We understand that the integration of a social system is most possible when, under the direction of a fundamental class, a strong hegemonic system emerges and consolidates itself, the management of which is entrusted to intellectuals (Portelli 1976). The latter are called upon to perform an "organisational" or connective function: [they must] organize the social hegemony of a group and its state domination, i.e. the consent given by the prestige of the function in the productive world and the apparatus of coercion for those groups that do not "consent," neither actively nor passively, or for those moments of crisis of command and direction in which voluntary consent suffers a crisis (Q 4, 476).

In the particular Italian social-historical affair, the subordinate groups were systematically subjected to paternalistic control that made them practically harmless and excluded them from every valid project of authentic cultural emancipation. Here returns the aforementioned problem of the lack of meeting between nation and people; and we must remember that "Gramsci attributes this lack of national-popular spirit to the country's fragmented history, to the cosmopolitan character of the intellectuals, and to their detachment from practical activity" (Green 2009, 70). The subordinate groups are therefore called upon to develop an operational and political strategy, developing their own stratum of organic intellectuals, "in order to have the ability to represent themselves and to affirm their own interests and political aspirations" (70). But it is not easy to bring out a group of independent intellectuals:

> it requires a long process, with actions and reactions, with adhesions and dissolutions and very numerous and complex new formations: it is the concept of a subordinate social group, without historical initiative, which expands continuously but inorganically, and without being able to go beyond a certain qualitative level which always falls short of possession of the State, from the actual exercise of hegemony over the whole society that only allows a certain organic balance in the development of the intellectual group.
>
> Q 16, 1860

In their condition of subordination, these groups seem unable to formulate descriptions of the world in which they live.

> The history of subaltern social groups is necessarily fragmented and episodic. There undoubtedly does exist a tendency to (at least provisional stages of) unification in the historical activity of these groups, but this tendency is continually interrupted by the activity of the ruling groups; it therefore can only be demonstrated when an historical cycle is completed and this cycle culminates in a success. Subaltern groups are always subject to the activity of ruling groups, even when they rebel and rise

up: only "permanent" victory breaks their subordination, and that not immediately. In reality, even when they appear triumphant, the subaltern groups are merely anxious to defend themselves (a truth which can be demonstrated by the history of the French Revolution at least up to 1830).

Q 25, 2283–4

Subordinate groups often see the world from the perspective of the dominant one. The conception of their own situation is therefore partial, inconsistent, disjointed and essentially lacking that necessary awareness of the local contexts of oppression in the ambit of the wider political and economic realities, without which all hope of becoming a counter-hegemonic force is in vain (Crehan 2002). It must indeed be considered that

> the supremacy of a social group manifests itself in two ways, as "domination" and as "intellectual and moral leadership." A social group dominates antagonistic groups, which it tends to "liquidate," or to subjugate perhaps even by armed force; it leads kindred and allied groups. A social group can, and indeed must, already exercise "leadership" before winning governmental power (this indeed is one of the principal conditions for the winning of such power); it subsequently becomes dominant when it exercises power, but even if it holds it firmly in its grasp, it must continue to "lead" as well.

Q 19, 2010–1

To achieve a solid hegemony, a reform of the intellectual and moral direction, ideological as well as political, is indispensable, one capable of creating the conditions favorable to integral changes of the social structure and thus allowing the civil elevation of the lower classes (Santucci 2010). For this purpose, two conditions are necessary for Gramsci: "an organic crisis; the presence of a new social formation (generally the party) which affirms the integral autonomy of the lower classes, becomes capable of hegemony, 'of new historical and institutional values,' and creates a contrasting historical bloc, a *state in a nutshell*" (Pizzorno 1975, 119).

It should be noted that the concept of "hegemony" is to be understood above all as a synonym of direction – political, intellectual, moral – and that the "hegemonic struggle" is exactly the opposite of "hegemonism," that is a conquest of supremacy at any cost, by any means, peaceful or violent. In the Gramscian perspective, in fact, by "hegemonic struggle" we must understand "the articulation of differences and conflicts in essentially political and cultural terms, or political as cultural, or cultural as political or, if you will, in ideological terms, in the sense that Gramsci gives to the concept of ideology. Hegemonic struggle is synonymous with peaceful or non-violent competition between both allies and adversaries, but combines, or can be combined with, the antagonistic and military aspects of political and social struggle" (Baratta 2007, 38; Cospito 2004).

At this point one thinks of the "regulated society" which provides for the reabsorption of political society into civil society (Q 5, 662), the transition from the realm of necessity to the realm of freedom (Q 14, 1728–30).

In the Notebooks, the design aspect of the question is clarified with a strong reference to the creation of a new intellectual class

> The problem of creating a new stratum of intellectuals consists therefore in the critical elaboration of the intellectual activity that exists in everyone at a certain degree of development, modifying its relationship with the muscular-nervous effort towards a new equilibrium, and ensuring that the muscular-nervous effort itself, in so far as it is an element of a general practical activity, which is perpetually innovating the physical and social world, becomes the foundation of a new and integral conception of the world. The traditional and vulgarised type of the intellectual is given by the man of letters, the philosopher, the artist. [...] The mode of being of the new intellectual can no longer consist in eloquence, which is an exterior and momentary mover of feelings and passions, but in active participation in practical life, as constructor, organiser, "permanent persuader" and not just a simple orator (but superior at the same time to the abstract mathematical spirit); from technique-as-work one proceeds to technique-as-science and to the humanistic conception of history, without which one remains "specialised" and does not become "directive" (specialised and political).
>
> Q 12, 1551

In this way, Gramsci indicates a possible route, a strategy to interrupt the bureaucratic domain (Filippini 2015, 2017); to break that conservative rationality linked to the ranks of traditional intellectuals and functional to the status quo. Reactivating, in this way, new political possibilities and social redemptions.

6   Final Considerations

As can be deduced from the analysis completed so far, Gramsci often uses his analytical categories jointly, frequently making connections between one concept and another – this is the case, for example, for historical bloc, hegemony, ideology and organic function – and moves towards the description of the dynamics that operate in social systems "becoming": differentiation and integration. But he does not stop at the description. This is accompanied by a political project aimed at orienting the directions of change and defining, in a revolutionary way, its "possible society."

As much as this work deserves further study, not possible here, the elements put in place allow us to perceive in Gramsci the personality traits of a special social analyst or, to use Alvin Gouldner's expression, (1977) a "partisan sociologist."

It is obvious that this partisanship must be interpreted. If we assert the canons of "avalutativity," or freedom from value judgement, then Gramsci is anything but avalutative. On the contrary, he considers evaluation as a fundamental part of analysis that cannot be separated from criticism and, therefore, evaluation enters into the general logic of knowledge. In this sense, the meaning of "reality" is drawn from observation; but observation cannot fail to be selective and therefore "biased." And this is the first point to underline, essentially of an epistemological and methodological nature.

However, there is something more decisive: the option for social justice and, therefore, for the search for the obstacles to be removed and the opportunities to be strengthened for its full realization. Naturally, since we are dealing with human and social facts, all this brings with it a set of elaborations that tend to represent the complexity and interdependence of phenomena, and even the contradictions that the immanent dialectic of living and living together expose with particular clarity.

In the consideration of society, that is of every society in every phase of its history, the intensely problematic and, indeed, dramatic human factor penetrates everywhere and gives Gramsci that anti-dogmatic attitude that allowed him to overcome the vicissitudes of Marxism and continue to be vital in the culture of emancipation and rights. Retracing Gramsci's lesson with judicious selectivity of concepts and diligent clarifications is a valuable aid in countering conservative irrationality, linked by Gramsci to the ranks of traditional intellectuals so functional to the *status quo*. Golden pages, in short, for the possibility of redemption from a painful historical reality that only the indifferent are allowed to judge fatal. Gramsci would not have allowed them this either, those towards whom, at twenty-six, he had aimed sharp arrows in that splendid, now well-known article published in The Future City: "I live, I am a partisan. Therefore, I hate those who do not take sides, I hate the indifferent" (Gramsci 1917, 1).

References

Badaloni, Nicola. 1975. *Il marxismo di Gramsci.* Torino: Einaudi.

Badaloni, Nicola. 1987. "Filosofia della praxis." In *Gramsci. Le sue idee nel nostro tempo,* edited by Carla Ricchini, Eugenio Manca and Luisa Melograni, 93–5. Roma: L'Unità.

Baratta, Giorgio. 2007. *Antonio Gramsci in contrappunto. Dialoghi col presente.* Roma: Carocci.

Cerroni, Umberto. 1992. "Marx e Gramsci." *I Quaderni. Trimestrale Dell'Istituto Gramsci Marche,* no. 4: 31–48.

Cospito, Giuseppe. 2004. "Egemonia." In *Le parole di Gramsci,* edited by Fabio Frosini and Guido Liguori. Roma: Carocci.

Crehan, Kate. 2002. *Gramsci: Culture and Anthropology.* London: Pluto Press.

D'Orsi, Angelo. ed. 2005. *Gli storici si raccontano. Tre generazioni tra revisioni e revisionismi.* Roma: Manifestolibri.

D'Orsi, Angelo. 2014. *Gramsciana. Saggi su Antonio Gramsci.* Modena: Mucchi Editore.

Ferrara, Alfredo. ed. 2015. *Prospettiva Gramsci. Dialoghi tra il presente e un classico del Novecento.* Bari: Caratteri Mobili.

Filippini, Michele. 2015. *Una politica di massa. Antonio Gramsci e la rivoluzione della società.* Roma: Carocci.

Filippini, Michele. 2017. *Using Gramsci. A New Approach.* London: Pluto Press.

Filippini, Michele, and Massimo Rosati. 2013. "Introduzione. Ampliare il canone: la sociologia e Gramsci." *Quaderni Di Teoria Sociale,* no. 13:11–21.

Frosini, Fabio. 2003. *Gramsci e la filosofia. Saggio sui «Quaderni del carcere.»* Roma: Carocci.

Gallino, Luciano. 1975. "Gramsci e le scienze sociali." In *Gramsci e la cultura* contemporanea, edited by Pietro Rossi. Roma: Editori Riuniti.

Gouldner, Alvin W. 1977. *Per la sociologia.* Napoli: Liguori.

Gramsci, Antonio. 1917. "Indifferenti." In *La Città futura.* Torino: Federazione Giovanile Socialista Piemontese.

Green, Marcus. E. 2009. "Subalternità, questione meridionale e funzione degli intellettuali." In *Gramsci le culture e il mondo,* edited by Giancarlo Schirru. Roma: Viella.

Luporini, Cesare. 1987. "La metodologia del marxismo nel pensiero di Gramsci." In *Letture di Gramsci,* edited by Antonio. A. Santucci, 70–1. Roma: Editori Riuniti.

Marx, Karl. 1859. *Per la critica dell'economia, Editori Riuniti, Roma, 1969.* Roma: Editori Riuniti.

Paci, Massimo. 1992. "Gramsci e i classici della sociologia." *1 Quaderni. Trimestrale Dell'Istituto Gramsci Marche,* no. 4: 7–29.

Paci, Massimo. 2013. *Lezioni di sociologia storica.* Bologna: il Mulino.

Pastore, Gerardo. 2011. *Antonio Gramsci. Questione sociale e questione sociologica.* Livorno: Belforte.

Pastore, Gerardo. 2018. "Gramsci, Antonio." In *The Wiley-Blackwell Encyclopedia of Social Theory,* edited by Bryan S. Turner, 1002–4. New Jersey: Wiley-Blackwell.

Pizzorno, Alessandro. 1975. "Sul metodo di Gramsci: dalla storiografia alla scienza politica." In *Gramsci e la cultura contemporanea. Atti del Convegno internazionale di studi gramsciani tenuto a Cagliari il 23–27 aprile 1967,* edited by Pietro Rossi. Roma: Editori Riuniti-Istituto Gramsci.

Portelli, Huhues. 1976. *Gramsci e il blocco storico.* Bari: Laterza.

Prestipino, Giuseppe. 2000. *Tradire Gramsci.* Milano: Teti Editore.

Razeto Migliaro, Luis, and Pasquale Misuraca. 1978. *Sociologia e marxismo nella critica di Gramsci. Dalla critica delle sociologie alla scienza della storia e della politica.* Bari: De Donato.

Santucci, Antonio A. 2010. *Antonio Gramsci.* New York: Monthly Review Press.

Toscano, Mario A. 2002. *The Sociological Spirit.* Pisa: Pisa University Press.

Toscano, Mario A. 2010. "Società e sociologia in Italia per una lettura critica tra storia e cronaca." In *Mosaico Italia. Lo stato del Paese agli inizi del XXI secolo,* edited by Annick Magnier and Giovanna Vicarelli. Milano: FrancoAngeli.

Vacca, Giuseppe. 1999. *Appuntamenti con Gramsci.* Roma: Carocci.

Vacca, Giuseppe. 2017. *Modernità alternative. Il Novecento di Antonio Gramsci.* Torino: Einaudi.

CHAPTER 3

The Historical Sociology of Long-Term Social Change

Notes on the Contribution of Christopher Chase-Dunn to World-System Analysis

Domenico Maddaloni

1   Introduction

World-systems analysis originated in the early 1970s as a new research perspective on long-term social change. This approach merges classical elements, such as historical materialism or the school of the *Annales*, with new analytical categories. It tries not only to understand why and how the social world changes in a *longue durée* perspective, but also to critically examine the traditional structures of thought, and to contribute in the development of alternatives for a more democratic and more egalitarian society. The "founding father" of this perspective is Immanuel Wallerstein who, together with some other scholars such as Andre Gunder Frank, Samir Amin, Terence K. Hopkins and Giovanni Arrighi, has provided the basic elements for the development of this field of research (Wallerstein 1979; Hopkins and Wallerstein et al. 1982; Amin et al. 1982; Wallerstein 1983, 1984, 1991, 1995, 2004).

The aim of this chapter is to discuss the historical-comparative approach developed by the sociologist Christopher Chase-Dunn in the general framework of world-systems analysis (Chase-Dunn and Hall 1997; Chase-Dunn and Anderson 2005; Chase-Dunn and Lerro 2013). This approach was developed in the second half of the 1990s and aims to compare the modern world-system, based on the capitalist world-economy, with other world-systems that have preceded it over the centuries. This comparison is used to identify patterns of reproduction and transformation shared by every historical world-system. In section 2, I will discuss the theoretical foundations of the approach and its main features as they can be identified in Wallerstein's work. In section 3, I will address the basic elements of the perspective developed by Chase-Dunn (in cooperation with the anthropologist T. D. Hall) on the pathway opened by Wallerstein. In section 4, I will debate on some main features of Chase-Dunn's thinking, in order to show its critical relevance for a better understanding of long-term social change, thus contributing to merge the fields of sociology and historiography in a single world-historical-ecological social science. Finally, I will try to draw some conclusions on the role that the approach proposed by Chase Dunn can play in the development of this type of social science, in a dialogue with other social research perspectives.

2   The World-System Analysis: Genesis and Original Features

In his more recent essay on the fundamentals of his perspective on world-systems analysis, Wallerstein (2004) maintains that this field of study emerged between the 1960s and 1970s. The approach is based on some developments that deeply innovated both traditional disciplines – economics, sociology, political science, but also anthropology and oriental studies – and the new-born field of area studies. The latter had emerged in the post-World War II era as a tool of both scientific knowledge and political rhetoric in favor of the West and in particular the United States, which had acquired a hegemonic role in the international economic and political arena (10–1).

The first change was a growing intermingling among different research fields and academic disciplines. In turn, this led to a growing awareness of the artificial nature of the distinctions among the fields of knowledge regarding the social world and human cultures (Wallerstein 1991). The second one was the appearance of some debates that highlighted the need for a new way of thinking about the social world in its spatial and temporal coordinates. The first of them was on the concepts of *core* and *periphery* developed by the United Nations Economic Commission for Latin America (ECLA) and their revision by dependency theory. Together with the debate among Marxist scholars on the utility of Marx's concept of "Asiatic mode of production," or "oriental despotism," they gave a strong contribution to the overcoming of the unilinear evolutionism on which the previous theories of development were based. The third debate which Wallerstein refers to is the discussion among Western historians on the transition from feudalism to modern capitalism. It contributed to the idea that the unit of analysis to be used in the research on social change is not the single State, but the complex system formed by all the cultures or polities among which there is a stable division of labor. Moreover, there was "the debate about 'total history' and the triumph of the *Annales* school of historiography in France and then in many other parts of the world" (Wallerstein 2004, 11). This debate gave an important contribution to the overcoming of idiographic historiography in favor of research on long-term continuity and change patterns in broad social contexts, defined as "world-systems." Finally, Wallerstein highlights the influence exerted by Karl Polanyi's work on the distinction between three forms of economic organization which he called reciprocal (a sort of direct give and take), redistributive (in which goods went from the bottom of the social ladder to the top to be then returned in part to the bottom), and market (in which exchange occurred in monetary forms in a public arena). (17)

In the conflictual political scenery and the effervescent intellectual climate of the late 1960s and early 1970s, Immanuel Wallerstein's world-systems approach proposes a new way of understanding the social world and its change. The starting point of the world-systems approach may be identified in an episte-mological claim. The most appropriate unit of analysis to explain the events occurring in the social world cannot be derived *a posteriori* from the obser-vation of historical events. The latter often draws artificial boundaries among interdependent cultures. The borders that separate neighboring political units – and with them the multiple flows of goods, people and ideas that cross them – are very often taken as invariable reference points in social as well as historical research. On the contrary, they are not a product of nature, but of history – a history that includes them in a larger whole. In accordance with his-torical materialism, Wallerstein therefore maintains that the unit of analysis must be identified following the spatial contours of the division of labor rul-ing the most part of human subsistence and social reproduction. These spatial contours can coincide with the geographical limits and/or political borders of a single culture; or they can go beyond, so as to include a plurality of cultures and polities (Wallerstein 2000, 71–105).

When the division of labor does not go beyond the boundaries of a single culture and the economic and political relations among cultures are erratic, we have *mini-systems* – this is the case of geographically isolated hunting, gather-ing or fishing societies. On the contrary, when the labor division involves many cultures, then a second-order system appears – this system is called *world-system*, even if it does not cover the whole world (71–105).

According to Wallerstein, in order to understand the structure and dynam-ics of this system, it is therefore necessary to develop an approach that can view it as a totality in itself. He maintains that human history has witnessed the birth, development, decline and disappearance of many world systems (71–105; see also Ellwell 2006, 73–8).

For Wallerstein and his followers, the basic principle of structuring the whole system is either political or economic. In the first case, we have *world-empires*, that is political domains emerging around a culture showing basically a military force capable of imposing itself on satellite territories. In the second case, we have *world-economies*, which are transnational mercantile networks associated with inter-state systems. The continuous "cooperative competition" among these states usually ends in the relative dominance of the most powerful one. In a geographical perspective, world systems show also a competition among central, semiperipheral and peripheral areas which produces a hierarchy of dependence on systemic dynamics. This tripartite structure and its internal dynamics is also the basis of some of the structural changes producing a vertical mobility among the involved areas. Two examples of this are the growing importance of the eastern part of the Roman Empire in its last centuries of life, on one side, and the rise of East- and South Asia in the modern capitalist world economy, on the other (Chase-Dunn 2006a; Sanderson 2006).

As for the developmental logic of these two kinds of world-system, the approach maintains that every world-empire is subject to a dilemma. On the one hand, it strives to ensure the standard of living of the imperial elite and the upper classes (courtesans, the military, bureaucrats, and the landowners). On the other, it is constantly forced to protect itself against the risks coming both from lower classes and subject peoples (internal opponents) and from the enemies outside its boundaries. In addition, world-empire rulers must keep under control the upper classes, which may have aspirations for political autonomy or even claims to the supreme authority. Sooner or later, therefore, the world-empire is forced to face a military and/or a fiscal crisis, which in turn can result in a decline or even a collapse. Hence the idea of a circularity of historical time, shared by the ideologies developed by the upper classes of the world-empires.

World-economies, instead, appear where there is a systemic balance based on a 'competitive cooperation' among the polities that are part of them (chiefdoms, city-states, monarchies, etc.). The world-economy grows insofar this balance is preserved, but when the balance is broken by the growing power of a state or by the invasion by a neighboring empire, the system collapses. Therefore, the circularity of historical time can be found also in world-economies, but with one exception. The deviant case is the world-economy of Western Europe that emerged in the 16th century. It was based on colonialism, imperialism and a 'balance of powers' that lasted long enough to allow its expansion to the whole world (Wallerstein 2000, 71–105; a discussion on this point is in Turner 2003, 174–81). From this point on, Wallerstein focuses on the analysis of the modern capitalist world-economy. As is well known, Wallerstein's analysis has been criticized,[1] but his attempt to create a new "world-historical social

---

1 Theda Skocpol, for instance, suggested that, rather than focusing on a 'single world-system' as a unique unit of analysis, it would be better to conceive this world-system as emerging from overlapping but relatively autonomous structures – class structures, trade networks, state

science" has strongly contributed to the reinvigoration of historical sociology (Robinson 2011) and attracted a large number of scholars.

3   World-System Analysis and Long-Term Social Change: Chase-Dunn's Approach

Differences among world-systems scholars relate to many analytical dimensions, such as: the relative importance of the dynamics involving core areas; the role of political actors as opposed to economic actors; the importance of ecological, demographic, or technological variables in defining the fundamental structure of the whole system; or even the number of world-systems historically identifiable. In this latter "continuist-transformationist" debate (Straussfogel 1998), which developed during the 1990s, two basic views emerged. Scholars like Frank and Gills insisted that in human history there has been only one single world-system, basically a trade network who lately developed as a division of labor and an interstate system (Frank and Gills 1993). Other scholars were instead more prone to highlight the discontinuities among the social formations emerging as a result of the agricultural and urban revolutions, together with some continuities with simpler, more archaic, social systems. On this latter side of the debate we find Chase-Dunn's approach. We refer in particular to *Rise and Demise* (Chase-Dunn and Hall 1997),[2] in which the theoretical contours of what the authors define as *institutional materialism* are outlined (see also Chase-Dunn 2006a).

For Chase-Dunn and Hall a world-system can be defined as

> an inter-societal network in which interactions – e.g., trade, war, intermarriage or information – are important for the reproduction of the internal structures of the composite units and importantly affect the changes that occur in these local structures.
>
> CHASE-DUNN and HALL 1997, 28

---

structures, and geopolitical systems. Moreover, she maintains that Wallerstein's argument is teleological: "Repeatedly he argues that things at a certain time and place had to be a certain way in order to bring about later states or developments that accord (or seem to accord) with what his system model of the world capitalist economy requires or predicts" (Skocpol 1977, 1088).

2 Chase-Dunn had already worked on the capitalist world-economy in a world-system perspective (Chase-Dunn 1998) and he had already developed the main structure of *Rise and Demise* when he associated himself with the anthropologist T. D. Hall, who contributed to its final release mostly working on some case studies related to kinship-based world-systems (Sanderson 2002).

Like in Wallerstein's thinking, the spatial configuration of world-systems is based on the categories of core / semi-periphery / periphery. However, their internal structure is no longer identifiable with an inter-societal division of labor, which allows them to overcome an apparent weakness in Wallerstein's approach. Rather, they propose a typology of "modes of production," or system developmental logics, as they also call it:

1. *kin-based modes of accumulation,* in which social labor, distribution, and collective accumulation are mobilized by means of normative integration based on consensual definitions of value, obligations, affective ties, kinship networks, and rules of conduct – a moral order;
2. *tributary modes,* in which accumulation of surplus product is mobilized by means of politically institutionalized coercion based on codified law and formally organized military power;
3. *capitalist modes,* in which land, labor, wealth, and goods are cornmodified and strongly exposed to the forces of price-setting markets and accumulation occurs primarily through the production of commodities using cornmodified labor; and
4. *socialist modes,* a hypothetical class of logics in which major policy, investment, and allocation decisions are controlled democratically by the people they affect according to a logic of collective rationality. (30)

According to Chase-Dunn and Hall, one of the most important features of these modes of production are the effects they induce on both the social and the spatial structure of the whole social system. Kin-based modes and socialist modes create nothing more than a simple differentiation among social layers and geographical areas. Tributary modes and capitalist modes, instead, result in the birth and consolidation of hierarchical structures, both at a social level (classes) and a territorial level (core, semi-periphery, and periphery). On this point, it has also to be said that in the Chase-Dunn's thinking the role of the semi-periphery has a special relevance, as semiperipheral areas sometimes play the role of seedbed of change (78–89; see also Bair and Werner 2017; Moghadam 2017).[3] Drawing on preceding works on social-historical change by Trotsky (1932), Gerschenkron (1962), Service (1971) and Quigley (1979), he

---

3 According to Chase-Dunn and Hall, semi-periphery include "1. regions that mix both core and peripheral forms of organization; 2. regions spatially located between core and peripheral regions; 3. regions spatially located between two or more competing core regions; 4. regions in which mediating activities linking core and peripheral areas take place; and 5. regions in which institutional features are intermediate in form between those forms found in adjacent

contends that "semi-peripheral areas are likely to generate new institutional forms that transform system structures and modes of accumulation" (Chase-Dunn and Hall 1997, 79). Anyway, these changes happen in a very different way according to both the structural features of the whole system and those prevailing in the semi-peripheral area.

Among the types of world-system identified by Chase-Dunn and Hall, the oldest (and simplest) are *kinship-based systems*. In this most basic kind of social systems, the most important inter-societal constraints are based on kinship, and there is a core-periphery polarization not leading to a stable hierarchical structure. Kinship-based systems are followed by *tributary world-systems*, in which a surplus is created and the core acts as its main collector via some kind of a tax system. For Chase-Dunn and Hall there are several (sub-)types of tributary world-systems:

(a) *primary world-systems*, based on the state, in which the relationship core/periphery is basically similar to city/countryside (e.g., the city-states of ancient Mesopotamia);

(b) *primary empires*, or large-scale polities based on a common geographical and cultural background (e.g. ancient Egypt, the Chinese Empire);

(c) *polycentric world-systems*, or networks among states, cities, and 'backward' semiperipheral or peripheral regions (e.g., the Near East, the Aztec empire);

(d) *state-based merchant world-systems*, featuring high levels of labor division and market production (e.g., the ancient Rome).

Finally, according to the authors, we have the *modern capitalist world-system*, mostly based on capitalist enterprise and market production, which gradually emerged between the end of the 15th century and the beginning of the 16th century. This has spread throughout the world and its functioning logic is based on the unlimited accumulation of capital. (41–56)

For Chase-Dunn and Hall, the ecological, demographic and economic factors are at the basis of both the rise and the fall of each world-system. On this point, they follow the theoretical pathway opened by Marvin Harris in his books on *The Rise of the Anthropological Theory* (Harris 1968) and *Cultural materialism* (Harris 1979). For Harris, the basis of any human social system is its ecological

---

core and peripheral areas" (1997, 78). Semi-peripheral areas tends to be dominated by the core, but they at the same time tend to dominate peripheral regions.

context, which imposes inescapable limits. These relate to (a) the availability of resources for survival and reproduction and to (b) its resilience to the environmental degradation which is mostly produced by human activity. These factors are also at the origin of the main processes of institutional innovation and vertical mobility in each kind of world-system. However, unlike Harris, who assume rational choice as the basis of innovation and cultural evolution, Chase-Dunn and Hall's world-systems derive – as we have seen – from a plurality of functioning logics, which are based on kinship, the surplus gained by an imperial structure, or capitalist accumulation. Moreover, these different logics greatly affect the social self, the personality, and the substantive contents of the 'rational choice' the actors practice in each social context (on this point see also Chase-Dunn and Lerro 2013, 50–72).[4]

Chase-Dunn and Hall's typology of social systems is an interesting feature of their theorizing. However, even more interesting is their attempt at identifying a causal model which could be used in the comparative analysis of large-scale social change. They define it *iteration model*, because it is based on processes of circular and cumulative causation (Myrdal 1957). These multiple feedback loops make possible the reproduction, but also the change of the peculiar institutional pattern shown by each world-system (Chase-Dunn and Hall 1997, 99–117). Following Harris, the starting point of their theory of large-scale social change are

> The contextual substrata of human social change [namely] those demographic and ecological facts that are built into the natural universe. [...] Human beings are part of the biosphere and human culture is built upon the bumpy surface of biological, topographic, geological, and climatic variation. Variations in these media impose constraints on what can be erected and on the sustainability of the constructions.
>
> The species-specific biological constraints on human behavior are less limiting than for all other animals because of the unusually large proportion of the human brain that is composed of unpreprogrammed (non-instinctive) cortex. This unprogrammed mentality makes it possible for individuals to take up the latest cultural "software," and for the species it

---

4 According to Chase-Dunn and Lerro, the social self is "an institution, an invention that is produced by the world historical action of individuals and the possibilities and constraints that larger social structures provide. As social structures evolve so does the social self" (2013, 1). On this point, they state, "Just as hunting- gathering societies, horticultural societies, agricultural states, and industrial capitalist societies have very different technologies, economies, and political and sacred systems, they also possess different concepts of the self" (68). On the process of construction of the social self, see Chase-Dunn, Lerro 2013, 50–72.

makes rapid and flexible cultural adaptation possible. Thus, cultural evolution is much faster than biological evolution. Still, constraints remain embedded in both our brains and our bowels: Both need clean water and shelter. Constraints are in our mind, too. Most of them are socially constructed, and thus can be reconstructed. (99–100)

The iteration model[5] shows that the fundamental path of systemic change has to be identified in the loops of interaction between a number of factors. The first and most basic of them is (1) *population growth*, considered as a long-term trend in the human species. Sooner or later, population growth will result in a process of (2) *intensification*, that is, the exploitation of an ever-increasing amount of matter and energy for human and social subsistence and reproduction. Intensification leads to both resource depletion and environmental pollution, that is (3) *environmental degradation*. At the same time, these processes also lead to a growing (4) *demographic pressure*, because of the increased costs of subsistence and reproduction induced by environmental depletion and pollution.

This basic loop leads to the alternative between (5a) *migration* to unexplored territories, which has gradually prompted humans to take over the whole planet, and (5b) *circumscription*, that is, the invasion, conquest and exploitation of the land of other peoples.[6] These latter processes produce (6) patterns of *conflict and domination* – from the reduction of strangers into slaves to the conquest and submission of the natives –, not excluding various patterns of peaceful coexistence if the groups succeed in developing complementary activities.[7]

At this point, we can see the formation and consolidation of (7) *hierarchical structures* concerning the production, reproduction, regulation and legitimization of both the whole system and its local, relatively autonomous, parts (local/regional/national 'societies'). In turn, these hierarchical structures may definitely overcome the more ancient and simpler kinship-based systems, tending towards two basic patterns: (7a) *tributary world-systems*, and (7b) *capitalist world-systems*.

---

5 Here, again, Chase-Dunn and Hall draw on a earlier theoretical model, developed by Marvin Harris. In his famous book *Cannibal and Kings* (Harris 1977), he had already identified a long-term historical cycle, based on a sequence of intensification-depletion-renewed intensification.

6 The concept was firstly coined by the American anthropologist Robert L. Carneiro, who used it in order to explain the process of early State formation (Carneiro 1970, 2012).

7 On this point, Chase-Dunn and Hall's work has apparently been influenced by the Chicago school theorizing on human ecology.

Another basic development made by Chase-Dunn and Hall on the way of rethinking the world-systems approach is their concept of world-historical *shortcuts* (Chase-Dunn and Hall 1997, 109–17). The iterative character of the model above, in fact, does not imply the constant and invariable repetition of the same structures and dynamics, because the possibility of technological and organizational innovation is always open. These innovations can result in shortcuts introducing structural changes in the model. More specifically, shortcuts-producing innovations refer to processes of *State formation* and *capitalist development*. These innovations, therefore, concern war, administration, communications, transport, and – last but not least – the production of goods. Some of these processes can be related also to changes in the sources of energy that are socially available – human work, wind, water, animal power, non-renewable sources, to end with the latest developments in renewable sources. These processes create a shorter circuit among (a) demographic pressure, (b) technological change, and (c) the production, reproduction and transformation of world-systemic hierarchies (see also Chase-Dunn 2006a; Sanderson 2006; Sanderson 2007, 214–8).

To summarize Chase-Dunn's argument, the main pathway of change in human history starts from demographic growth and the consequent imbalance between population and natural resources. This results into several unexpected consequences: migration, warfare, and above all technological and institutional changes in both economic and political domains. These major structural innovations result also in changes, both in the essential features of the categorical and corporate units (Hawley 1986, 67–72)[8] which can be found at the meso level, and in the mutual (mostly hierarchical) relationships among them. In turn, these units act as an interface between the world-system as a whole and daily social interaction at a micro level.

However, this major path of large-scale social change has some shortcuts, as we have seen. These shortcuts are based on the State and later, also on capitalist enterprise. They are capable to move the ecological limits of the world-system forward. The world where only kinship-based systems existed, the world where social life was based on bands of a few individuals and the available technology was limited to hunting and gathering, could not be populated by more than a few million human beings (Burger and Fristoe 2018). In the world shaped by global capitalism the human population has reached and surpassed 7 billion,

---

8 According to Hawley, corporate units are defined by "symbiotic relationships" of mutual dependence among the actors that constitute them (for example: families, cities, organizations). Instead, categorical units are defined by "commensality relationships" among actors aware of their common interests (for example, classes or status groups).

although – unlike in ancient times of kinship-based systems – the living conditions of these people are extremely unequal. Shortcuts also change the very nature of the fundamental relationship between population and resources. New factors, such as the ecological impact of production techniques and the degree and type of opulence in consumption, may change the parameters of the basic relationship. Together with the global expansion of the modern capitalist world-system, these changes have led us to think as if those limits do not exist – or, this is the mainstream thinking on the subject even today.

Shortcuts, therefore, intensify their action insofar the world-system changes its fundamental structure and developmental logic, moving from a tributary production mode to a capitalist production mode (Chase-Dunn 2006a). This is the case of the modern capitalist world-system, in which there are increasing tendencies to reduce population pressure through the demographic transition. The latter is triggered by three major structural changes: (a) the ever-increasing use of non-renewable energy sources, which enormously extends the opportunities for production and distribution of goods; (b) the development of a labor market in which the working class and the middle classes (but also women) acquire some degree of power; (c) the introduction of increasingly effective and efficient contraceptive techniques, which tends to separate sexuality from procreation. On this point, however, Chase-Dunn note cautiously that these major changes seem to concentrate their effects in the central areas of the global system (Chase-Dunn 2006a).[9]

Moreover, Chase-Dunn maintains that these changes produce two unprecedented problems on a world scale: increasing pollution, on one side, and the spread of opulent consumption, on the other. In the long run, according to Chase-Dunn, shortcuts cannot obliterate the wider circuit of cumulative causation, along which the modern capitalist world-system will meet its ecological limits.[10] On the point, Chase-Dunn and Lerro state that

> The main problem is that the scale and scope of environmental degradation has increased so greatly that very powerful institutions and social

---

9   This statement is rather questionable. It is true that the trend to the exhaustion of non-renewable energies makes it impossible to spread their use on a global scale. It is also true that the other revolutions mentioned above are taking place in ever larger parts of the world (Sen 1999).

10 Before this happens, anyway, the inequality structures at work both at a systemic and a regional and local level may create environmental crises mostly in semiperipheral and peripheral areas, keeping, to a large extent, environmental problems away from the core (Jorgenson 2004).

movements will be required to bring about a sustainable human civilization. Capitalism may not be capable of doing this, and so those theoretical perspectives that point to the need for a major overhaul may be closer to the point than those that contend that capitalism itself can be reformed to become sustainable.

> CHASE-DUNN and LERRO 2013, 233

4   On Chase-Dunn's Theorizing about Large-Scale Social Change

The attempt made by Chase-Dunn and his collaborators in developing a new perspective on world-systems is very complex. Our brief review allows us to highlight only a few aspects that make the thought of Chase-Dunn rather unique in the context of contemporary sociology.

First of all, Chase-Dunn is one of the few thinkers in today's sociology that qualifies his approach as *materialist*.[11] According to Chase-Dunn and Lerro,

> Institutional materialism explains human sociocultural evolution as an adaptive response to demographic, ecological, and economic forces in which people devise institutional inventions to solve emergent problems and to overcome constraints. Institutional inventions include ideological constructions such as religion as well as technologies of production and power. (13)

In this effort of explaining the social world and its change, institutional materialism includes theoretical and empirical contributions from almost every social science. This meta-theoretical option has been influenced not only by historical materialism but also by Marvin Harris' cultural materialism, and more indirectly by Spencer's and Sumner's thinking about change and evolution in human societies. Harris' attempt to merge Marxian and Spencerian

---

11   However, he is not the only one, as evidenced by the flowering of a growing literature on 'new materialisms' (see, for instance, the table in https://simplysociology.files.word press .com/2018/01/overview-of-new-materialism-approaches3.pdf. Last retrieval: February 3, 2019). Anyway, most of the work made by "new materialists" (mainly influenced by such thinkers as Deleuze, Guattari, Latour, Braidotti and so on) is more a development and a deepening of critical theory. Therefore, it seems to be quite a long way from an attempt at theory and research on the social world based on methodological assumptions widely shared by interdisciplinary communities of scholars and scientists and in a more-than-local perspective.

thinking in an analytical model based on an ecological-demographic determinism provided a deep, albeit questionable, foundation for the work made
by Chase-Dunn and Hall, that can therefore be seen also as a better attempt at
bringing the environment back in macro-sociological theorizing (Sanderson
2007, 214–8; Maddaloni 2015).

This leads us to a second main feature of Chase-Dunn's thinking on large-
scale social change, its *evolutionary* character. Given the negative reputation
generally attributed to the older *evolutionist* theories in the social sciences, it
should be noted that for Chase-Dunn and Hall the word 'evolutionary' is by no
means synonymous with "evolutionist." On this point, for instance, they maintain that

> by "evolution" [we do not] presume a unilinear, progressive, continuous
> process of change from simple to complex society. History is usually dis-
> continuous, conjunctural, and somewhat open-ended. Nevertheless, cer-
> tain long-run patterns are observable. We hope that an explanation of
> these patterns may improve our collective chances of survival.
>
> CHASE-DUNN and HALL 1997, 3

They admit that some of these changes may be cumulative, resulting in more
complex institutional frameworks. For instance, "human interaction networks
have been increasing in spatial scale for millennia as new technologies of
communications and transportation have been developed" (Chase-Dunn and
Anderson 2005, xi). Nevertheless, even these processes are included in patterns of uneven development which can only be explained by a multilinear,
conjunctural and probabilistic model of large-scale social change. A model
which is similar to those developed by evolutionary biology and anthropology
in recent times.[12] Nor the evolutionary approach developed by Chase-Dunn
and collaborators has anything in common with conventional ideas on "progress." First of all, as Chase-Dunn and Lerro state, "Progress is not a scientific
idea in itself, because it involves evaluations of the human condition that are
necessarily matters of values and ethics" (2013, 11). Even if we can share some

---

12   On this point, we think that the contribution made by scholars such as Niles Eldredge,
     Stephen J. Gould or Elizabeth Vrba to the renewal of evolutionary theory should be con-
     sidered as very important also by social scientists. Their concepts of punctuated equilib-
     ria, exaptation or hierarchical structures have changed our idea of evolution, turning it
     into an uneven and discontinuous bricolage, a "transformation of the possible, a variation
     on known themes, a skillful tinkering on the existing, a different use and regulation of the
     same structural information" (Pievani 2008, 125).

ideas about the desirable ends for the human action, however, we have to recognize that many innovations have positive effects on someone's wellbeing
but negative effects on someone else's wellbeing – and the latter may be many
more than the former, as occurred in the agricultural and urban revolutions
(Lenski 1966; Harris 1979). In addition, as we have seen, every world-system
will eventually meet its ecological limits, which could even result in a societal
collapse (Tainter 1988; Diamond 2005).

A third feature of Chase-Dunn's thinking we can discuss here is its effort
in developing a robust analytical *methodology* for historical social science.[13]
The first step on this way is his strong option for "The comparative method
[which] allows us to establish causality, albeit less certainly than the experimental method" (Chase-Dunn and Lerro 2013, 5). Together with the use of a
probabilistic logic, the comparative method allows the definition of models
of social change in which several causal tendencies can be properly identified. More specifically, a comparative and probabilistic approach is developed
by Chase-Dunn and collaborators in order to deepen our understanding on
the evolution of the intersocietal networks also known as "world-systems."
Moreover, his insistence on greater analytical rigor in world-systems analysis,
and, more specifically, on explicit modeling as a research strategy (when data
are available) has attracted an increasing attention from many scholars working in this perspective (Babones and Chase-Dunn 2012, 127–60). This turn in
the evolutionary analysis of world-systems may lead this research field even
closer to complexity theory (Grimes 2017). Building mainly on Chase-Dunn's
work as a bridge between natural and social/cultural sciences, the latter author
maintains that we can now

> use complexity to explain how entropy builds structures on a physical
> level, then how those same dynamics created life, drove evolution, and
> continue to drive social complexity from our nomadic roots to our cur-
> rent global strife. (678)

Finally, we have to mention another important feature of Chase-Dunn's thinking about world-systems – his *political commitment*. Always consistent with
his political identity as a democratic socialist,[14] he has constantly investigated

---

13   Chase-Dunn's focus on clarifying the methodological aspects of his research work is
      widely reflected in the space devoted to conceptual definitions, working hypotheses and
      research techniques in his larger works (Chase-Dunn and Hall 1997, 11–56; Chase-Dunn
      and Lerro 2013, 1–72).

14   The young Chase-Dunn actively participated in the protests against the Vietnam War,
      which culminated in what he refers to as "the world revolution of 1968" (Chase-Dunn 2017).

on the actual possibilities to build a more democratic, more egalitarian international economic and political order (Chase-Dunn and Hall 1997, 239–46; Boswell and Chase-Dunn 2000; Chase-Dunn 2006b, 92–102). Anyway, he remains aware that a global democratic order is just one possibility among many others. The future evolution (or de-evolution) of the modern capitalist world-system is open – and we cannot be reassured by any comforting belief that what we will find tomorrow will be better than what we have today (Chase-Dunn and Lerro 2013, 362–7).

5   Some Final Remarks

To conclude, a first question to ask ourselves may be: Do we still need "grand" theories on large-scale social change? We now live in a "post-modern" culture that seems to have dismissed the great narratives (Lyotard 1984). In the same field of social sciences, approaches aimed at the local, micro level are largely prevalent today. Anyway, the same theory on the end of great narratives is itself a narrative. Moreover, if we work only at a micro level, and the macro level is left unguarded, we leave the field free for the defenders of the neo-liberal order of the world (like Francis Fukuyama, for instance: Fukuyama 1992). Social sciences, therefore, should not easily dismiss the attempt at building a relatively stable cognitive framework in which even local events can find a better and wider understanding.

Others may find the attempt made by Chase-Dunn and his collaborators at re-bridging natural and social sciences through institutional materialism outdated and perhaps disturbing. In our "post-modern" academic world, reality is widely perceived as a social construction (Berger and Luckmann 1967). This statement is often understood as if we, as sociologists, no longer need any reference to human needs, to the real ecological and societal conditions under which they occur, and to the ways these needs are met, resulting into networks of inequalities and power. Under this perspective, "the most important thing to do" is a critical study on the processes by which a cognitive order emerges, reflecting conditions and dynamics whose nature and evolution remain largely unexplored.

Nevertheless, many scholars have been attracted by Chase-Dunn's research program, in the more general context of world-system analysis. They insist on the continuing relevance of an analytical perspective on "really existing" power structures – including "really existing neoliberalism"[15] – and their inter-relations at multiple levels. A perspective that can be based on the accumulation of knowledge produced by scientific practice. For these scholars, the attempt made by Chase-Dunn and his collaborators at merging world-system analysis and a renewed evolutionary perspective is a tempting option. It offers a broad and robust approach – *a world-historical eco-social science*, we may perhaps define it – to research into large-scale social change. It may not be free from any criticism (see for instance Turner 2017),[16] but it seems to us that it allows to overcome many shortcomings in early theorizing on world-systems, thus improving our understanding of the world we live. By doing this, Chase-Dunn's institutional materialism can help us to convert from passive recipients of world-systemic change to active subjects of social transformation.

References

Amin, Samir, Giovanni Arrighi, Andre Gunder Frank, and Immanuel Wallerstein. 1982. *Dynamics of Global Crisis*. London: MacMillan.

Babones, Salvatore J., and Christopher Chase-Dunn (eds.). 2012. *Routledge Handbook of World-System Analysis*. Oxon-New York: Routledge.

Bair, Jennifer, and Marion Werner. 2017. "New Geographies of Uneven Development in *Global Formation*: Thinking with Chase-Dunn." *Journal of World-Systems Research* 23 (2): 604–19.

Berger, Peter Ludwig, and Thomas Luckmann. 1967. *The Social Construction of Reality: A treatise in the sociology of knowledge*. New York: Anchor Books.

Boswell, Terry, and Christopher Chase-Dunn. 2000. *The Spiral of Capitalism and Socialism: Toward Global Democracy*. Boulder: Lynne Rienner.

---

15   By "really existing neoliberalism" we mean a mix of ideas and practices aimed at putting politics at the mercy of the economy, the economy at the disposal of finance (Gallino 2011), and finance at the feet of a small transnational capitalist class (Sklair 2001).

16   More specifically, Turner – another evolutionary sociologist – suggests that the world-systems paradigm no longer reflects today's realities and provides what he retains as a broader conceptualization of social evolution based on inter-societal systems. According to Turner, "core, periphery, and semi-periphery are not consistently found across a broad range of inter-societal systems, beginning with those among hunting and gathering societies and moving to the current capitalist inter-societal system. Furthermore, the often-implied view that the current geo-economic global system has replaced geo-political systems is overdrawn because geo-economics and geo-politics constantly intersect and interact in all inter-societal systems" (2017, 639). Anyway, Turner's criticisms are much more on the original world-system approach as developed by Wallerstein than on Chase-Dunn's evolutionary world-systems perspective.

Burger, Joseph Robert, and Trevor S. Fristoe. 2018. "Hunter-gatherer population inform modern ecology." *Proceedings of the National Academy of Sciences* 115 (6): 1137–39.

Carneiro, Robert Leonard. 1970. "A Theory of the Origin of the State." *Science* 169 (3947): 733–8.

Carneiro, Robert Leonard. 2012. "The Circumscription Theory: A Clarification, Amplification, and Reformulation." *Social Evolution & History* 11 (2): 5–30.

Chase-Dunn, Christopher. 1998. *Global Formation.* Lanham: Rowman & Littlefield.

Chase-Dunn, Christopher. 2006a. "World-Systems Theorizing." In *Handbook of Sociological Theory*, edited by Jonathan H. Turner. New York: Springer.

Chase-Dunn, Christopher. 2006b. "Globalization: A World-System Perspective." In *Global Social Change. Historical and Comparative Perspectives*, edited by Christopher Chase-Dunn and Salvatore J. Babones. Baltimore: The Johns Hopkins University Press.

Chase-Dunn, Christopher. 2017. "Social Science and World Revolutions." *Journal of World-Systems Research* 23 (2): 733–52.

Chase-Dunn, Christopher, and Tomas D. Hall. 1997. *Rise and Demise: Comparing World-Systems.* Boulder: Westview Press.

Chase-Dunn, Christopher, and Bruce Lerro. 2013. *Social Change. Globalization from the Stone Age to the Present.* London-New York: Routledge.

Chase-Dunn, Christopher, and Eugene N. Anderson. eds. 2005. *The Historical Evolution of World-Systems.* New York-Basingstoke: Palgrave MacMillan.

Diamond, Jared. 2005. *Collapse.* New York: Viking.

Ellwell, Frank W. 2006. *Macrosociology. Four Modern Theorists.* Boulder: Paradigm.

Frank, Andre Gunder, and Barry K. Gills. eds. 1993. *The World-System. Five Hundred Years or Five Thousand?* London: Routledge.

Fukuyama, Francis. 1992. *The End of the History and the Last Man.* New York: The Free Press.

Gallino, Luciano. 2011. *Finanzcapitalismo. La civiltà del denaro in crisi [Finanzkapitalismus. The civilization of money in crisis].* Torino: Einaudi.

Gerschenkron, Alexander. 1962. *Economic Backwardness in Historical Perspective.* Cambridge, MA: Harvard University Press.

Grimes, Peter E. 2017. "Evolution and World-Systems: Complexity, Energy, and Form." *Journal of World-Systems Research* 23, (2): 678–732.

Harris, Marvin. 1968. *The Rise of Anthropological Theory. A History of Theories of Culture.* New York: Cromwell.

Harris, Marvin. 1977. *Cannibals and Kings. The Origins of Culture.* New York: Vintage.

Harris, Marvin. 1979. *Cultural Materialism. The Struggle for a Science of Culture.* Walnut Creek: AltaMira Press.

Hawley, Amos H. 1986. *Human Ecology: A Theoretical Essay.* Chicago: The University of Chicago Press.

Hopkins, Thomas K., Immanuel Wallerstein et al. 1982. *World-Systems Analysis: Theory and Methodology*. Beverly Hills: Sage.

Jorgenson, Andrew K. 2004. "Uneven Processes and Environmental Degradation in the World-Economy." *Human Ecology Review*, no. 11: 103–17.

Lenski, Gerhard E. 1966. *Power and Privilege. A Theory of Social Stratification*. Chapel Hill: The University of North Carolina Press.

Lyotard, Jean-François. 1984. *The Postmodern Condition: A Report on Knowledge*. Minneapolis: University of Minnesota Press.

Maddaloni, Domenico. 2015. "Bringing the Natural Environment Back In: Concepts and Models for the Understanding of Macro Social Changes." *The International Journal of Interdisciplinary Environmental Studies* 10 (3): 1–12.

Moghadam, Valentine. 2017. "The Semi-Periphery, World Revolution, and the Arab Spring: Reflections on Tunisia." *Journal of World-Systems Research* 23 (2): 620–36.

Gunnar, Myrdal. 1957. *Economic Theory and Underdeveloped Regions*. London: Methuen.

Pievani, Telmo. 2008. "Exaptation. Storia di un concetto [Exaptation. History of a Concept]." In *Exaptation. Il bricolage dell'evoluzione [Exaptation. The Bricolage of Evolution]*, edited by Steven Jay Gould and Elisabeth Vrba. Torino: Bollati Boringhieri.

Quigley, Carol. 1979. *The Evolution of Civilizations*. Indianapolis: Liberty Press.

Robinson, William I. 2011. "Globalization and the sociology of Immanuel Wallerstein: A critical appraisal." *International Sociology*, no. 1: 1–23.

Sanderson, Stephen K. 2002. "How Chase-Dunn and Hall Got It Almost Right. Review of Christopher Chase-Dunn and Tom D. Hall *Rise and Demise*." *Social Evolution and History*, no. 1(1): 171–176.

Sanderson, Stephen K. 2006. "Social Change." In *21st Century Sociology. A Reference Handbook*, edited by Clifton D. Bryant and Dennis Peck. Sage: Thousand Oaks.

Sanderson, Stephen. 2007. *Evolutionism and Its Critics. Deconstructing and Reconstructing an Evolutionary Interpretation of Human Society*. Boulder: Paradigm.

Sen, Amartya K. 1999. *Development as Freedom*. Oxford-New York: Oxford University Press.

Service, Elman R. 1971. *Cultural Evolutionism: Theory and Practice*. New York: Holt, Reinhart and Winston.

Sklair, Leslie. 2001. *The Transnational Capitalist Class*. New York: Wiley.

Skocpol, Theda. 1977. "Wallerstein's World Capitalist System: A Theoretical and Historical Critique." *American Journal of Sociology*, no. 5: 1075–90.

Straussfogel, Debra. 1998. "How Many World-Systems? A Contribution to the Continuationist/Transformationist Debate." *Review* 21 (1): 1–28.

Tainter, Joseph. 1988. *The Collapse of Complex Societies*. Cambridge: University Press.

Trotsky, Lev. 1932. *History of the Russian Revolution*, vol. 1. New York: Simon & Schuster.

Turner, Jonathan H. 2003. *The Structure of Sociological Theory, 7th Edition*. Belmont: Wadsworth.

Turner, Jonathan H. 2017. "Principles of Inter-Societal Dynamics." *Journal of World-Systems Research* 23 (2): 639–77.

Wallerstein, Immanuel. 1979. *The Capitalist World-Economy.* Cambridge: Cambridge University Press.

Wallerstein, Immanuel. 1983. *Historical Capitalism.* London: Verso.

Wallerstein, Immanuel. 1984. *The Politics of the World-Economy. The States, the Movements and the Civilizations.* Cambridge: University Press.

Wallerstein, Immanuel. 1991. *Unthinking Social Science: The Limits of Nineteenth Century Paradigm.* Cambridge: Polity Press.

Wallerstein, Immanuel. 1995. *Historical Capitalism, with Capitalist Civilization.* London: Verso.

Wallerstein, Immanuel. 2000. *The Essential Wallerstein.* New York: The New Press.

Wallerstein, Immanuel. 2004. *World-Systems Analysis: An Introduction.* Durnham: Duke University Press.

CHAPTER 4

The Great Oscillation

*Historicism, Polanyi's Double Movement, and Embedded
Dynamics of Capitalism*

Cory Blad

Karl Polanyi's work is far more than a single, albeit magisterial, book. That said, two of the most influential concepts in global political economic theory, *embeddedness* and the *double movement*, emerge from The Great Transformation as lasting indicators of the simple complexity of Polanyi's historical analyses. The concept of *embeddedness* (and the mirror of *disembeddedness* that results from market liberalization) alone arguably bolstered the fields of economic anthropology (Polanyi 1957; Halperin 1984) and economic sociology (Arrighi 1994; Block and Somers 2014). His concept of the *double movement*, however, provides a distinct path toward understanding Polanyi's contributions to not only historical political economy, but also the ways in which specific global political economic developments, such as the ideology of neoliberalism, can be understood in both contemporary and historical contexts. The *double movement* as unique in that it maps, and offers causal explanations for, both collective and regressive elements of global political economy in the postwar period.

Giorgio Resta, in the posthumously published *For a New West*, argues that Polanyi's sustained relevance is the product of his requisite demand that historical conditions and approaches be understood in comparative context (Polanyi 2014, 3). That is, concepts developed in the 1940s should be critically evaluated in any contemporary context based on those same contemporary conditions. This analytical testing requirement may appear obvious in a positivist sense, but taking Polanyi's suggestion to heart opens an opportunity to understand how the double movement has retained substantial relevance as the ideological hegemonic context of the postwar shifted from demand-side, embedded liberal to supply-side neoliberal capitalism. Interestingly, the concept demonstrates remarkable flexibility in historical context, particularly when we are able to examine both the direct application (i.e., presence) and indirect circumvention (i.e., presumed absence) of the double movement dynamics. In other words, the double movement retains its explanatory capacities whether it structuring in the mechanical functioning of a respective political economic moment or perceived to be absent in those same machinations. The former superficially describes the embedded liberal era (arguably 1944–1971), while the latter clearly describes the current market dominance of the neoliberal era.

This conceptual flexibility is central to the lasting utility of the double movement. It's theoretical compatibility with Keynesian demand-side economics typifies the ways in which the double movement explains capitalist continuity despite intractable structural tendencies toward crisis and material inequalities. The irony, of course, is that this was not the original intent of the double movement concept as initially developed by Polanyi. The static historicity of the original concept emerged from a specific epoch at the end of the Second World War and offered a prescient analysis of what would become the embedded liberal Bretton Woods monetary system. As noted by Mark Blyth, "... the great transformation was seen to be a one-way process" typified by "welfare states within an institutional order that heavily regulated the movement of capital and scope of markets, mark(ing) a permanent change in the institutional makeup of capitalism" (2002, 4).

The permanence of this great transformation was to provide a lasting solution to the constant tension of the double movement – a compromise of sorts that would rely on the state to mitigate the emergent adversities of liberal capitalism. The obvious problem with this assumption was the collapse of the Bretton Woods system in 1971 and the plotted resurgence of liberal capitalism in the form of institutionalized neoliberalism out of those respective ashes. For Blyth, this "counter double movement" of coordinated intellectual and business interests is reflective of a sustained conceptual dynamism, although the apparent "reversal" of the double movement to deemphasize social protectionism is cited as justification for jettisoning the double movement as an analytical framework (6).

Blyth's call to move beyond an historically restrictive concept is certainly understandable, however many have similarly recognized the underlying conceptual dynamism inherent in the double movement. While Polanyi's intent may have been to describe a singular historical shift in institutional capitalist orientation, the reversion of policy coordination efforts to liberal capitalism has actually intensified attention to the sustained utility of the double movement – not necessarily to explain the "reversal" to neoliberal hegemony, rather the explosion of counter movement effects produced as a result. This chapter chronicles the historical and theoretical impact of the double movement and highlights the ways in which a limited historical prognostication has surged in theoretical value as a result of broad global neoliberalization initiatives.

The following section briefly recounts the well-told story of the double movement concept, with particular emphasis on the historicity of the concept. This historicity is complicated in the subsequent three sections that examine the rise of the Bretton Woods-facilitated system of "embedded liberalism," the resurgence of liberal capitalist hegemony, and the tenuous political economic context of late neoliberalism, particularly following the 2008 financial crisis. The chapter concludes with a call for continued work on integrating Polanyi's creative insights into future political economic theories, particularly as they relate to the state and democracy in an era of excess and uncertainty.

1   Double Movement and It's Popularity

This relationship between liberal (or liberalizing) capitalism and the worsening of economic hardships was a central feature in the political economic theory of Karl Polanyi. His classic, *The Great Transformation,* builds off an evidenced critique of emergent Austrian School economic theories, specifically, their claim that capitalism is inherently "self-regulating" (Polanyi [1944] 2001, 32). In sum, Polanyi's critique rested on two important points. First, the expansion of market principles from particular exchange practices (or quite literally, the activities taking place in an actual marketplace) to encompass and drive social organization was a theoretical impossibility. Taken alone (as did the Austrian School and as do contemporary neoliberals), it is certainly possible to understand market dynamics as conditioning behavior of participatory actors and encouraging action in collaborative fashion that could be construed as *social.*

However, several problems become immediately apparent. The most important of these theoretical problems for Polanyi was the fact that market-based social assumptions ignore an important constituency: Non-beneficiaries. Liberal capitalist assumptions, whether (neo)classical (*homo economicus*) or Austrian (*homo agens*), emphasize the process of active market transactions with little attention to those who are excluded from active market participation or those who are adversely affected by "proper" market activities.

In actuality, there are countless factors that can restrict market access, bias market activities, and otherwise disrupt the supposed universality of market beneficence. Polanyi's critique recognizes this lack of empirical universality, which leads to the next obvious question of what might occur when non-beneficiaries are excluded or adversely affected by market activities. The answer is that they seek protection from material hardships resulting from societal market integration by either state policy or extra-state action.

Second, Polanyi argued that the self-regulating market society is historically or empirically problematic due to the fact that (a) there is no historical evidence that self-regulating market societies are a normative, or natural, social condition and (b) the naturalistic claims of liberal capitalist proponents belie a deep and power laden intentionality. That is, the self-regulating market society was (and remains) a construction of self-interested capitalists in search of expanded capital accumulation opportunities (Polanyi 2001, 146–7). In both critiques, assumptions are made that exclude the potential for broad societal reaction to the systemic inegalitarian distribution of capital – but also opportunities for and access to benefits stemming from capital accumulation.

This critique provided the foundation for a broader theoretical understanding of capitalist dynamics that would become his dynamic model of the *double movement*. Polanyi agreed with broadly understood contentions that capitalism necessitates inequalities (see 84, 108) but went further in examining the impact of liberalization on this requisite condition. His historically embedded critique showed that liberalization (or, the sustained push by capitalist beneficiaries for expanded capital accumulation opportunities) exacerbated hardships (138, 145); that is, capitalism explicitly motivates growth, which leads beneficiaries to call for increased "freedom" from (regulatory) conditions deemed to hinder said growth. The novelty of Polanyi's approach was to examine the social effects of liberalizing capital accumulation – specifically the reaction of non-beneficiaries.

As liberalization facilitates the reduction of labor and production costs (thus enabling increased profit), the effects of said capital growth has a commensurate negative effect on those actively engaged in labor/productive activities. Stagnating or depressing wages, job losses, and inflation pressures all exacerbate material hardships which motivate broad demands for protection from authoritative social institutions – namely, the state. Viewed in this inclusive fashion, the social effect of excessive economic liberalization is a "protectionist counter-movement" demanding the state mitigate resulting material hardships (79–80, 151, 210). The tension between these countervailing demands is constant – the result of sustained (and purposive) liberal efforts to expand capital accumulation that expands inequalities, exacerbates hardship conditions and thus results in commensurate protectionist demands.

Two key aspects of the double movement are essential here. The first is the role of the state as a mediating institution. State institutions (and actors) are required to satisfy demands for *both* capital accumulation and social protection (162; Block and Somers 1984, 68; see O'Connor 1973 for a similar argument). Invariably, institutions and actors that are perceived to privilege one side of the double movement over the other or those unwilling or unable to meet growth or protectionist demands will lose legitimating support. Specifically, we would expect state institutions and actors unable/unwilling to meet protectionist demands to suffer a decline in legitimacy – this is particularly salient point in the contemporary era of neoliberalization. To what extent has state support for neoliberalization resulted in political delegitimation? This is a question to which we will return.

Secondly, Polanyi identified clear cross-class characteristics with respect to protectionist demands (Polanyi 2001, 159–60). While economic inequality and material hardships are easily discernable among traditional laborers, Polanyi argues those adversely affected by changes in monetary or trade policies will also demand protection (161, 214). For example, a producer who is confronted with increased competition and price depression due to trade liberalization will likely demand protection from said policy. As a result, class becomes a less essential determinant of counter-movement participation. Again, this is contingent on the beneficiary status of the respective constituent: Those who face adversities resulting from liberalization will demand protection – this does not imply counter-movement coordination among aggrieved groups; however, he clearly illustrates the potential for cross-class mobilization.

2   Embedded Liberalism

The emergence of broad political economic consensus around the quasi-Keynesian policies that emerged from the 1944 Bretton Woods Conference would serve as the operational justification for Polanyi's concept of the double movement (published in the same year, in an amusing coincidence). The collapse of the gold standard orthodoxy in the ashes of economic depression and war led many to the understanding that state-led development and demand-side facilitation of consumption was an effective means of mitigation popular dissatisfaction with the resultant economic hardships that stubbornly persist as companions to liberal market capitalism. Also consistent with Polanyi's understanding of the double movement, however, was the persistence of liberal economic demands and the centrality of the state as a mediating institution (Block and Somers 1984; Blad 2019). Thus, a coexistence of sorts would allow for a mitigation of economic hardships without destroying the growth requisite of market capitalism.

In short, the Bretton Woods Agreements established international currency value coordination, ultimately pegging national currencies to the US dollar's subsequent valuation based on gold (set at $35 per ounce). Institutional support for this new international currency valuation system was to be managed by the International Monetary Fund (IMF) with support from the International Bank for Reconstruction and Development (World Bank). The goal of these systemic agreements was to reestablish stability in global trade, regulate speculative investment, and circumvent the nationalist isolationism of the Depression era. What evolved out of these agreements was an expansion of the demand-side economic practices that would underscore postwar welfare capitalism (Esping-Andersen 1999) and an episodic dominance of state-led programs designed to enhance consumptive capacities of respective national populations in advanced capitalist countries – the so-called "Atlantic Fordism" (Jessop 2002) of the embedded liberalism (Ruggie 1982) – until the early 1970s.

The macroeconomic compromise of the Bretton Woods Monetary System reflected the dual tensions of the double movement. Liberal capitalist proponents argued for a return to free trade policies that would enhance growth. In the past, global trade was facilitated by the common adherence to gold standard currency valuation; however, the restrictive context of gold essentially eliminated monetary policy as a social protectionist alternative. The shift to a national currency valuation tied to a single gold pegged currency (the US dollar), allowed more flexibility with regards to state-level monetary intervention. Built on the foundation of US "dollar hegemony," international trade grew nearly 300% in the twenty years following World War Two (Ashworth 1987, 285).

This international monetary system, alone, neither met national protectionist demands, nor single-handedly redressed local economic hardships resulting from war and economic depression. In North America and Europe, the emergence of a state-centric, Keynesian approach to public spending designed to maximize local consumption through reduced household service expenditures (i.e., health care, education, pensions, child care) and increases in disposable household income driven by increases in manufacturing and infrastructure employment (not to mention institutionalized labor market and collective bargaining protections).

The model is representative of the Bretton Woods period of "embedded liberalism" – in which state institutions maintained local monetary control and emphasized the development of "demand-side" economic strategies. The Bretton Woods agreements facilitated national economic autonomy under the aegis of American dollar hegemony, while the development of social welfare expenditures demonstrated a dedication to class-compromise. In short, it appeared that Polanyi's prediction of a "New World" in the post-war era was coming to fruition:

> Out of the ruins of the Old World, cornerstones of the New can be seen to emerge: economic collaboration of governments and the liberty to organize national life at will ... the end of market economy may well mean effective cooperation with domestic freedom.
>
> POLANYI 2001, 262

While this shift was reflective of Polanyi's predictions based on a singular historical shift in the double movement, there is a dynamic aspect of double movement relationships that is present but indirect in Polanyi's account. The mediating context of the double movement is also predicated on the understanding of self-interested oscillations that typify capitalist relations. While the double movement may have been seen by Polanyi as ending with the shifts toward embedded liberalism in the 1950s, a less historicist reading of double movement dynamics highlights the sustainability of the model – if the focus returns to social conflict inherent in capitalist relationships.

Przeworski is particularly clear in his representative work focusing on the necessary reciprocity of benefits between both capital and labor interests. His comparative review of Jurgen Habermas and Claus Offe's contributions to this ongoing problem identify specific problems with regards to both capitalism and state responses. With respect to the former, he identifies Offe's work on "decommodification" or the inherent trend towards disembedding labor and profit from structurally-governed market relationships (Przeworski 1990, 74). Once relationships of production become decommodified, the material benefits formerly distributed through market regulation become disproportionately allocated, threatening both respective material conditions and subsequently capitalist legitimation. This tendency is only mitigated by the actions of state institutions, which are required to intervene both for the purpose of maintaining conditions amenable for positive capital accumulation, but also for the purpose of maintain popular legitimate support for the very practice of capitalist social organization. In his summation of Habermas: "Hence the objective of the state under late capitalism: maximize capital accumulation under the *constraint* of maintaining legitimacy" (76, my emphasis).

While this is certainly not a novel observation, it does raise important questions with respect to the process of legitimating political authority, particularly in an era of perceived state "decline." Habermas is particularly relevant with respect to his understanding of the tenuous role of the state in maintain the legitimacy of capitalism and itself. As expected, Habermas understands the role of national populations as significant arbiters of authority, but in a distinctly reciprocal sense: "Taking the long view, the only kind of democratic process that will count as legitimate ... will be one that succeeds in an appropriate allocation and a fair distribution of rights. But to remain a source of solidarity, the status of citizenship has to maintain a use-value: it has to *pay* to be a citizen ..." (Habermas 2001, 77, emphasis in original).

Habermas' account is focused on a broader political application of reciprocal legitimation, but he does not minimize the fundamental importance of
economic protectionism: "As markets drive out politics, the nation-state
increasingly loses its capacities to raise taxes and stimulate growth, and with
them the ability to secure the essential foundations of its own legitimacy" (79).
Put simply, the base of legitimate political authority, particularly that of state
institutions, is rooted in a capacity to meet the economic protectionist demands
of local populations – either through the assurance of equitable growth distribution or through more direct protectionist measures such as subsistence subsidies or market/labor defenses. Taken with Przeworski's understanding of the
state as a manger/mitigator of capitalist distribution, we can therefore develop
a theoretical understand of a mediating state: attempting to ensure positive
capital accumulation while also meeting economic protectionist demands
from national populations in the face of the corrosive tendencies inherent in
capitalist structural operation.

We have, of course, seen this theoretical perspective before in Karl Polanyi's
understanding of the state as a mediator of the double movement. Polanyi's
original conceptualization of the double movement emphasises (as the title
would suggest) the *dual* pressures of global market integration and national
popular resistance (Polanyi 2001, 79–80).

3   Neoliberalism

The collapse of the Bretton Woods system in 1971, resulted from a combination
of factors including the overprinting of US dollars to satisfy global demand, as
well as the emergence of a parallel market ("Eurodollar market") trade in US
currency outside of the United States. The sustainability of an international
monetary system based on an overvalued currency led to obvious crises of con-
fidence and led to a series of shifts and withdrawals (not the least of which
was the removal of the US dollar gold peg in 1971) that ended broad economic
policy coordination.

In the wake (or perhaps hastening the demise) of this Keynesian-inspired
system, was the neoclassical, monetarism of Milton Friedman, bolstered by
many disciples of Polanyi's oft-target, Ludwig von Mises. The emergence of
what would be termed, neoliberalism, rejected the state-centric regulatory
capacities of the Bretton Woods era and ushered in a resurgence of free market
capitalism based on assumptions of growth through deregulation, circumvention of collective bargaining, and a championing of private capital (to name
but a few). This turn to privileged and protected market hegemony represented

substantial effort on the part of vested capitalist class actors (Harvey 2011) and reinforced by emergent think tanks and other privately funded producers of ideological strategy and support for this broad-scale effort to delegitimize state-centered regulation (Desai 2006).

These efforts were, of course, disseminated to national populations through various political avenues (Reagan's oft-cited proclamations of the "evils" of government, for example), but also through concerted efforts to shift popular expectations away from the state. The promotion of self-reliance and individualized engagement with broader social institutions, including the economy. These claims of "liberation of the market" from the regulatory context of the embedded liberal period were, of course, matched by sustained declines in household financial health predicated on rising costs in sectors either formerly regulated and supported (health care, education, housing) or exacerbated by stagnating real wages. The "successful politics of wage repression" (Harvey 2011, 21) facilitated elite and corporate growth opportunities, while many others experienced regressive or stagnating capacities to meet the cost burdens for increasingly expensive services – an historical eventuality identified by Polanyi as a product of the adversities resulting from liberal capitalist operations and prompting demands for protection from those same market-driven adversities (Polanyi 2001, 151). Streeck cites Michel in noting that "81.7 per cent of the increase in the United States between 1983 and 2009 went to the top 5 per cent, while the bottom 60 per cent *lost* the equivalent of 7.5per cent of the total asset increase" (2017, 53–4, emphasis in original). The realities of neoliberal capitalist reform were rooted in stagnation and adversity of popular majorities in all neoliberal national states. The result of these predictable outcomes, neoliberal proponents were required to justify these adverse conditions and somehow deflect responsibility for their resolution *away* from the state.

Wendy Brown highlights the vernacular transition to "entrepreneurialism" as a neoliberal adaptation to these eventualities of liberal capitalism. In short, this ideological influence promoted "responsibilization" (or assuming individual responsibility for social needs such as child care and health care), a celebration of contract labor through such vehicles (pun intended) as the gig economy and marketized ideations of "hustling" as acceptable means of circumventing wage insecurity, and finally demands that a return to familial responsibility for addressing cost increases for child care, education, retirement, and other needs (which, of course, privileges conservative notions of patriarchal "traditional family" responsibilities and exacerbated burdens on women) (Brown 2019, 38–9). Brown's efficient overview of these framed promotions of positive (neoliberal) responses to inevitable financial hardships is deeply reflective of both the aforementioned intentionality of the neoliberal project as well as the transformative nature of neoliberal capitalism, itself. As Douglas Holmes' description of the transformative impact of "fast capitalism" (essentially synonymous with neoliberal or late capitalism) summarizes these efforts as: "a corrosive productive regime that transforms the conceptual and the relational power of 'society' by subverting foundational moral claims, social dimensions, and material dispensations" (Holmes 2000, 5).

All of this reflects the holistic context of Polanyi's critique of liberal capitalism – the reliance on market equilibrium and equitable distribution supposedly found in pure capitalist markets, while the reality of exacerbated inequalities and material adversities for the majority within respective national populations. As a result of this inherent critique of contemporary neoliberalism, the double movement has found renewed interest as an explanatory concept (Levien and Paret 2012); however, this resurgence belies the aforementioned historical specificity of Polanyi's original concept. Polanyi's interpretation of the postwar shifts toward Keynesian-Fordist implied an inevitable path toward a social democratic telos (Burawoy 2003). The systemic collapse of the liberal capitalist infrastructure following depression and war would ultimately begin the process of re-embedding markets in response to popular countermovement demands. The certainty of Polanyi's belief was evident: "Undoubtedly, our age will be credited with having seen the end of the self-regulating market" (Polanyi 2001, 148).

This teleological prediction has not reduced the popularity of Polanyi's analysis or its potential to explain the resurgence of liberal capitalism in the 1980s, however it has led many to question the efficacy of its conclusions. Gareth Dale notes the substantial increase in (neo) Polanyian analyses of neoliberalism as being particularly focused on the explanatory role of the double movement. These approaches shift from the historical rigidity of the double movement to emphasize the dynamic potential of the double movement as an almost ever-present swing between liberal and protectionist countermovement trends that Dale refers to as "pendular forces" (2012, 14–5). His critique of both the neo-Polanyian treatment of neoliberalism and specifically, the pendular thesis, is both reasonable and limiting.

On the one hand, Dale (among others) argues that the countermovement tendencies identified during the neoliberal era – e.g., the so-called "Pink Tide" in Latin America, antiglobalization movements, and global movements against persisting economic inequality – are unduly inclusive. That is, any action that could be perceived as running counter to the unfettered operation of markets was subsumed under the label of "protectionism" and thus integrated into the dynamic analytical framework of the double movement. More to the point, the diversity of such state actions often serves to reinforce neoliberal goals and cannot be universally assumed to be protectionist. In his words: "Does it make sense to lump together the alterglobalization movement with xeno-phobic reactionaries – and does this not play into the hands of the those who seek to discredit the former by conflating it with the latter? How precisely does one determine whether an act of economic protection – for example, the state provision of export guarantees to armaments firms – is contributing to mar-ketization or to the protectionist counter movement?" (Dale 2010, 219). Dale raises important questions about the consequences of conceptual conflation; a critique of the double movement that is all the more salient when we look at the literature and assumptions of a perceived move to a "postneoliberal" era that emerged following economic crises from 1998 through 2008.

4   Postneoliberal Possibilities and Failures

For many, the crises of late capitalism represented a clear sign of systemic breakdown. The prevalence of movements focused on market-driven condi-tions including economic inequality, environmental sustainability, systemic racism, and more seemed to confirm, for many, that a protectionist counter-movement was gaining power to reverse the market swing of neoliberalism. Returning to Dale's (2010) quote above, the rise in exclusionary nationalist sentiment and political mobilization during the same time also indicates a dangerous new element that is somehow related to the reactionary effects of liberalization since the 1980s. The former point (the demise of neoliberalism) has been shown to be highly problematic, however the latter point (resurgent exclusionary nationalism), I would argue, highlights the continued value of the double movement as a dynamic concept that requires more theoretical embedding.

4.1   *Postneoliberal Possibilities?*
The term emerged as an analytical concept following the most recent global economic recession. The term begins to appear in 2008 (Challies and Murray) and expanded significantly the following year notably in a special issue of *Development Dialog* (cf. Brand and Sekler 2009; Altvater 2009; Ceceña 2009). A cursory look at scholarship that seeks to articulate and define postneoliber-alism belies an obvious link to earlier empirical motivations, specifically the "Pink Tide" of neoliberal critics elected in South American countries after 1998 (Grugel and Riggirozzi 2012; Kaltwasser 2011; Macdonald and Ruckert 2009; Sader 2009) and to describe more heterodox responses to the East Asian finan-cial crisis (Akçali et al. 2015; Demirovic 2009).

Indeed, the very question of a "post" neoliberalism was motivated by both popular and systemic challenges culminating in the crisis years after 2007 which prompted some to declare the end of neoliberalism as a dominant political economic ideology (Stiglitz 2008; Wallerstein 2008). The problem is, of course, that few of the scholars proclaiming the death of neoliberalism were complete in their proclamations and most were cautious in their conclusions – in fact, the bulk of work on a "postneoliberal" reality is defined by this ambiguity over the current state of neoliberal efficacy. Consensus has developed around the notion that neoliberal ideology has reached a tipping point of sorts (Farmer and Noonan 2011; Peck et al. 2010; Sandbrook 2011; Springer 2015) but deep empirical problems persist – not the least of which is the sustained authority of neoliberal policies and institutions.

The challenge seems to be rooted in a deep disconnect between occasions of social and cultural rejection of neoliberalism and inertial (and often willful) political policy support for market fundamentalist solutions. Protectionist demands, anti-inequality mobilization, and populist dissatisfaction in contemporary advanced capitalist societies highlight public dissatisfaction with the effect of neoliberal economic policies. Coupled with demonstrable structural economic failures after 2007, it stands to reason that free market fundamentalism inherent in neoliberal ideology would be difficult to revive. However, market centric policy responses to seem to have not only survived the purge, but emerged stronger. Ordoliberal austerity, for example, was presented as a singular alternative to debt crises wrought by deregulation and excessive financialization – despite deep public resistance to deepening hardships for the benefit of a global elite financial class.

Smith's (2008) understanding of mid-recession neoliberalism as "dominant, but dead" characterizes this policy/public disconnect. Aalbers similarly struggles with the reality that "the ideology of neoliberalism may have failed, but that neoliberal practice is alive and kicking" (Aalbers 2013, 1083). Peck offers a conceptual understanding of this phenomenon by understanding neoliberal policies as "entering a zombie phase ... The brain has apparently long since ceased functioning, but the limbs are still moving, and many of the defensive reflexes seem to be working too. The living dead of the free-market revolution continue to walk the earth, though with each resurrection their decidedly uncoordinated gait becomes even more erratic" (Peck 2010, 109).

In such an ambiguous climate, how can we begin to discuss the concept of "post" neoliberalism? I would argue that advanced capitalist societies have entered a period of transition out of neoliberal dominance, but that this is a precipice transition essentially to nowhere. The problem facing political actors and organizations – as well as non-political financial actors such as the IMF who clearly recognize the distributional and punitive failures of neoliberal-ism (Ostry et al. 2016) – is that while most see this failure, there is no viable political economic alternative in place to serve as a destination point during this transitional period. As such, traditional political actors have struggled to defend failed ideologies and policy models, argued for a return to a Keynesian past, or circumvented political economic realities by offering a mélange of contradictory protectionist alternatives while sustaining a rhetorical belief in the fundamentals of market capitalism. More to the point, the critique of overt conceptual breadth made by Dale is reinforced by Streeck, who argues that not only has neoliberalism become culturally accepted as a normative reality (Streeck 2017, 31), but that neoliberal states have come to rely on public debt as a mechanism of both maintaining legitimacy, but also in facilitating financial growth (xix–xxi). Thus, we are back to the question of whether state actions seen as bolstering public finances through debt accumulation are really mark-ers of state funding of financial elites.

While it is difficult to see how neoliberalism meets its end in the current cli-mate of financial capital dominance, it is clear that we are not living an a post-neoliberal reality. It's undefined "zombie" state notwithstanding, there is little evidence of a paradigmatic alternative and certainly no evidence that a dem-ocratic socialist consensus, as envisioned by Polanyi, is on the verge of imple-mentation. That said, I would argue that this critique of the double movement is built on a restricted, instrumentalist notion of the state as a vehicle for cap-italist interests. If we step back and view the state as a mediating institution, perhaps working to mitigate the inherent conflict of an active double move-ment, this allows for far more engaged role for the double movement as an analytical tool to better understand the contemporary crisis of late capitalism.

4.2   State Legitimation in Late Capitalism

As Block and Somers note, a Polanyian conceptualization of the state is as a dynamic mediator: "The state was necessarily both a universal, representing the interests of society against the market, and a class state, pursuing the agen-das of the capitalist class, since the reproduction of capitalist relations was necessary to preserve the society. The state became, in short, the crystalliza-tion of the contradictory impulses of nineteenth century development" (Block and Somers 1984, 68).

The role of the state was then to mediate and manage the integration of national market liberalization (Polanyi 2001 147, 216). The mechanisms availa-ble for the state to meet these mediation requirements were largely economic in nature. The primary mechanism was control over monetary policy, which allowed states to adjust local prices in times of increased foreign competition or scarcity (214). The two other forms of economic protectionism, "land and labour," are linked to the regulatory influence of states in managing labor laws and enabling social protections that ensured at least a minimal level of survival as well as agricultural subsidies that remain in force to this day. In sum, the role of the state in tempering the effects of the dually-supported liberal market system was essential and took the form of restricted economic protectionism, particularly notable in the postwar embedded liberal era.

The key question then becomes how state-centered political authority can maintain legitimation in the face neoliberal dominance? In the minds of many, including many of those already referenced, it cannot maintain traditional levels of authority. However, it seems that in the face of clear analytical evidence supporting the visible sustenance of state institutions the question of "traditional" authority seems misplaced. While neoliberal reforms have clearly retasked state institutions in forms ranging from decentralization to welfare/workfare adaptations to sheer regulatory abdication, it is also clear that the state is still a necessary authoritative institution. As capitalism, writ large, is unable to legitimate itself, so too does its contemporary global iteration suffer from this structural limitation. The transformative and microcosmic effects of economic globalization mirror those of liberal capitalism: Expanded capital accumulation and exacerbated adversities resulting from aggravated socioeconomic inequalities. Perhaps Barrow puts it best with the contention that states are "principle agents of globalization" (Barrow 2005, 123), which reinforces his argument that without the support of state institutions globalization would be unable to sustain itself. More specifically, Barrow frames this sustained need for state authority in familiar terms: "... within the new global political economy, state elites must still manage the contradictory pressures of (global) accumulation and (national) legitimation" (125).

Thus, the state is both retrenching yet necessary in the contemporary era. Given the contradictory demands inherent in the double movement – it is difficult to see how this could be otherwise in the context of sustained "late capitalism." The question, therefore, must center on that of legitimation. As states face severe pressure on economic protectionist capacities, the threat is not simply to populations adversely affected by neoliberalization, but also to political legitimation, itself. With reduced capacities (or even desires) to meet local protectionist demands through economic means, the material foundations for reciprocal legitimation are restricted, at best. In this neoliberal context, political entities – including state institutions – are increasingly turning to alternative legitimation strategies as traditional economic means wither.

I argue here (and elsewhere) that this legitimation gap is increasingly circumvented through the integration of monolithic nationalist political rhetoric and practices (see Blad 2019; Blad and Koçer 2012). As the economic protectionism so prevalent in the embedded liberal period becomes less viable as a result of ubiquitous, albeit uneven, neoliberalization nationalist politics play an increasingly viable role – not simply as a result of a power vacuum commonly implied (see Castells 2004; Piven 1995) but as an intentional legitimation strategy in the restrictive context resulting from neoliberal adaptation. The imbrication of nationalism as political legitimation becomes an important strategy in support of neoliberal ends. In the case of neoliberal political legitimation however, the process is two-fold. Not only must neoliberal political entities find a way to obtain legitimate authority without relying on economic protectionist means, but they must also work to legitimate the project of neoliberalism as well. To the latter end, it becomes important to link ongoing legitimation efforts with the diminution of formerly dominant ones. This ideological othering (see Cammaerts 2012; Göl 2005) is a strategic mechanism in the discursive struggle for hegemonic position. Nationalism has certainly played a central role in the history of this longer process of normative political construction – yet it is the relationship between strategic political legitimation and the project of creating a normative neoliberal context that highlights the role nationalist politics plays in the contemporary era.

Based on these theoretical assumptions, we can postulate the following. First, as political entities embrace neoliberalism, the ability to obtain legitimate authority through claims of economic protectionism become less viable. While neoliberals consistently support economic arguments for an elusive market equilibrium, the effects of "actually existing neoliberalism" exacerbate persisting inequalities, maintain wage stagnation, and reduce the role of the state in social service provisions across class-lines. These adversities (of relative and varying intensity) limit the ability of neoliberal political actors to convince legitimating constituents of the protectionist potential of deregulated market capitalism.

Second, as a result, we should expect viable neoliberal political actors to increasingly turn to nationalist political strategies to define respective policies and platforms. Thus, nationalist symbolic discourse comes to be a constructed association as neoliberal political actors seek alternative means of legitimate authority. Put simply, the paucity of legitimation options available to neoliberal proponents facilitates the drive to wrap political rhetoric in nationalist ideological and symbolic garb. We can see this tendency in efforts on the part of state actors of various political alignments. While Reagan capitalized on a resurgent traditionalism found in relatively novel evangelical and Republican alliances in the United States (see Heclo 1986), the Labour Party of New Zealand could also be seen reviving the Waitangi Treaty in 1984 as a means of establishing control over a national cultural definition while simultaneously inaugurating massive deregulation efforts in both the United States and New Zealand (see Kelsey 1991; Larner 2002). The former case is clearly predicated on a monolithic, exclusionary national cultural definition, while the latter highlights a more bicultural national identity formation, but the causal motivations are the same: In an environment of decreased material support – in lines with neoliberal reform – alternative means for establishing and maintaining political legitimacy needed to be found.

The post 2008 political economic environment has seen these strategic efforts taken to the extreme. While efforts to recapture material means of economic protectionism are certainly apparent, neoliberal actors are increasingly confronted with the reality that the "rising tide" of free market integration certainly has not lifted all boats ... and largely resulted in broad dissatisfaction based off of real material adversities. For many, the early work of nationalist symbolic imbrication has resulted in a cultural affiliation with particular political parties and rhetoric, sometimes ensuring political support despite the lack of clear material benefits. This implies a lack of awareness and intentionality, however, and is belied by the active abandonment of formerly protectionist parties as they acquiesced to neoliberal goals and policies in the 1990s. So, while one might support a Republican or Tory political platform based off of a perceived historical alignment with patriotic symbols and definitions (often racialized), others may be new converts drawn to the cultural legitimation of nationalist rhetoric found in Trumpist anti-immigration vitriol or Brexit exclusivity after first being abandoned by Democratic, Labour, or Social Democratic parties as they embraced neoliberal reforms. Key here is the sustained viability of double movement dynamics. In both cases, national populations are seeking support in the face of worsening economic conditions, yet many see little reason to vote for traditional labour-oriented, working class political alliances that were often abandoned with the rush toward free market growth and neoliberal reform movements throughout the advanced capitalist world in the 1990s. One could certainly argue that the neoliberal alternatives to which many shifted their political support was even less likely to result in material protective support, but the broad success of outsider politicians and clear shifts in rhetoric to circumvent traditional "politics as usual" underscores the motivation (or desperation) on the part of many to find anyone who might alter the status quo. In this sense, the Trumpist Republican Party, Five Star, the UKIP, and even various Pirate Parties can be understood as being products of this desire for alternative political leadership.

The sustained power of neoliberal practices – if not ideals – exacerbates this trend toward nationalist, populist political alternatives, but also the resurgence of social democratic efforts to rekindle past state-led economic protectionist alternatives. These are not equivalent movements in any context; however, their common foundations in relative economic adversities, worsened by market fundamentalism, must be recognized. More to the point, without such a recognition, it becomes nearly impossible to either understand the role of material adversities (perceived and real) in nationalist political mobilization (as well as the elite *capacity* to mobilize support using exclusionary national-ist means) or effective means to counter this historically dangerous political legitimation strategy. Movements, state institutions, and ideas are consistently coopted by capitalist interests and vested actors. Dale's concern for concep-tual conflation is important, but I would argue that through the Polanyian lens of state mediation potential and the persistence of economic protectionist motivations continues to offer analytical and strategic possibilities in a time of perceived intransigence and division. It may be worth considering that sus-taining motivational divisions may be equally helpful to those who seek to dis-credit the social democratic alternatives by conflating them with nationalist mobilization.

References

Aalbers, Manuel B. 2013. "Neoliberalism is Dead ... Long Live Neoliberalism!" *International Journal of Urban and Regional Research* 37 (3): 1083–90.

Akçali, Emel, Lerna K. Yanik, and Ho-Fung Hung. 2015. "Inter-Asian (Post-) Neolibera-lism?" *Asian Journal of Social Science* 43 (1–2): 5–21.

Altvater, Elmar. 2009. "Postneoliberalism or Postcapitalism? The Failure of Neoliberalism in the Financial Market Crisis." *Development Dialogue*, no. 51 (January): 73–88.

Arrighi, Giovanni. 1994. *The Long Twentieth Century: Money, Power, and the Origins of Our Times.* London: Verso.

Ashworth, William A. 1987. *A Short History of the International Economy Since 1850.* London: Longman.

Barrow, Clyde. 2005. "The Return of the State: Globalization, State Theory, and the New Imperialism." *New Political Science* 27 (2): 123–45.

Barrow, Clyde. 2016. "Faustian States: Nationalist Politics and the Problem of Legiti-macy in the Neoliberal Era." In *Global Culture: Theories and Paradigms Revisited*, edited by Vincenzo Mele and Marina Vujnovic. Leiden: Brill Academic Publishers.

Blad, Cory. 2019. "Searching for Saviors: Economic Adversities and the Challenge of Legitimacy in the Neoliberal Era." In *Social Welfare Responses in a Neoliberal Era*, edited by Mia Arp Fallov and Cory Blad. Leiden: Brill Academic Publishers.

Blad, Cory and Banu Koçer. 2012. "Political Islam and State Legitimacy in Turkey: The Role of National Culture in Neoliberal State-Building." *International Political Sociology* 6 (1): 36–56.

Block, Fred. 1984. "Beyond the Economistic Fallacy: The Holistic Social Science of Karl Polanyi." In *Vision and Method in Historical Sociology*, edited by Theda Skocpol. Cambridge: University Press.

Block, Fred, and Margaret R. Somers. 2014. *The Power of Market Fundamentalism*. Cambridge: Harvard University Press.

Blyth, Mark. 2002. *Great Transformations: The Rise and Decline of Embedded Liberalism*. Cambridge: University Press.

Brand, Ulrich, and Nicola Sekler. 2009. "Postneoliberalism: Catch-all Word or Valuable Analytical and Political Concept? –Aims of a Beginning Debate." *Development Dialogue* 51 (1): 5–14.

Brown, Wendy. 2019 *In the Ruins of Neoliberalism: The Rise of Antidemocratic Politics in the West*. New York: Columbia University Press.

Burawoy, Michael. 2003. "For a Sociological Marxism: The Complementary Convergence of Antonio Gramsci and Karl Polanyi." *Politics & Society* 31 (2): 193–261.

Cammaerts, Bart. 2012. "The Strategic Use of Metaphors by Political and Media Elites: The 2007–11 Belgian Constitutional Crisis." *International Journal of Media and Cultural Politics* 8 (2–3): 229–49.

Castells, Manuel. 2004. *The Power of Identity*. 2nd ed. Malden: Blackwell Publishing.

Ceceña, Ana Esther. 2009. "Postneoliberalism and its Bifurcations." *Development Dialogue*, no. 51 (January): 33–44.

Challies, Edward RT, and Warwick E. Murray. 2008. "Towards Post-neoliberalism? The Comparative Politico-economic Transition of New Zealand and Chile." *Asia Pacific Viewpoint* 49 (2): 228–43.

Dale, Gareth. 2012. "Double Movements and Pendular Forces: Polanyian Perspectives on the Neoliberal Age." *Current Sociology* 60 (1): 3–27.

Dale, Gareth. 2010. *Karl Polanyi*. London: Polity Press.

Demirovic, Alex. 2009. "Postneoliberalism and Post-Fordism: Is There a New Period in the Capitalist Mode of Production." *Development Dialogue*, no. 51 (January): 45–57.

Desai, Radhika. 2006. "Neoliberalism and Cultural Nationalism: A *danse macabre*." In *Neoliberal Hegemony: A Global Critique, edited by Dieter Plehwe, Bernhard Walpen, and Gisela Neunhöffer*. New York: Routledge.

Esping-Andersen, Gøsta. 1999. *Social Foundations of Postindustrial Economies*. Oxford: University Press.

Farmer, Stephanie, and Sean Noonan. 2011. "Post-Neoliberalism or Deepened Neoliberalism? The Chicago Public Transportation Service and Elite Response during the Great Stagnation." *Perspectives on Global Development and Technology* 10 (1): 73–84.

Göl, Ayla. 2005. "Imagining the Nation Through 'Othering' Armenians." *Nations and Nationalism* 11 (1): 121–39.

Grugel, Jean, and Pía Riggirozzi. 2012. "Post-neoliberalism in Latin America: Rebuilding and Reclaiming the State after Crisis." *Development and Change* 43 (1): 1–21.

Habermas, Jürgen. 2001. *The Postnational Constellation: Political Essays.* Cambridge: MIT Press.

Halperin, Rhoda H. 1984. "Polanyi, Marx, and the Institutional Paradigm in Economic Anthropology." *Research in Economic Anthropology,* no. 6: 245–72.

Harvey, David. 2011. *The Enigma of Capital and the Crises of Capitalism.* New York: Oxford University Press.

Heclo, Hugh. 1986. "Reaganism and the Search for a Public Philosophy." In *Perspectives on the Reagan Years,* edited by John L. Palmer. Washington D.C.: The Urban Institute.

Holmes, Douglas R. 2000. *Integral Europe: Fast Capitalism, Multiculturalism, and Neo-Fascism.* Princeton: University Press.

Jessop, Bob. 2002. "Liberalism, neoliberalism, and urban governance: A state–theoretical perspective." *Antipode* 34 (3): 452–72.

Kaltwasser, Cristóbal Rovira. 2011. "Toward post-neoliberalism in Latin America?" *Latin American Research Review* 46 (2): 225–34.

Kelsey, Jane. "Rogernomics and the Treaty of Waitangi: the contradiction between the economic and Treaty policies of the fourth Labour government, 1984–1990, and the role of law in mediating that contradiction in the interests of the colonial capitalist state." PhD diss. University of Auckland, 1991.

Larner, Wendy. 2002. "Neoliberalism and Tino Rangatiratanga: Welfare Restructuring in Aotearoa/New Zealand." In *Western Welfare in Decline: Globalization and Women's Poverty,* edited by Catherine Kingfisher. Philadelphia: University of Pennsylvania Press.

Levien, Michael, and Marcel Paret. 2012. "A Second Double Movement? Polanyi and Shifting Global Opinions on Neoliberalism." *International Sociology* 27 (6): 724–44.

Macdonald, Laura, and Arne Ruckert, eds. 2009. *Post-neoliberalism in the Americas.* Houndmills: Palgrave Macmillan.

O'Connor, James. 1973. *The Fiscal Crisis of the State.* New York: St. Martin's Press.

Ostry, Jonathan D., Prakash Loungani, and Davide Furceri. 2016. "Neoliberalism: Oversold." *Finance & Development* 53 (2): 38–41.

Peck, Jamie. 2010. "Zombie Neoliberalism and the Ambidextrous State." *Theoretical Criminology* 14 (1): 104–10.

Peck, Jamie, Nik Theodore, and Neil Brenner. 2010. "Postneoliberalism and its Malcontents." *Antipode* 41 (s1): 94–116.

Piven, Frances Fox. 1995. "Globalizing Capitalism and the Rise of Identity Politics." In *Socialist Register 1995: Why Not Capitalism?,* edited by Leo Panitch. London: Merlin Press.

Polanyi, Karl. 1957. "The Economy as Instituted Process." In *Trade and Market in the Early Empires*, edited by Karl Polanyi, Conrad Arensberg and Harry Pearson. Glencoe: Free Press.

Polanyi, Karl. (2001 [1944]). *The Great Transformation: The Political Economic Origins of Our Time*. Boston: Beacon Press.

Polanyi, Karl. 2014. *For a new West: essays, 1919–1958*. Cambridge: Polity Press.

Przeworski, Adam. 1990. *The State and the Economy under Capitalism*. London: Harwood Academic Publishers.

Ruggie, John. 1982. "International Regimes, Transactions, and Change: Embedded Liberalism in the Postwar Economic Order." *International Organization* 36 (2): 379–415.

Sader, Emir. 2009. "Postneoliberalism in Latin America." *Development Dialogue* 51 (1): 171–79.

Sandbrook, Richard. 2011. "Polanyi and Post-neoliberalism in the Global South: Dilemmas of Re-embedding the Economy." *New Political Economy* 16 (4): 415–43.

Smith, Neil. 2008. "Neoliberalism is Dead, Dominant, Defeatable–then What." *Human Geography* 1 (2): 1–3.

Springer, Simon. 2015. "Postneoliberalism?" *Review of Radical Political Economics* 47 (1): 5–17.

Stiglitz, Joseph. 2008. "The End of Neoliberalism?" *Project Syndicate Commentary*, (July). Retrieved November 12, 2020. https://www.project-syndicate.org/comment ary/the-end-of-neo-liberalism?barrier=true.

Streeck, Wolfgang. 2017. *Buying Time: The Delayed Crisis of Democratic Capitalism*. 2nd edition. London: Verso Books.

Wallerstein, Immanuel. 2008. "The Demise of Neoliberal Globalization." *MRZine*, (February). Retrieved November 12, 2016. http://www.mrzine.monthlyreview.org.

CHAPTER 5

Depth in the Inexhaustible Surface of Things
Postmodernism and the Fetishism of Commodities

Enrico Campo and Alfonso Maurizio Iacono

The metaphor that I like is that of lifting the veils that obscure or hide what is going on. The task of scientific study is to lift the veils that cover the area of group life that one proposes to study. The veils are not lifted by substituting, in whatever degree, preformed images for firsthand knowledge. The veils are lifted by getting close to the area and by digging deep into it through careful study.

BLUMER 1969, 39

• • •

Four centuries after the "solutions" of the Renaissance and three centuries after Descartes, depth is still new, and it insists on being sought, not "once in a lifetime" but all through life.

MERLEAU-PONTY 1964, 180

• • •

It is only after you have come to know the surface of things [...] that you venture to seek what is underneath. But the surface is inexhaustible.

CALVINO 1999, 51

•
• •
•

1 Introduction

Why return to the discussion on the relationship between the modern and post-modern now that the debate seems to have lost vitality even for proponents of postmodernism?[1] We believe it necessary because the debate carries with it traces of unresolved issues that have tormented modernity and that are still of political relevance today. We are referring to the ecological crisis and, more generally, to the difficulty of finding an adequate narrative for our times that permits us to understand the challenges and is, at the same time, open to otherness and does not claim to be a universal or totalizing discourse.

The debate on postmodernism is particularly articulated and rich and has crossed disciplinary and national borders. From the very beginning any attempt to try and restore unity to what is instead fragmentary by nature has been looked upon with suspicion. Thus, any claim offering a complete or ordered narrative of postmodernism contradicts one of its essential premises.[2] Yet, perhaps paradoxically, now that such a debate has lost its disruptive charge and seems to have exhausted itself, it appears easier to provide a narrative of postmodernity than modernity: that is, it is easier to narrate a current of thought in which rejection of "grand narratives" is one of its essential issues (Franzini 2018). At the same time, we must recognize that modernity itself has a structure that is necessarily ambiguous, beginning with its very etymology. Defining a period as modern, as *Neuzeit,* and therefore an epoch of novelty and change, means renouncing any attempt to repair its constitutive character univocally and definitively. Modernity has a dialogical structure; it is animated by dialectical tensions that are not resolved in a definitive synthesis. Despite this, it also presents a need to bring it back to unity, a need to create order through conceptual and all-encompassing representative schemes, possibly through universal and progressive philosophies of history. One of the great merits of postmodernism consists in its having definitively shown the illusory – and politically dangerous – nature of such claims, unmasking any attempt to reduce the ambiguity of modernity by resorting to a foundation: there is no chance to "make whole what has been smashed." (Benjamin 2007, 257) On the other hand, some of the results of postmodern thought tend to defuse the dialectical and dialogical tension that animates the constitutive elements of modernity, which have given us fragmentary thought in exchange that struggles to become a bearer of meaning. We are referring in particular to the excesses of the linguistic paradigm that have led to an ontological devaluation of reality, reduced to a mere sign (Iofrida 2019).

The aim of our contribution is to reactivate some of these tensions and display their dialogical character. One of these has had an essential historical and

---

1 Although the chapter is the result of a collective work, the first two sections have been written by Enrico Campo, while sections 3, 4 and 5 by Alfonso Maurizio Iacono.

2 For a very broad, transdisciplinary mapping, see Susen (2015).

definitional function: the distinction between use value and exchange value which has already been discussed in Jean-François Lyotard's [1924–1998] well-known book *The Postmodern Condition* [1924–1998]. In it the French philosopher predicts the coming of a new form of capitalism in which information has a primary role in the devaluation, if not the cancellation, of use value. Our hypothesis – which we will develop in the next section – is that this outcome is based on an overly sharp contrast between the two dialectical poles and an epistemological perspective that makes a simplistic distinction between "appearance" and "reality," between representation and the represented, or – more important for our aims – between surface and depth. Two other great interpreters of postmodernity – Daniel Bell [1919–2011] and Fredric Jameson, whom we will discuss in the next section – clearly grasp this epistemological issue and interpret postmodernity, respectively, as a "crisis of distance" and a *pastiche of* images. Though they start from opposite political positions, they both connect the ends of a certain epistemological model – paradigmatically represented by a linear perspective that identifies depth with distance – to the definitive defeat of use value in favor of exchange value. Yet, as we will try to show in the third section, according to Karl Marx [1812–1883] it is impossible to completely erase use value: its dialectical tension is always present and cannot be cancelled altogether. Finally, in light of this awareness, in our conclusion we will try to lay the foundations for future research that identifies *another kind of* depth that is no longer linked to the opposition between appearance and reality and to the perspectival concept of distance. We will therefore attempt to hypothesize a different relationship between surface and depth through the concept of overlap, starting from Paul Cézanne [1839–1906] who, according to Bell, definitively dissolved perspective depth. We want to identify a different kind of depth that rejects equating surface with falseness, and instead aims to preserve the dialogic tension between surface and depth.

2   Work vs Consumption, Desire vs Need

As already mentioned, one of the central issues addressed in the debate on postmodernism has been a change in the balance between the poles of use value and exchange value. The reflection on postmodernism in this case more directly meets the contemporary debate on post-industrial society and concerns the centrality of information, knowledge and therefore language. This tendency, which we might call "dematerializing," has led to a surreptitious opposition between use and exchange value, as if the former were the only truly authentic form of value and the latter merely its symbolic distortion. This opposition can (often implicitly) lead one to imagine a nostalgic prior state in which it was clearly possible to distinguish between original needs, indicated by use value, and induced desires:

> The notion of the consumer so distributing his income as to maximize satisfactions that originate with himself and his environment was not inappropriate to an earlier stage of economic development. When goods were less abundant, when they served urgent physical need and their acquisition received close thought and attention, purchases were much less subject to management. And, on the other side, producers [...] did not need to persuade – to manage demand.
>
> GALBRAITH 1972, 217

From this point of view, the more subjects limit their desires and remain in touch with their "original" needs, the more autonomous they are. Clearly, the subject who is postulated by these visions, realizes this autonomy in a Robinsonian way by distancing himself from things and others, with whom he has, if anything, an instrumental relationship with respect to his own ends (Sennett 1976; Iacono 2016).

Theories that have interpreted the emergence of post-industrial society in terms of a progressive dematerialization have therefore emphasized the extension of consumption's sphere of influence over that of production and have identified the former with marketing strategies and advertising. Solid industrial reality is replaced by a *pastiche* of images of which the objective referent has been lost. It is the reign of surface over depth in the substance of reality: "the primacy of style over substance has become the normative consciousness" (Ewen 1988, 2). Many of these authors clearly refer to *The Consumer Society* (1998) by Jean Baudrillard [1929 – 2007] in which the French philosopher offers an original reinterpretation of the Marxian fetishism of goods: the object of consumption is viewed as the expression of a system of signs and was then subjected to semiotic analysis. The great merit of Baudrillard's work was in clarifying how the meaning of a single consumer object depends on the broader ("global, arbitrary, coherent") symbolic system to which it belongs: a system that, in Baudrillard's view, "substitutes [the] social order of values and classification." (Baudrillard 1998, 79; Lunt and Livingstone 1992). Although Baudrillard explicitly criticized the idea of an "original" use value devoid of any symbolic distortion, he autonomized the world of objects to such an extent that it became a system of "self-referential signs" that totalize collective existence: "Just as the wolf-child became a wolf by living among wolves, so we too are slowly becoming functional. We live by object time: by this I mean that

we live at the pace of objects, live to the rhythm of their ceaseless succession
... we live, sheltered by signs, in the denial of the real." (Baudrillard 1998, 25,
34) In this process of self-referential signs, the use value of objects essentially
becomes irrelevant:

> Outside the field of its objective function, where it is irreplaceable,
> outside the field of its denotation, the object becomes substitutable in
> a more or less unlimited way within the field of connotations, where it
> assumes sign-value. Thus, the washing machine serves as an appliance
> and acts as an element of prestige, comfort, etc. It is strictly this latter
> field which is the field of consumption. All kinds of other objects may be
> substituted here for the washing machine as signifying element. In the
> logic of signs, as in that of symbols, objects are no longer linked in any
> sense to a definite function or need. (76–7)

This typically postmodern approach is based on the removal or underestima-
tion of both the concrete social practices expressed and the meanings given to
this world of objects, as well as the relationships and material production processes, to the extent that the practices of use and contexts of production disappear or are relegated to the background (Appadurai 1986). As a consequence,
social relationships and commodities are reduced to an automatic adherence
to the messages conveyed by adverts. The subject in this vision is reduced to
a spectator-user of the signs and images offered up by advertising discourse,
from which a series of contradictions are inherited. Within this vision, in fact,
the processes of constructing a postmodern identity are nothing but a mirror
of the paradoxical logic of consumption, which implies the potentially infinite
stimulation of desires, destined to remain systematically unsatisfied in the
face of the limited purchasing power of consumers. It is a logic that, on the
one hand, induces a need to differentiate oneself in order to celebrate one's
uniqueness and, on the other, allows one to express this uniqueness through
consumption and thus has mass-produced goods as a reference point. Subjects
must "perform their identity through commodities as difference from commodities" (Sassatelli 2007, 150). That is "consumers are encouraged to acquire
and display material possessions in order to feel differentiated from others,
and advertising promotes products and brands in such a way that their perceptions of uniqueness are enhanced. [...] the idea that uniqueness can be
achieved through mass-produced and mass-consumed goods is a paradox in
and of itself." (Dittmar 2007, 212–13).

These paradoxes have been expressed using different formulas, which all
refer to the field of both collective and individual pathology: generalized

hysteria (Baudrillard), schizophrenia (Jameson), narcissism (Lasch) or bulimia (Bordo). Even when it is explicitly argued that postmodernism is now the only possible historical horizon, it seems to return often to a nostalgic image of "modern" processes of identification, conceived of as being exclusively based on work and in which there could be an original and undistorted relationship with objects. It is only within this undistorted context could "real" needs be satisfied.

> The best defenses against the terrors of existence are the homely com-
> forts of love, work, and family life, which connect us to a world that is
> independent of our wishes yet responsive to our needs. It is through love
> and work, as Freud noted in a characteristically pungent remark, that we
> exchange crippling emotional conflict for ordinary unhappiness.
>
> LASCH 1979, 248

This approach is based on a contradiction that was thought to be unresolvable between work and consumption, desire and need, use value and exchange value. The former are conceived of as deep and the latter as superficial: "the dominance of surface over substance must be overcome. There must be a reconciliation of image and meaning, a reinvigoration of a politics of substance." (Ewen 1988, 271) Yet, while acknowledging that the logic of work and consumption tend to clash, we argue that they should not be thought of as two separate spheres that belong to completely different and opposing logics. This same contradiction, in fact, inherits and revives both the Smithian and Hegelian vision of work as a dilation of desire, and consumption as the realm of (always partial) satisfaction of desires sustained by advertising discourse. Instead, we maintain that the two logics present a much more complex relationship: consider for example that consumption is very often configured as a form of unpaid domestic work, rather than the fulfillment of the realm of desire (Sassatelli 2007).

As mentioned earlier, we propose looking at these oppositions from an epistemological point of view: they all share a rigid interpretation of the relationship between appearance and reality, between true and false. For these authors, postmodernism represents a full awareness that representation can no longer faithfully correspond to the represented and the modern is nostalgically viewed as that historical moment in which such a correspondence was still possible; the era of grand narratives and of the profound as opposed to the surface of things. Not surprisingly, Bell, one of the most lucid interpreters of postmodernity, discusses the transition towards postmodernity in terms of a "crisis of distance," that is, a crisis of the model which, beginning with the

invention of the Renaissance perspective, permitted a "faithful" reproduction
of reality.

3   Postmodernism: between an "Eclipse of Distance" and Pastiche

What does Bell mean by an "eclipse of distance"? Influenced by Meyer Schapiro
[1904–1996], Bell analyzes modernism – the connotations of which more closely
resemble what we tend to call "postmodernism" and are part of the analysis of
what he calls post-industrial society – through the concept of style. Bell believes
modernity can't be defined by means of a single principle. Modernity is characterized by variety and syncretism, whereas classical western culture was based
on continuity and tradition. "Modernity – he writes – has been defined as 'the
tradition of the new'" (Bell 1976, 100), but an interesting aspect of his apocalyptic neoconservative[3] view of Postmodernism is his observation that "there
is no center; there are only peripheries" in contemporary times. (104) It is a
world in which the visual prevails and where dramatization dominates over
conceptualization above all. This type of dominance has ousted depth as distance which was what distinguished the Renaissance in particular with Leon
Battista Alberti's [1404–1472] theory on linear perspective. "The painting of the
Renaissance – Bell writes – in the principles laid down by Alberti, was 'rational'
not only in that it applied formal mathematical principles to the depiction of
a scene (e.g., the role of proportion and perspective), but also in that it sought
to translate into art a rational cosmography of space as depth, and time as
sequence." (108) Bell refers to the famous *De pictura* from *1435*, the book that
inaugurated high definition in the human faculty and capacity to reproduce
images and that exerted enormous influence throughout western culture and
beyond. In this book, Alberti combines the well-known image of a window
to give a sense of framing with the mathematical method by which he taught
the reproduction of images on a two-dimensional plain while giving the illusion of depth (i.e., the third dimension).[4] According to perspective theorists,
the frame had a fundamental epistemological and conceptual importance. It

---

3   Ceserani (1997) links the apocalyptic and neoconservative vision of *Postmodernism* that Bell
    has with that of Toynbee and Wright Mills, as well as, from a different perspective, that of
    Baudrillard.
4   The following year, 1436, he published the vernacular version of the book dedicated to Filippo
    Brunelleschi. Brunelleschi, together with Donatello and Masaccio, laid the foundations in
    Florence during the 15th century which, about two centuries later, with Descartes, would lead
    to modernity.

is what delimits the window and, consequently, what gives meaning to the representation. What lies within the window enclosed by the frame is a construction based on the illusion of depth which, in turn, is organized through geometric measurements. We are particularly interested in pointing out how all of this was already present in Alberti's *De pictura*, where the centrality of man was offered, from a philosophical point of view by Protagoras' saying that man is the measure of all things, and from a visual point of view by the vanishing point. It was thus a "modern" subjectivity at the time that would later have further and more conscious expressions (think of Descartes for example [1596–1650]).

In Bell there is a nostalgia for the rational and severe lost world of the Renaissance, where there was correspondence between worlds, where a foreground was geometrically inscribed, thanks to the device of the frame, in linear perspective and depicted in the instances of a temporal sequence in progression. Underneath all this was a fundamental cosmological image: "depth, the projection of a three-dimensional space, created an 'interior distance' which provided a simulation of the real world; narrative, with the idea of a beginning, a middle, and an end, gave a chronological chain to sequence, providing a sense of progression and conclusion."(Bell 1976, 109) In this perfect, utopian world of the past, the spectator created *theoria*, and *this* meant distancing oneself from an object or experience which allowed one to establish the time and space necessary to absorb and judge one or the other.

After many centuries, the epistemological and aesthetic scenario inaugurated by Alberti acquired an epistemological awareness with Paul Cézanne [1839–1906]. Cézanne rejected *mimesis,* but above all did so without depth at least in terms of distance: "in his aesthetics, he made the famous dictum that all the structures of the real world are variations on the three basic solids, the cube, the sphere, and the cone. And his pictorial space was organized in planes to emphasize one or another of these forms." Painting was therefore no longer an illusion of depth of the third dimension over the other two, "but a single surface in which the element of immediacy was dominant."(111) From a cognitive rather than aesthetic point of view, according to Bell, we were witnessing a passage, later affirmed by the Cubists in the wake of Cézanne, from a single point of view to a multiplicity of viewpoints and from the interpretation of a scene to feeling it emotionally. All this was disrupted by what he calls Modernism but which, as mentioned before, can be identified with Postmodernism. The impression it gives is that while the Renaissance conception of rationalism was based on the prevalence of correspondence and depth, in Postmodernism emotion and sensation prevail. Although Bell never explicitly quotes Walter

Benjamin [1892–1940], he clearly takes up his analysis of modernity as an age of novelty and the experience of shock.

As a consequence, Bell identifies the decay in Postmodernism with the end of correspondence, depth, and distance and the rise of immediacy, sensation, and emotion. "The eclipse of distance, as an aesthetic, sociological, and psychic fact, means that for human beings, and for the organization of thought, there are no boundaries, no ordering principles of experience and judgment. Time and space no longer form the coordinates of a home for modern men." (119) The idea that depth must be associated with distance, an idea that Jameson would resume despite having opposite political intentions from Bell, represents the collapse of one of the cornerstones of Modernity. Jameson addressed the issue of depth in *Postmodernism* by underlining how the contemporary age, both narcissistic and self-referential, has lost the concept of depth that is schematized into five points: 1) inside-outside; 2) essence-appearance; 3) latent-manifest; 4) authenticity-inauthenticity; 5) Signifier-Signified (Jameson 1991). These are well-known polarities which, when seen in this light, presuppose the idea of oppositions based on the relationship of distance between foreground and background precisely in the perspective terms defined by Alberti and the Renaissance. This relationship was linked to the opposition between true/false. If we view these oppositions within a conception of depth characterized by distance, then the external, the apparent, the manifest, the inauthentic, and the signified may all represent the deceptive aspect of their opposites essentially in Platonic terms. By placing the external, the apparent, the manifest, the inauthentic, and the signified in the foreground their truth lies in the depths of their opposites where a correspondence between representation and reality might finally be realized. Skipping this scenario, the alternative, according to Jameson, is *pastiche*, a term he borrows from Adorno and which, in its blank emptiness, constitutes the perfect expression of advanced post-industrial and post-modern capitalism, where countries "are now a field of stylistic and discursive heterogeneity without a norm" (Jameson 1991, 17). For Jameson, *pastiche* corresponds to *simulacrum* (cf. Gilles Deleuze, Baudrillard and before that Guy Debord [1931–1994]), that is the copy of an original that never existed (Plato). Jameson writes: "the culture of the simulacrum comes to life in a society where exchange value has been generalized to the point at which the very memory of use value is effaced, a society of which Guy Debord has observed, in an extraordinary phrase, that in it 'the image has become the final form of commodity reification.'" (18) *Pastiche* thus implies the loss of history at the same moment it becomes an imitation of ironically juxtaposed texts or images or music.

In this scenario Jameson concludes: "all modern culture [...] tends to turn upon itself and designate its own cultural production as its content." (42) This is made possible by the loss of *depth* in contemporary culture and the tendency of exchange value to erase the memory of use value. He, like Baudrillard, argues that exchange value becomes so autonomous it no longer requires use value, an idea which, we have tried to argue, is based on the theory of knowledge that identifies depth with distance. But can use value ever be *completely* erased? Our hypothesis is that Marx never intended as much, not because he remained anchored to the dichotomy of essence-appearance (which Jameson identified as a characteristic of Modernity), but because there was not necessarily a contraposition between depth and surface and he did not necessarily associate depth with distance – not even in the theory of commodity fetishism.

4   Things "Appear as What They Are"

In postmodernism, the fetish character of commodities has increased their aesthetic power. A commodity has a dual function: it must be useful and it must be exchangeable. It is the result of two social processes: a commodity is produced by cooperative labor and it is saleable, in that it incorporates social value, which, in a capitalist society, is exchange value. The social-symbolic is incorporated into the exchange value. When the exchange value exceeds the use value, the aesthetic dimension of the object has the better of the cooperative – working process that produces the use value. The spectacle of the commodity hides the labor and the character absorbs the actor(s) within itself and cancels them. It is this absorption of the actor by the character that gives this sense of fetishism to the commodity. But how does this substitution process take place? In relation to commodity fetishism, Marx underlines how things "appear as what they are." (Marx 1996, 84) We can then deduce that the critical analysis the young Marx developed with Engels on ideology and false consciousness, in the case of commodity fetishism, should not be included, as mentioned above, in the "appearance-essence" dichotomy, and is therefore not part of that concept of *depth* that characterized Modernity for Jameson. Marx, with regard to commodities and their fetish character, has a concept of depth compatible with the statement that things "appear as what they are." In fact, use value and exchange value are both on the surface, overlapping and intersecting. A commodity in its phantasmagorical form is not based on the metaphor of distance and, above all, is not based on the concept of truth in which its essence lies behind it, so to speak, hidden by appearances and which, for this reason, assimilates appearance as a deceptive illusion and, consequently, creates the illusion of deception. On the contrary, if "things appear as what they are," then truth is to be found in the interweaving of appearances, just as depth must be discovered on the surface.

The relationship between use value and exchange value, between the object and the commodity, we repeat, has nothing to do with the modern dichotomies of depth indicated by Jameson.[5] In the section on "the character of fetish and its arcane," Marx points out that the most suitable analogy for understanding the fetishism of commodities is not the dark room, which he had already evoked with Engels in *German Ideology*, but instead religion, a phantasmagorical form which does not reverse the image, but precisely by representation, *exceeds* what is being represented by representing it again. What exceeds does not reverse itself but distorts, finding resemblance in what is different (Merleau-Ponty 1964). The use value is hidden in the exchange value as depth is hidden on the surface, in the sense that it is invisible and visible at the same time. Exchange value manifesting itself as use value and thus representing it, almost exceeds it according to the terms in which, as defined by Richard Wollheim [1923–2003] regarding Walter Pater, a representation exceeds the thing represented by representing it (Wollheim 1974). In this there is no distance, there is no concealment, there is no essence distant and hidden from appearance. There is no copy without the original, there is no simulacrum: it is in the exchange value that we must look for the use value, just as the invisible must be sought within the visible. Applying the status of falsehood to the fetishism of commodity, by identifying appearance with falsehood and essence with truth, is an error. The truth is in the interweaving of appearances, the invisible found within the visible.

Social relationships "appear as what they are": relationships among things between people, and social relationships among things. Commodities therefore conceal nothing. If the world appears upside down then there is no essence hidden behind the deceptive appearance, but nor is there a simulacrum, a copy without an original, a representation without a referent. Use value has not disappeared, it has become the servant of exchange value and, as such, has separated itself from the human cooperation (social labor) that produced it. In fact, Marx states that the commodity becomes something sensitively *supersensible* (*sinnliche übersinnlichen Ding*). He uses this expression

---

5 When Marx envisions a society of associated free producers, he invokes the transparency of relationships between people and things. It is here that his ambivalence arises, and he contradicts himself. Transparency does not eliminate the opacity of relations even when a society of free cooperators rather than a society of spectators, is established (he imagines that it will be established).

"sensitively supersensible" upon mentioning the dancing table of the séances that was fashionable at that time and which were also object of Flaubert's irony in *Bouvard and Pécouchet*. We find the concept of "supersensible" in Kant, in Schiller, in Hegel, but in *Capital* it theatrically sums up the relationship created between *use value* and *exchange value* or, to put it differently, the intertwining of the material and immaterial dimensions of an object that becomes a commodity. Jacques Derrida [1930–2004] plays on the spectral aspect of the commodity, but the idea of something supersensible which is also *sensuous*, more than something spectral, seems to lead to a body or a face that is deceiving, by presenting and hiding at the same time an alterity. The image of the ghost recalls the theme of the *simulacrum*, that is, of a copy that has no original and therefore no referent. However, when Marx refers to the table as a commodity that is "sensitively supersensible," placing emphasis on the adverb "sensitively," he emphasizes materiality, that is, a referent that is not an original, but a support that cannot but presuppose a corporeal dimension. What, then, is meant here by "immaterial"?

David Harvey underlines two characteristics of value: that is it both in motion and immaterial. As such, capital flows are compared to the water cycle and its immateriality refers to its definition as *socially necessary labour time*. This implies forms of social relationships that cannot be empirically measured: "Historical materialism, Harvey writes, recognizes the importance of immaterial but objective powers of this sort. We typically appeal to them to account for the collapse of the Berlin Wall, the election of Donald Trump, feelings of national identity or the desire of indigenous populations to live according to their own cultural norms. We describe features such as power, influence, belief, status, loyalty and social solidarity in immaterial terms. Value, for Marx, is exactly such a concept." (Harvey 2018, 5) Harvey cites a passage from Marx's *Grundrisse* to sustain his theory: "it then again occurs to them that capital is in one respect *value*, i.e. something *immaterial*, indifferent to its physical consistency"(Marx 1986, 235).[6]

In this case immateriality is specified by the fact that the *value* is uninterested in the matter. In other words, it is safe to say that *value* as an *exchange value* is immaterial because it is uninterested in *use value*. The unconcern of exchange value towards use value does not at all mean that exchange value has

---

6   Marx quotes Jean-Baptiste Say (the quotation is in French): "*Le capital est toujours d'une essence immaterielle,* puisque ce n'est pas la matiere qui fait le capital, mais la valeur *de* cette matiere, valeur qui n'a rien de corporel" (*Traité d'économie politique,* 3rd ed., vol. II, Paris, p. 429 – "*Capital is always immaterial by nature,* since it is not matter which makes capital, but the value of that matter, value which has nothing corporeal about it").

lost its material dimension, instead it means that it arises abstractly in relation to any possible use value. In any case, it cannot help but have a relationship with use value. Essentially, exchange value never loses its use value referent, even if the latter may vary. The word immaterial is defined as that which keeps a relationship with what is material and does not disappear in the mists of the spirit. It is true, as indicated by Harvey, that realities such as power or belief are immaterial, but it is also true that they exist only when they are defined in a material way. Power and belief are in the same situation in Plato's triangle which can be thought of as an idea, but which can only be represented as *that* triangle someone draws on a piece of paper. As Bateson says, immaterial information depends on the difference that exists between the white color of the paper and the blue of the ink but the immaterial idea of *difference*, which provides us information, is ensured by the paper and ink which are material. To represent Power, it is always *that* power with material supports (the throne, the crown, the tiara). To represent belief, it is *that* belief equipped with material supports (voice, language, writing, recording).

From this point of view, commodity as exchange value becomes fetish when the material and immaterial exchange roles and social relationships become objectified as things. It is no longer immaterial exchange value that has material use-value as its referent, but it is material use-value that represents immaterial exchange value. The commodity appropriates the social relationships that produced it and therefore enters the scene.

5   Depth Is Hidden on the Surface

If we consider the scenario used by Marx to explain the magic of commodity by referencing the dancing tables by means of the definition "sensitively supersensible," then perhaps we can better understand the sense of the analogy proposed by Aldo Giorgio Gargani [1933–2009], between the fetish character of the commodity described by Marx and language and, more generally, the question of the intertwining of the material and immaterial. Although Gargani never directly addressed the question of postmodernism, his research denounced that specific condition of the crisis of modernity that simultaneously announced itself as postmodernity.

With respect to the complex intertwining of the material and immaterial, Gargani never gave up the idea that the immaterial always has something material as its basis and referent: "Similarly," he writes, "the materials of language are vibrations of the air or some other physical medium, or, for example, ink blots on paper; however, as soon as these physical quantities come to constitute, through the rules of formation and transformation arranged by use, a language, they are no longer mere vibrations of a physical medium, nor mere ink marks on paper, but they become objects provided with a meaning, they rise to that statute of logical sublimation in which a material object is crossed by the vital breath of meaning; also for these objects we could say that the incomparable event of a 'sensibly supersensible property' has taken place."(Gargani 1975, 43–4) In other words, according to Gargani, the uses and decisions acquired by a community, the behaviors of people within a determined form of life, that is, the "constructive conditions"(Gargani 1975, 44) that have transformed physical and material means into the symbols of language, present themselves as distorted in the object form as if they were the internal properties of symbolism. The use of language is crystallized in the meaning and the latter is presented as an internal property of symbolism that takes the form of an object model that is characterized according to the grammar of object-designation. Therefore, the uses of language that depend on the forms of life and their history are presented as objective data, as fetish, as something that stands in the place of something else and in so doing distorts it. But not because it stands in the background, nor because it is enough to remove the veil creating the distortion in order to find correctness of knowing and the foundation of truth – Nietzsche reminds us that truths are metaphors which we have forgotten how to use – but because in our acting, doing, deciding we forget that use is the Marxian result of social histories or Wittgensteinian forms of life.

Gargani moved in the wake of research that sought another kind of depth: not the rejection of reason but the search for a different way of representing it. An awareness of the possibility that both meanings and commodities can take on the characteristics of fetish should not, however, lead one to regret a supposedly original state of full correspondence nor seek out a way to restore its foundations. At this point in our journey, it is important to clarify: once the claim of achieving a perfect correspondence between representation and reality is revealed to be illusory, that is, once the fetishistic character of the foundations are recognized, it is not a question of finding others that are cleansed of fetishization, and neither should everything be reduced to information, difference, or language, as is the case with certain strands of postmodern thought. Our thesis is that the typical postmodern opposition between depth-as-distance and acceptance of the juxtaposition of disparate elements (*pastiche*) is actually a false dichotomy: it is possible to identify another kind of depth, one that is not tied to either an ultimate foundation or distance.

The problem concerns the forms of relationships, the ways in which elements are ordered, arranged, and organized. Linear perspective is a model of pictorial relationship that generates a 3D illusion of depth on the two-dimensional surface of a painting, which produces *a type of* depth. *Pastiche is a kind of* relationship that produces a collection of elements juxtaposed on the same plain. Depth has to do with pictorial perspective, with distance, with the appearance-essence relationship, with the idea of the future. *Pastiche* abolishes perspective, distance, and future by placing everything on the same (two-dimensional) plain. According to Jameson, and Bell too, once distance disappears, it is necessary to renounce depth as well in that it is linked to a linear perspective. Yet, depth is a relationship that does not necessarily need distance, at least not in the terms established by linear perspective and so not in the terms indicated by Bell. In fact, as Raymond Ruyer [1902–1987], and with him Maurice Merleau-Ponty [1908–1961], showed, the problem of depth is axiological, it is related to value, and consequently does not have to be related to distance. As discussed above, Bell affirmed how the "crisis of distance" that characterizes postmodernism is realized on an artistic level with Cézanne: which was, according to him, the end of depth and the dominance of immediacy and the multiplication of points of view. However, Bell does not realize that Cézanne, by refusing depth as distance in the terms paradigmatically given by Alberti, does not dissolve it at all, but seeks another form of depth no longer associated with distance. This search can be thought of as an attempt to identify *a* different *kind of* depth linked to overlapping – an expression used by Merleau-Ponty and Rudolf Arnheim [1904–2007]: a different kind of relationship from both the depth linked to distance and to juxtaposition.

The idea of overlapping unhinges the opposition between appearance and reality: depth is to be sought not elsewhere, nor far away, nor beyond what appears, but, as Cézanne in his Montagne Sainte-Victoire, in the interweaving of appearances, because the invisible lies in the networks of the visible just as exploitation, in Marxian terms, can be found in the plots of commodity and its visibility. For Cézanne, in fact, depth does not lie in the background, but in the fabric that constitutes, one might say, what is seen in the foreground. The difference between representation and the represented does not consist in a spatial relationship between front and back, foreground and background, but rather in a relationship where depth lies on the surface in an overlap. In this case, representation is not *less than* something which is *more* – the original – nor is it something autonomous from the original (copy without an original: simulacrum), rather it is something *more* that depends on the relationship with what is *less* (i.e. the original). In this way Cézanne and the Impressionists questioned *the forms of representation* hidden in the illusion of perspective, and thus showed the conventional, but not arbitrary, character of the organization of visual space into foreground and background. It is a depth that reveals the constructive act of the observer who, guided by the artist, decides what is in the foreground and what is in the background. It is a depth without distance. In this sense, overlapping does not conceal the conventional nature of the distinction between foreground and background: what is "foreground" for one social group or culture may represent a background element for another culture. Therefore, in the concept of overlapping, the social and political character of this distinction is made explicit, without denying its cognitive specificity; it is always possible to reverse the relationship through a "Gestalt switch" and move what was previously in the background to the foreground (Zerubavel 2015).

Overlapping makes the relationship between surface and depth more complex, because it breaks identification of the surface with appearance and of depth with essence (or foundation): it even paints the surface with essence, and appearance is no longer only appearance. If then, depth is in the textures of the surface, truth is not beyond appearance or what is visible, but rather hidden in plain sight (to borrow the title of Eviatar Zerubavel's (2015) book.) Italo Calvino [1923–1985] also expressed a similar concept in his *Six Memos* in which he quotes a phrase from Hugo von Hofmannsthal [1874–1929]: "Depth must be hidden. Where? On the surface." He had already had *Palomar* say: "only after having known the surface of things ... can one push oneself to look for what lies beneath. But the surface of things is inexhaustible." (Calvino 1999, 51). Calvino puts together Hofmannsthal's phrase with a statement from Ludwig Wittgenstein's [1889–1951] *Philosophical Researches*: "what is hidden ... is of no interest to us." However, he says he does not wish to be so drastic: "I think we are always searching for something hidden or merely potential or hypothetical, following its traces whenever they appear on the surface [...] The word connects the visible trace with the invisible thing, the absent thing, the thing that is desired or feared, like a frail emergency bridge flung over an abyss." (1988, 77). Clearly Calvino's problem is the relationship between words and things, between language and reality, between surface and depth, continuously trying to preserve their dialectical tension.

References

Appadurai, Arjun, ed. 1986. *The Social Life of Things. Commodities in Cultural Perspectives.* Cambridge: University Press.

Baudrillard, Jean. 1998. *The Consumer Society: Myths and Structures.* Reprinted. Theory, Culture & Society. Los Angeles, CA: SAGE.

Bell, Daniel. 1976. *The Cultural Contradictions of Capitalism.* New York: Basic Books.

Benjamin, Walter. 2007. *Illuminations*. Translated by Harry Zohn. New York: Schocken Books.

Blumer, Herbert. 1969. *Symbolic Interactionism: Perspective and Method*. Berkeley, CA: University of California Press.

Calvino, Italo. 1988. *Six memos for the next millennium*. Cambridge: Harvard University Press.

Calvino, Italo. 1999. *Mr Palomar*. London: Vintage.

Ceserani, Remo. 1997. *Raccontare Il Postmoderno*. Torino: Bollati Boringhieri.

Dittmar, Helga. 2007. *Consumer Culture, Identity and Well-Being: The Search for the "Good Life" and the "Body Perfect."* Hove and New York: Psychology Press.

Ewen, Stuart. 1988. *All Consuming Images. The Politics of Style in Contemporary Culture*. New York: Basic Books.

Franzini, Elio. 2018. *Moderno e postmoderno: un bilancio*. Saggi. Milano: Raffaello Cortina editore.

Galbraith, John Kenneth. 1972. *The New Industrial State*. New York: New American Library.

Gargani, Aldo Giorgio. 1975. *Il sapere senza fondamenti*. Torino: Einaudi.

Harvey, David. 2018. *Marx, Capital and the Madness of Economic Reason*. Oxford: University Press.

Iacono, Alfonso Maurizio. 2016. *The History and Theory of Fetishism*. New York: Palgrave Macmillan.

Iofrida, Manlio. 2019. *Per un paradigma del corpo: una rifondazione filosofica dell'ecologia*. Macerata: Quodlibet.

Jameson, Fredric. 1991. *Postmodernism. Or the Cultural Logic of Late Capitalism*. Durham, NC: Duke University Press.

Lasch, Christopher. 1979. *The Culture of Narcissism: American Life in an Age of Diminishing Expectations*. New York: Norton & Company.

Lunt, Peter, and Sonia Livingstone. 1992. *Mass Consumption and Personal Identity*. Buckingham: Open University Press.

Marx, Karl. 1986. "Economic Manuscript of 1857–1858." In *Marx Engels Collected Works*. Vol. 28. London: Lawrence and Wishart.

Marx, Karl. 1996. "Capital Volume I." In *Marx Engels Collected Works*. Vol. 35. London: Lawrence and Wishart.

Merleau-Ponty, Maurice. 1964. "Eye and Mind." In *The Primacy of Perception: And Other Sssays on Phenomenological Psychology, the Philosophy of Art, History and Politics*, edited by James M. Edie, translated by Carleton Dallery, 159–90. Evanston, IL: Northwestern Univ. Press.

Sassatelli, Roberta. 2007. *Consumer Culture: History, Theory and Politics*. Los Angeles: SAGE Publications.

Sennett, Richard. 1976. *The Fall of Public Man*. Cambridge: University Press.

Susen, Simon. 2015. *The Postmodern Turn in the Social Sciences*. Basingstoke: Palgrave Macmillan.

Wollheim, Richard. 1974. "Walter Pater as a Critic of the Arts." In *On Art and Mind*, edited by Richard Wollheim, 155–76. Cambridge: Harvard University Press.

Zerubavel, Eviatar. 2015. *Hidden in Plain Sight: The Social Structure of Irrelevance*. New York: Oxford University Press.

CHAPTER 6

Method, History, and Society

The Main Road by Werner Sombart

Roberta Iannone

1   History and Sociology: a Long Story

"History is blind without sociology and sociology is empty without history."
We all know this methodological aphorism (Topitsch 1975, 110), as we all know
that, as Braudel stated (2003, 89), sociology and history represent "an only
adventure within the soul"?

Still, when dealing with statements everybody knows, they will hardly be
obvious, accepted by the totality of people, or uniformly understandable and
understood. To say, people will hardly forget that the dialogue between historians and sociologists is an "of deaf" one (Burke 1982, 8)[1] On the other hand,
we must not forget that in the past, sociology, and historiography "absurdly
divorced" (Pellicani 2005, 9), especially in Italy.

Thus, although a clean, irreconcilable break between history and sociology
would nowadays be considered by (luckily) most of the people as an "epistemological blasphemy" (Pellicani 2005, 10), historians and sociologists are still
continuing to try and sabotage this "wedding between subjects." Such liaison
is continually being jeopardized, especially as for sociology, by a reading oriented towards present and tending to melt with the most trivial survey.

In such cases, "contingency" stops being an era or the last segment of modernity to become culture, science and to look like a methodological, mainly
epistemological soul of scientific theory and research. In such cases, "contingency" does not only look like a breakthrough (Mongardini 2009), a new cultural, social, psychological and political dimension of our times. Nor it simply
becomes the new condition of action and decision, in its causes and effects,
willing to cancel the weight and the role of history, of past, of the stream of
social change, but it rather becomes a cognitive paradigm.

---

1   Here Burke (1982, 8) quotes the famous statement by Braudel "Sociology and history do not
    speak the same language yet. The resulting dialogue is, as stated by Ferdinand Braudel, an 'of
    deaf' one."

When this happens, far be it from effectively combatting the astray from a scientific point of view, sociology, rather a certain sociology, adapts to it and even accommodates in the blind tunnel of moment, refurbishing and making it look better through readings, which might be evocative but lack in historical breath.

Still, in such a moment – when contingency turns into era, zipping time into the current culture – sociology should reflect on the limits and dangers of this late modern condition and favor both critical and historical readings about social change. On the other hand, turning contingency into sociology interpretative criterion, does not only mean foreclosing, from the very root, every deep knowledge of social phenomena, but even distorting sociology from its original ratio, from its intimate nature of grammar through which reading the big history book and turning it into an "interdisciplinary subject" rather than into a mere "self-subject."

On the other hand, this is how sociology originates. "Sociology rises when social change turns into matter. And the matter with social change can only be analyzed following an historical retrospective" (Orsini 2005, 17). This is the inheritance from sociology, but this is, most of all, the inheritance from Werner Sombart and German historicism.

2   On the Traces of Werner Sombart

The famous "debate on the method" which, starting from mid-19th century involved and somehow kept an eye on almost all historical and social sciences – since, as we all know, not only did it aim at defining the specific task of each and any of them, but also the effectiveness of the related research procedures – established a more "advanced," "proper" border for each and any of the above mentioned sciences, and in particular for historiography and economy, but it even gave life to our subject as we know it today, to say a not merely positivist sociology. As we all know, this occurred when German culture refused English and French Positivism, which was not sociology as such. At that point, as highlighted by Pietro Rossi (1956), two different paths could possibly be taken: surrendering to the obvious lack of such subject or founding it on new grounds. In other words, refusing 'that one' sociology and declaring the death of tout court sociology. Such solution was coherent with the assumptions of a historical school which had always been trying to make every social science flow into historiography and history understanding; or "defining the setting sociology can take and its links with historiography and social sciences following other bases" (Rossi 1956, 12).

No doubt Sombart expresses the latter vision and there might even be no need to clarify it, as this was an uncompromising element of his works. His relationship with history was so central that, besides being remembered as economist and sociologist, he was considered as a historian even at his time. During a speech he gave in 1917 on Scholler's death, he clearly stated that a knowledge "Which does not have its roots into the maternal alveolus of philosophy and history is a cognition connected to a purpose, a knowledge, a technology which cannot aim at being noble Science" (quote in Kellenbenz 1964, 11).

With these words, Sombart meant to remind of the example given by Schmoller but, as Kellenbenz (1964) points out, these words remind of the example of Sombart himself.

So, the reasons why Sombart called himself a historian, were deeper than the self-evident ones produced by Savous, that is to say "because he focused on past facts" (quote in Sapori 1955, 1094), and as Armando Sapori pointed out, he called himself "historian" and asked history scholars to call him that way. During a famous congress held in Pisa in 1933 he said:

> [...] Italy is where I found a comprehension higher than anywhere else. I found it in Luzzato first of all: not only he translated my *Capitalism,* he also called it history work with no restrictions. Italian judgement, which did not leave a bitter taste in my mouth, came from documents stored into your rich files: isn't constantly criticizing a work through a document considering it a history work?.
>
> Quoted in SAPORI 1944, 16–7

3   Werner Sombart and Historical Sociology

Detecting historical sociology in the mare magnum of Sombart production might lead to two different issue orders:
1.   Historical – geneticist classification;
2.   The relationship between theory and history through an interdisciplinary path.

3.1   *Historical – Geneticist Classification*
As for the first point, in *Soziologie* (Sombart 1936), his most important essay dedicated to Sociology, Sombart provides a *historical-geneticist classification of the subject* which is interesting as it places "historical trend" among sociology founding trends, close to:

- giusnaturalistic and normative trend;
- sociology as natural science (and hence fiscalism, biologism and psychologism);
- philosofical sociology;
- formal sociology
- what he himself calls "German sociology."

He traces both limits and credits for each and any of the above. The one Sombart calls "German" sociology is interesting, as it provides elements of historical sociology even before the author calls it so.

Considering that Sombart attributes "German sociology" to three founding fathers, namely von Mohl, von Stein and Marx, which is the limit of such trend that reconciles history even though it is not historical sociology? Sombart answers it has limits as:

1. in some cases, it is all about "social history" rather than sociology (as in the case of Stein and Marx' s theories about capitalism).

2. elsewhere, rather than practicing sociology, metaphysics (which he considers as bad) is put in action (as when historical criteria are adopted as general principles).

3. in further cases, social theories are partial or incomplete, despite their sociological effectiveness, if considered as "categories of the historical movement."

Social history, metaphysics, incompleteness, and partiality are thus little by little defining themselves as risks historical sociology should beware of.

Nonetheless, Sombart still thinks that actual historical trend or sociology – as orientation setting the different structural conditions of society in chronological order – is something different. It was present when the subject was born and even before, in the ideas of Smith, Ferguson and Millar, its English forerunners and in the French ones as well, namely Montesquieu and Condorcet, to get to its highest peak in the 20th century, when sociology became a different way to make history (see Mongardini 1970).

Considering the above, we can say that Sombart sees sociology as a different way to make history.

When thinking about his contemporaries, Sombart says that Alfred Weber was the one who "saw the cultural process as independent from the social one and from the civilization process" (Allodi 1986, 259).

However, such tributes did not prevent Sombart from setting the limits of the historical orientation of his time, and tended to make sociography out of sociology, depriving it from its side of theoretical science of social phenomena.

3.2   *The Relationship between Theory and History Through an Interdisciplinary Path*

The relationship between theory and history is the fundamental nucleus through which the Author frames historical sociology. Or rather, the junction through which Sombart frames tout court sociology, through the debate over method and the more general insertion of such reflections oriented towards the knowledge Vico forerun. We are referring to the cognitive attitude which will give contents to the discussion on historiography of 19th and 20th century and on Italian and German historicism.

Such relationship between history and theory was clarified by Vico through an interdisciplinary road starting from history, going through economy, and getting to sociology.

It starts from history since, as we know, Sombart's thought was deep inside the division which shifted, on the one hand, the representatives of theory economy, and on the other the representatives of the young historic school of economy, to say on the one hand people who claimed the need to use very general, deductive method and on the other those who claimed the importance of the particular and of the inductive method: to say the division between Wagner and Schmoller followers.

As we know, Sombart, attended meetings given by both and, together with M. Weber, he would have to overcome such dichotomies, both on a methodological and of concrete research level, and we can say that the way to sociology was led by overcoming such dichotomy between history and economy.

No doubt he made a constant effort to make a connection between the two links, or overcome such dualism believing that

> Historiography which does not mean to be mere fact telling, cannot help using a theory – conceptual system, while sociology which does not want to build abstract theory buildings, cannot help placing its statements on a certain space – time context.
>
> Treccani Online Encyclopedia 2020,
> http://www.treccani.it/enciclopedia/sociologia/

Such approach is likely to have led to science even before sociology as the author thought that (he himself wrote it, quoting Aristotle) "nulla scientia nisi de universalibus": making science always means particularly focusing on universal categories, otherwise it is not science but scientific descriptivism (Allodi 1986, 266).

If we limited to the fundamental aspects of such theory and history path originating from history and economy and ending into sociology, they could be summed up as follows:

1. first of all, Sombart reverses the relationship classic scholars set between theory and empiria: to classic scholars who stated that "concrete economics comes in to supplement the pure economics" (following Keynes), Sombart opposes the conviction that economic theory is not an end in itself, but it explains concrete economy, as the very essence justifying an economic science is "understanding," the *verstehen*, man's life within community, and such problem cannot be faced, we cannot make a science out of economic life without theory (Bruguier, quote in Sapori 1944, 31).

2. Secondly, he thinks about theory as critical theory.

    > It is not pure economy, which abstract laws are, as the laws of natural sciences, mere uniformity observation, then pseudo laws: it is a critical theory, *verstehende*, melting with historical reality through interpretative concepts, *Wesenbegriff*, in its essence, in the meaning of things, *Sinngesetz*, based on logical aprioristic relationships, effective for the building of rational schemes. (32)

3. If we were to find the concept/construct Sombart appoints for the creation of a connection point between theory and history, no doubt this would be the "economic system." A concept/construct Sombart will focus very much on, making it very peculiar, if not little explicable. Considering the above, we wonder why this Author is not mentioned amongst the founding fathers of the system sociological context (see De Nardis 1996).

It is a "system" that cannot be compared, *sic et simpliciter*, neither to the organicist conception inspired by Comte and Spencer, nor to the one inspired by Marx, nor to the one by Pareto, nor, finally to the functionalistic one by Parsons or to the systems general theory inspired by Luhmann.

Sombart states that, in comparison to the issue we are dealing with about the relationship between theory and history, the economic system can make history without setting theory apart. Sombart will say about his master Schmoller:

> The difference between me and him is the constructive element in the organization of the material, the radical premise of a unitary explanation, the structure of all historical events within a social system; in short, the specifically theorical element.
>
> CAVALLI 1967, 35

As Cavalli points out, Sombart did not miss the chance to argue with professional historians, the ones he called "members of the historians corporation" (35), who think they can deal with history without using theory. He rather thinks that

> Every human fact can have a historical meaning if it is considered as part of a whole, if it has its own place within a system. Reality does not foresee detached, isolated human facts, but each and any of them is a link in the chain, a simple unit within a series. History does not know single human facts as connected within systems, as enabling to appreciate theirs values (think about Roman Empire, Renaissance, etc.): history is always the study of a given phenomenon, but sees and evaluates the peculiarity of a fact only if it knows its unitary complex.
>
> BERTOLINO 1950, 344

Such unitary complex is then a "culture system," as the conjunctive tissue of historical facts is an idea in itself.

> As human mind shows off into the knowledge of reality in many fundamental forms, which make the great spheres of culture (such as Right, Art, Economy, State, etc.), historical facts cannot be understood unless they are given, through the complex they belong to, to a greater cultural system, in which they gain their ultimate meaning. (344)

Moreover, aimed at building economic history, such idea must be economic and not political, legal or of other nature, as Sombart thought.

Thus, to Sombart, the economic system deserves credit for catching and summing up the general aspects of historical facts and thus, the Author thinks it is a 'representative' category of economic facts within the historical stream (346): nonetheless, this does not oppose to the task of the historian to portray the individual, as he thinks that history cannot be made portraying only the individual, but even the general, to say: it can be made by catching general reality – the one Sombart calls "the never-individual reality" (347) in individuality. This is an interesting aspect, which is worth studying if we consider the best-known limit related to the concept of system, to say the one of static, conservative reading of social order, deprived of both conflict and power elements.

At this point, the difference Sombart makes between *individual* and *special* is interesting and such as, while special stands for the single event occurred once and which is not likely to occur again and so it is a pure individual fact, the individual fact is the one repeatedly occurring in time, and in a particular way; according to Sombart, such recurrence gives it a general aspect, although it is individual.

So, for the Author

> Rather than with special case, economic history mainly deals with frequent facts and situations somehow looking alike to each other and thus can be grouped together, given a common background, and treated as a whole.
>
> SOMBART, quote in BERTOLINO 1950, 347

Thus, according to Sombart, economic system would have many "credits": it would be both a conceptual and empiric category, one that would be both spiritual and material, both theorist and empiric, but it would be sociology most of all, passing through history and economy.

As Bertolino stated,

> the meaning of the statement by which economic history cannot be made without theory is more complex than the one coming from the meaning of the statement itself; as here we are seeking for help not only from economic theory, but from sociology as well.
>
> BERTOLINO 1950, 351

We know which limit critic saw into the concept of economic system given by Sombart: it is not always clear whether it can only be classified as "ideal type" in a Weber sense, and thus understood as mere methodological tool or, as clearly shown in the work *Die drei Nationaloekonomien* (1930), it is about the step M. Weber, unlike Sombart, never took, to say making such construct not only a knowledge tool, but even an "essence concept" (*wesenbegriffe*), able to catch the essence itself, the sense of phenomena.

Such aspect, as we know, is very discussed and exposed Sombart to the "metaphysic" critic (paradoxically the one he wanted to get the science rid of recalling facts and only facts). Scholars such as Cavalli think that would cancel the principle by which science cannot be evaluated. We could hardly disavow that Sombart always paid attention not to include into scientific research all those facts that, although looking science worth, were not, as they expressed value judgement. It is impossible not to remember that Sombart conceived metaphysics not together with the concept or reality of "essence," which are foundational to the comprehensive method, but where such essences are sought – as well as subjective and objective soul – outside the auditable experience. To say, using Sombart's words, "you aim at getting not the inherent sense of culture in its empiric giveness, but its transcendent sense, the sense of both humanity and the world" (Allodi 1986, 270).

Beyond such critics, it is mainly through the concept of economic system and its related soul (even with all its limits) that economic history detaches itself from every partial history (as it could be for the history of economic ideas, of technique and so on) to become "the history of the economic aspect of society" (Cavalli 1967, 41) and thus sociology. As for Sombart, from this perspective, sociology is everything but "the science of man social life, to which economy belongs to" (41).

4   No Theory, no History

What we stated should make clear that Sombart's sociology is placed at the meeting point of at least two translations of his thought, as Allodi shows:

> On the one hand, sociology cannot give up on its side of positive science, basing its knowledge on experience, *and thus it is till connected to the origins and to history* that characterizes it; on the other, it cannot give up to adapting to the particular object it studies, namely man as the method of nature science is not suitable to study him.
>
>   ALLODI 1986, 262

His "comprehensive economic science" comes from such crossroad and with it, on one side it overcomes the naturalism of classic economy, recovering the anthropological and cultural dimension of every economic phenomenon; on the other it bases its sociology, the so called *Noo-soziologie*.

Thus, sociology mainly comes from history and economy, but meanwhile and with no contradiction, it is an expression of that *science of culture* which is such as it studies phenomena based on "position" rather than "abstraction," to say within the context and the totality they belong to.

What happens to laws, then? They do not disappear; they rather change their features. They become sense sciences and among them – which he classifies as "irrational," "mathematic" and "essence" laws – the latter represent the essence of comprehensive sociology. Laws, or essence regularity, which are the ones referring to the link between *element* and *totality*, to say a needed link of a part to the totality (as it was for Husserl as well), and thus detect "the needed belonging to a given sense context, as the totality within soul is always connected to sense" (280).

In this context we need to read one of Sombart's most famous scientific anthems, to say "no theory, no history" to express the impossibility to detachedly follow either way. In this sense, Sombart methodology gets to:

- The impossibility to detect laws and regularity into the culture and society sphere
- The opportunity to deal with sociology as culture science starting from history and economy.

5   (Historical) Sociology as Science of Critical Soul

A methodological positivism, therefore, as he himself openly defines it in *Vom Menschen* (1938), invoking the 'facts' and intending a way to deal with reality denying the possibility that science can be practiced in relation to non-identifiable phenomena. But he is not subject to the traps and limits of positivism. On the contrary, he goes beyond and completely overcomes them when intending positivism in the light of naturalism and organism and, more generally, as the incorporation of the methods of the natural sciences into the social sciences. The whole work is based on the constant effort to go beyond the limits of a naïve reading of the organistic positivism, conceiving the spiritual activities of man according to the scheme of the natural becoming, and reducing the story of the spirit to a natural event. This type of interpretation was naïve as it caused positivism to betray itself and its own anti-metaphysical assumptions. By bringing back the consciousness, the aesthetic, the moral and the religious to incidental manifestations and epiphenomena of matter, it came to indulge perhaps in the coarsest metaphysic, the materialistic.[2]

Consequently, Sombart's work goes beyond positivism starting from positivism. He does that by reaping the benefits of an anti-positivist reaction begun in the late 19th century, which manifested itself in important theoretical objectifications by the early 20th century. This is the case of the neokantism and of the philosophy of values in Germany, of idealism in Italy, and of the assumptions attributable to Bergson in France. But it is especially the case of the trends opposing positivism in the name of a greater positivity in their interpretation of reality in a metaphysical and an anti-abstractionist sense: see, for example, the pragmatism of William James and F.C.S. Schiller (see Iannone 2011) and the intuitionism of H. Bergson. But it is especially the case of the aforementioned phenomenology of Husserl, whose influence is widely demonstrated in all the

---

2   This is the case of authors such as C. Vogt, L. Büchner, J. Moleschott and E.H. Haeckel.

works by Sombart (see Paci 1961; 1974; Cavalli 1969), even those preceding *Vom Menschen* (1938), as it is possible to read in Engel's work *Max Weber und Werner Sombart Lehre von Wirtschaftsgesetzen. Ein Beitrag zur Frage der Gesetzsbildung in den Geisteswissenschaften* (1933, quote in Cavalli 1969, 112), published in 1933.

In this sense, Sombart's idea of science provides a further implication pertaining to the division between the sciences of nature and the sciences of spirit.

Therefore, when it comes to science, the inevitable endpoint, is the science of the soul: that is, a type of science that, in relation to the objectives and proceedings, and in line with the whole previous epistemological tradition, is considered by Sombart as irreconcilably opposed to the natural sciences.

On the other hand, Sombart remarks that it is the subject of the treatise, the totality of the human being, which makes the mark of the science of the spirit obvious. Indeed, for the author, only the sciences of the soul can aspire to approximate the complexity of man.

The positive science that Sombart mentions is, therefore, neither a natural science nor an organicism one inherent to the human beings. "Making positivism" means reflecting on man according to the limits of understanding fixed by evidence and experience, no matter how inaccessible or historically complex this mission of knowledge is; it means refuting the application of the methods of natural science over man and society (Prestipino 1973).

> When Pascal defined the *esprit humain* "un sujet incapable d'ordre," he wanted to emphasize that the method (previously used) of the natural sciences to observe and identify laws, may be not applicable to it. The lack of results of the naturalistic "psychology" of the last century fully reiterated the truth of this statement, as we will see in the second part of the volume. A naturalistic (human) psychology does not exist, in the same way it does not exist as an anthropology considered as a natural science, of which this should be a part.
>
> SOMBART 1938, 276

Thus,

> the specificity of the cognitive method of the humanistic orientation, as compared with the scientific one, consists in the fact that first is aimed at the understanding of the complex circumstances it faces and that we define elations based on sense, while the cognitive method with a scientific approach (as the knowledge of nature remains foreclosed) consists in bringing back to the basic elements all the complex (compounded) phenomena, analyzing the mutual relation of these elements with respect

to regularity and to give expression to the so-called laws; a process that, within the humanities, is completely meaningless. (157)

The science of the soul is the science of "rational understanding" forced to move between the narrow limits left practicable by the transcendent forces on the one hand and by the forces of nature on the other. In other words, Sombart says that between the abyss of metaphysical thought and natural science,

> we aim at practicing the human sciences in a critical attitude. By "criti-
> cal" we mean that we plan to audit the different branches of knowledge,
> actively transmitting the knowledge on man, to examine what they can –
> and should – offer with respect to knowledge. (157)[3]

The clamor of the criticism current will highlight "the limitations inherent to all the scientific knowledge, where both the spheres of everyday experience and of faith begin, which is not the beginning but the end of all knowledge" (Sombart 1938, 157).

A science of the soul in a critical way: this is the definitive sense that, at the end of this itinerary, the author assigns to the work, rhetorically asking whether we should consider it a new science, a propaedeutic science, a universal science, or – the hypothesis he would go for – a fundamental science

> Including all the branches of science regarding man, a science which
> attributes a precise meaning to each of them and gives them a position
> in the cosmos of science, according to which everyone can orientate just
> like sailors looking at the North Star. (156)

In these passages, it seems that the positivist ambition to hierarchically organize science keeps coming back, as if this social science can draw strength from it.

---

3   In A. Bertolino's opinion on Sombart's methodology, the German scholar actually "does not adhere strictly and exclusively to the spiritualistic method (verstehend), which is the only conceivable thing in the philosophical system that he accepts and defends, but slips in proceedings relevant for the other methods. Moreover, with a strange inconsistency, he did not explicitly deny a responsibility to the metaphysical method, although it is a priori and proceeds through value judgments; besides, he did not deny a responsibility to the naturalistic method, although it constitutes an external knowledge of examined and generalized facts; he believes that both methods are partial and insufficient. He prefers the spiritualistic or cultural method because of its deeper logical appropriateness to the study of the human facts" (Barbieri et al. 1964, 177).

At this point, the "dualism of knowledge and faith, fact and value, objective and subjective" with which Ugo Spirito (1930, 329) deprecated without any appeal to the fundamentals of Sombart's elaboration, should be quite clear.[4] In fact, he believed that the massive positivist creed (329–30) to which Sombart always remained faithful, caused – although he was a man of high culture – "an absolute incapacity to acknowledge the development of contemporary thought" (329–30), completely compromising the historical prospective that even Spirito recognizes (see Acocella 1996-1997, 185–203). This is the so-called 'relativistic historicism', a historicism that, according to Spirito, has been interrupted during its evolution. A troubled historicism, a necessary troubled historicism, in order "to escape the doldrums of both the 'metaphysical' method and of the 'naturalistic' method of science (or at least the best itinerary able to suggest appropriate responses to the problem of science)" (193).[5]

Beyond these peculiar aspects, "Sombart's historicism is a controversial and not irrelevant chapter of Vico's incidence in the twentieth century" (203).

References

Acocella, Giuseppe. 1996–97. "Ugo Spirito e lo storicismo 'vichiano' di W. Sombart." In *Bollettino Centro di studi vichiani* XXVI–XXVII, 185–203. Napoli: Edizioni Scientifiche Italiane.

Allodi, Leonardo. 1986. "Attualità della sociologia noologica di W. Sombart." *Sociologia. Rivista di Scienze Sociali dell'Istituto Luigi Sturzo,* no. 20: 245–95.

---

4   Spirito refers particularly to Sombart's thought before this work, but his considerations seem extensible also to *Vom Menschen* (1938).

5   Later, interpreting the influence of Spirito on Sombart, Acocella wrote: "Exactly when he captures the most significant results of his speculation, Sombart appears incapable of reaching the turning point that Spirito considers essential in order to achieve the unity between science and philosophy, which – in his opinion – is the real turning point of the contemporary thought. The responsibility lies precisely in the 'philosophical assumptions' that are the basis of Sombart's argumentation" (Acocella 1996-1997, 199). Furthermore, Acocella directly mentions Spirito: "If, then, we want to re-define the speculative conception of Sombart, limiting ourselves to this second stage, we should look for the limitations in the same criticism to science characterizing the contemporary anti-intellectual philosophies. And the limits, then, can be found in the dualism of nature and spirit, which unfortunately impacts on science and philosophy as dualism of the same disciplines, and that suggests the insurmountability of the naturalistic conception of the natural sciences" (Spirito 1930, 331).

Barbieri, Gino, Alberto Bertolino, Maria Raffaella Caroselli, Hermann Kellenbenz, Giuseppe Luzzatto, Federigo Melis, and Giuseppe Mira. 1964. *L'Opera di Werner Sombart nel Centenario della nascita*. Milano: Giuffrè.

Bertolino, Alberto. 1950. *Esplorazioni della storia del pensiero economico*. Firenze: La Nuova Italia.

Braudel, Fernand. 2003. *Scritti sulla storia*. Milano: Bompiani.

Burke, Peter. 1982. *Sociologia e storia*. Bologna: il Mulino.

Cavalli, Alessandro. 1967. "Introduzione." In *Il capitalismo moderno*, edited by Werner Sombart. Torino: Utet.

Cavalli, Alessandro. 1969. *La fondazione del metodo sociologico in Max Weber e Werner Sombart*. Pavia: Università di Pavia, Istituto di Scienze Statistiche e demografiche, Istituto di Sociologia.

De Nardis, Paolo. 1996. *L'equivoco sistema. Soggetti, istituzioni e struttura sociale nelle prospettive funzionalistiche*. Milano: FrancoAngeli.

Iannone, Roberta. 2011. "Unità di cultura e costituzione di Europa. Storia e attualità europea nel pensiero di Werner Sombart." *Rivista di Studi Politici* 4 (23): 127–39.

Kellenbenz, Hermann. 1964. "Vita ed opera di Werner Sombart." In *L'Opera di Werner Sombart nel Centenario della nascita*, edited by Gino Barbieri, Alberto Bertolino, Maria Raffaella Caroselli, Hermann Kellenbenz, Giuseppe Luzzatto, Federigo Melis and Giuseppe Mira. Milano: Giuffrè.

Mongardini, Carlo. 1970. *L'epoca della società. Saggi di storia della sociologia*. Roma: Bulzoni.

Mongardini, Carlo. 2009. *L'epoca della contingenza*. Milano: FrancoAngeli.

Orsini, Alessandro. 2005. *In difesa della sociologia storica*. Milano: FrancoAngeli.

Paci, Enzo. 1961. *Tempo e verità nella fenomenologia di Husserl*. Roma-Bari: Laterza.

Paci, Enzo. 1974. *Fenomenologia e dialettica*. Milano: Feltrinelli.

Pellicani, Luciano. 2005. "Prefazione." In *In difesa della sociologia storica*, edited by Alessandro Orsini. Milano: FrancoAngeli.

Prestipino, Giuseppe. 1973. *Natura e società. Per una nuova lettura di Engels*. Roma: Editori Riuniti.

Rossi, Pietro. 1956. *Lo storicismo tedesco contemporaneo*. Torino: Einaudi.

Sapori, Armando. 1944. *Werner Sombart (1863–1941)*. Firenze: Le Monnier.

Sapori, Armando. 1955. *Studi di storia economica (secoli XIII, XIV, XV)*. Vol. 2. Firenze: Sansoni.

Sombart, Werner. 1930. *Die drei Nationalökonomien. Geschichte und System Lehre von der Wirtschaft*. München/Leipzig: Duncker & Humblot.

Sombart, Werner. 1936. *Soziologie. Soziologie: Was Ist Sie Und Was Sie Sein Sollte*. Sitzungsberichte der Preussischen Akademie der Wissenschaften, Berlin.

Sombart, Werner. 1938. *Vom Menschen. Versuch einer geistwissenschaftlichen Anthropologie*. Berlin: Duncker & Humblot.

Spirito, Ugo. 1930. "La nuova scienza dell'economia secondo Werner Sombart." *Nuovi studi di diritto, economia e politica* 6 (3): 381–91.

Topitsch, Ernst. 1975. *A che serve l'ideologia*. Bari: Laterza.

Treccani. n.d. "Sociologia." In *Treccani Online Encyclopedia*. Retrieved April 1, 2020. http://www.treccani.it/enciclopedia/sociologia/.

CHAPTER 7

Bourdieu and Elias, Historical Sociologists

Notes for a Comparison

Andrea Borghini

1   Introduction

1.1   *The Meaning of a Comparison*

Pierre Bourdieu and Norbert Elias can be considered, without a doubt, two "unique" figures in the contemporary sociological panorama: anti-dogmatics, anti-systemics, intolerants of any disciplinary barrier, allergic to those debates that fascinated many sociologists of their time – micro and macro, structure and action –, in favor of a diachronic and historical vision of the analysis of society, and particularly attentive towards highlighting the deep dynamics of power which guide and condition social change.

More specifically, the reasons for this uniqueness can be summarized as follows:

– A rare *mixture* of biography and social theory, which overcomes any kind of dualism or polarization, typical of classical biographical reconstructions. Bourdieu's life becomes nourishment for his analysis of society and for the elaboration of his social theory: take for example the *turning points* such as the Algerian experience or his participation in protests against neoliberal globalization, side by side with workers and farmers.

For Elias, biography and history, experiences and great structural changes represent the poles within which the key to his reflection on the historical-social world is formed, contributing, in a decisive manner, to founding his relational sociology and to creating epistemological constructs such as that of Figuration.

– An unconventional and non-rhetorical but authentic anti-dogmatism, testified to by their attitude towards the classics – Elias' criticisms of the Weberian ideal type or of the Frankfurt School, or Bourdieu's "iconoclastic" attitude towards the Marx-Durkheim-Weber triad; the sociological proposal that revolves around some "subversive" concepts such as that of configuration or process-oriented for Elias; or of field and capital and symbolic power for Bourdieu. The awareness and solidity of their vision can be deduced from some expressions which can be traced back to them: from Elias (1987) who accuses present-day sociology of having forgotten history and of having withdrawn into the present, to Bourdieu (2002, 43) who entrusts sociology with the task of freeing man from the chains of hypocrisy and rhetoric ("the sociologist is the one who finds the means to bring to light things that no one wants to know [...]. I wanted to be someone who would help provide tools for liberation. That's how I see myself, while the people who talk to you about freedom, freedom, freedom, are theatrical characters who say let's go, let's go, let's go, and stand still").

– What interests us more here is the orientation towards History and its relations with Sociology, which aims to revalue the connection, for example through processes of re-historicizing the biological world (Bourdieu 2001) or when the French sociologist defines the relationship between History and Sociology in this way: *"the separation of sociology and history is a disastrous division,* and one totally devoid of epistemological justification: all sociology should be historical and all history sociological" (Bourdieu 1992, 90).

Elias does use the metaphor of History as a long river that flows towards the sea but treats it as if its development were an unpredictable course, thus the voluntary absence of the search for an Archimedean point from which it is possible to understand the world surfaces – a search which, if undertaken, would be sterile as such a point does not exist.

For both authors, the focal point of the reflection – and of their life – is the combination of History as process-oriented, Sociology as vocation and Biography as soul and body.

The intellectual and cultural orientation that we have briefly outlined does not make them those formidable authors that they were, when considered individually, but is also valid when we consider them as a pair.

In fact, in a 2012 article, Bowen, together with other scholars, precisely underlines this aspect and brilliantly summarizes the reasons for the exceptional nature of the two authors, whom we have briefly presented: "Elias and Bourdieu can systematically overcome decades of misguided dichotomies in social thought, dichotomies such as those between individual and society, subject and object, the internal and the external, reason and emotion, the soul and the flesh" (Bowen, van Heerikhuizen, and Emirbayer 2012, 71).

Bourdieu and Elias demonstrate an extraordinary affinity given by the fact that "both relied heavily on the same triad of core concepts, and both deployed those concepts in a relentlessly relational and processual fashion" (71).

An affinity that certainly should not be overestimated, but which, upon careful investigation, reveals its full worth: "Elias and Bourdieu were exposed to the same intellectual currents during their formative years. They studied the works of Marx and Weber, felt the influence of philosophers such as Husserl, Cassirer, and Heidegger, and – perhaps most crucially – evinced a deep understanding of Durkheimian thought. In their biographies, one can also detect similarities. Both men felt in certain periods of their lives the sting of being outsiders. Both showed a tremendous energy in fighting their way into the castles of academic excellence. Both experienced, body and soul, how processes of inclusion and exclusion can restrict one's freedom of movement in various social fields. And, when the time came to collect the highest rewards the academic community has to offer, both discovered that such accolades do not alleviate the pain of scars for which there is no healing process. These parallels along biographical, social, and intellectual dimensions all help to explain the affinities between the two men" (71).[1]

We therefore believe that the elements briefly summarized here endorse our choice to offer a comparative reading of the two authors, and allow us to protect them from the risk of surrendering to the history of *post mortem* sociological thought, depriving them of that epistemological, content and moral coherence which was the intellectual and scientific mandate for an entire life of study, passion and activism.

In this sense, they are totally suited to be placed in a volume dedicated to Historical Sociology with a title such as *Beyond Dogmatism*, because, evidently, Bourdieu and Elias made anti-dogmatism their banner.

Furthermore, as we have already had occasion to underline, the intolerance towards ascribed sociological categories is the result, in turn, of an attitude towards History and its relationship with Sociology that fits perfectly within a 'non-paradigm' such as that represented by Historical Sociology, which even today, after decades of debates and publications, it is difficult to define once and for all.

In these few introductory pages we obviously cannot report the whole debate on Historical Sociology, but we will limit ourselves to emphasizing only this basic isomorphism and this mutual reference between the pair of authors and the approach. Where, on the one hand, Bourdieu arouses extensive

---

1   But obviously there is no shortage of distance, as Loyal points out: "It has been long recognized that there are parallels in their work. Both use a similar terminology of habitus and field, both subscribe to Cassirer's relational form of analysis, both have a strong Durkheimian social morphology underpinning their approach, and both share a similar political worldview – Republican socialism and radical social democrat respectively. Nevertheless, there are also differences in terms of their philosophical anthropology, the nature of the long-term analysis, the different contexts within which their work emerged – Algeria and the First and Second World War – and the divergent nature of the substantive sociological problems they engage with" (Loyal 2016, 1).

debates today, his reception or poor reception is discussed in some scientific and academic contexts and he is an thorny author in life[2] and unwanted in death,[3] Elias, on the other hand, is in some ways a heretic in that he wrote little in the first phase of his life, earning a certain consensus only very late and living it always and in any case with some embarrassment mixed with a sense of superiority,[4] sometimes, in some ways, even mocking a certain sociological hermeticism. Similarly, Historical Sociology, "the historicized (or temporalized) nature of society as a theoretical acquisition rich in methodological consequences for the social sciences does not yet seem adequately metabolized by contemporary sociology" (Paci 2019, 15). Over time, it has sparked an extensive debate, generating extreme positions, in one sense or another.[5] It is enough, among many others, to report what Delanty and Isin say according to whom "historical sociology occupies an ambiguous space between history and sociology" (Delanty and Isin 2003, 1).

In summary, Bourdieu and Elias, by vocation and conviction, are historical sociologists who shy away from crystallized categorization and exalt an approach that is not in itself very systematic. On the other hand, the approach, for historical reasons which we will mention below, is an approach which is already not very inclined to dogmatism and disciplinary orthodoxy and cannot but welcome two *outsiders* like Bourdieu and Elias.

In light of these initial considerations, in the following pages we would like to develop a comparative analysis between the two authors on the theme of Historical Sociology, defining the constitutive and peculiar features of their proposal. Obviously we cannot retrace their entire intellectual biography and all their works, but we will limit ourselves to using some of the most significant

---

2 It pleases us to report what Bourdieu describes in *The Sociologist and the Historian* about the risk of inviting him to debates. Addressing those who had invited him, he always warned them: "you don't realize what you're doing, you're asking me to do something dreadful, and it will be dramatic: there will be incidents, I'll provoke insults." And further: "and then what I feared really did happen: it was a genuine 'happening', and for the whole of the next week this was all that people talked about in the intellectual milieu of Brussels" (Bourdieu and Chartier 2015, 3).

3 See the essay by Angelo Salento (2010) on this aspect.

4 See Elias' description of the Frankfurt School members (Tabboni 1993, 50–1).

5 There are the pioneers like Abrams, according to whom it makes no sense to speak of sociology and history as two distinct disciplines, as both address the problem of human action in relation to structure issues and they do so by not being able to ignore a chronological framework; the "revolutionaries" like Calhoun who in Historical Sociology sees a tool for reorienting social thought in a historical key; the "deniers" like Goldthorpe, drastic in inviting the two disciplines to immediate divorce, as sociology is the study of the present, while the past must be left to history.

ones, with the aim of revealing Historical Sociology as a work method, choice of content, but above all as a vocation and intellectual style.

The work is organized into two parts.

The first concerns the contribution of Bourdieu and Elias to Historical Sociology in the terms previously indicated.

The second part includes a comparison between the two authors on a classic topic of Historical Sociology such as the theme of the State, its genesis, its historical trajectory, its function.

The latter topic lends itself particularly well to work as a key concept to reveal the peculiarity and relevance of their approach, for a series of reasons that critics have unfailingly pointed out.

– Both authors can be considered sociologists of power. We said it at the beginning and Bowen *et al.* (2012) reiterate this in their contribution, developing the comparative analysis of both through precisely the prism of power;

– The State, we know, is a key theme of Historical Sociology in all its development and our authors have extensively grappled with it. In addition, it is one of those topics for which Bourdieu was able to praise Elias, without, *ça va sans dire*, abdicating his own critical spirit.

– Finally, both have produced an interpretation of the State particularly in line with the recent developments in the debate on this institution.

At the end of this dense Introduction, we would like to reiterate what we are ultimately interested in providing to the reader. These are the *sui generis* key elements of Elias and Bourdieu in the debate on Historical Sociology. How the approach can be appreciated through them and, at the same time, how the intellectual style of these authors can be further highlighted through this. And, finally, how thanks to them, it is possible to carry out a serious sociological investigation of the State, which also allows us to understand the profound reasons for its *revival* which has been underway for some time now.

2   Part One. Historical Sociology as a Vocation: Bourdieu and Elias

2.1   *Pierre Bourdieu*

Bourdieu reaffirms his conception of sociology and history on several occasions, both in substantial terms and in terms of criticism of the French academic establishment. Already in the Introduction we mentioned the terminology used by the sociologist from Béarn when he states that it would be fatal to distinguish Sociology and History and that his mission is to develop a social concept according to which "history would be a historical sociology of the past and sociology would be a social history of the present" (Bourdieu 1995, 111).

This is not the place to undertake an exhaustive reconstruction of all his commitment as a historical sociologist. What we intend to do, as with Elias, is to underline the peculiarities of each one, drawing on both direct sources – some of their writings – and on those belonging to the critical literature.

There again, the introductory page of a 2011 article by Steinmetz (2011) would be enough to deny the accusations of non-historicity often addressed to Bourdieu.

For example, Bourdieu is a historical sociologist because of the nature of the tools he uses, the French cultural environment in which he lived and this helps to refute all those who relegate him to the role of sociologist of reproduction: "Bourdieu has been widely misunderstood as an ahistorical 'reproduction theorist' whose approach does not allow for diachronic change. In fact, *both* social reproduction and social change are at the very heart of Bourdieu's project. Bourdieu's main theoretical concepts – habitus, field, cultural and symbolic capital – are all inherently historical. Indeed, for Bourdieu, *every social object is historical.* More than any other French sociologist, Bourdieu allowed French sociology to historicize itself – to achieve a merger of history and sociology that had been discussed by Durkheim and the founders of the *Annales* School but never fully accepted by sociologists" (46).

And again, he was "one of the most forceful proponents of an epistemological tradition in which history and sociology are considered essentially the same thing [...]. Bourdieu described his own work as 'social history' [...] and praised Max Weber's 'extraordinary efforts to sketch a historical sociology or sociological history of religion, economics, and law.' The journal Bourdieu founded in 1975, *Actes de la recherche en sciences sociales*, was dedicated to the unity of sociology and history (and indeed of all of the social sciences). [...] Bourdieu has also had a pervasive influence on the work of professional historians [...], and is one of just ten sociologists included in the *Encyclopedia of Historians and Historical Writing*" (46).

Lastly, "each of Bourdieu's main theoretical concepts (habitus, cultural and symbolic capital, and field) is inherently historical, in three specific senses. First, these concepts designate objects or structures that exist in a specific time and place and that are not omnihistorical or universal – even if the range of their application is sometimes as broad as the entire sweep of modernity or capitalism. Second, each of these concepts is described as a form of incorporated history. Third, Bourdieu deploys his basic categories in ways that suggest an inherently historical or historicist social epistemology, one that is open to conjuncture, contingency, and radical discontinuity" (54; see also Steinmetz 2018).

Based on these last statements by Steinmetz, Bourdieu would be a historical sociologist, paradoxically timeless as he offered suggestions and lines of research close to what has been defined as the third wave of Historical Sociology (Adams *et al.* 2005), the so-called sociology of events (Sewell 2005).

Steinmetz obviously does not hide some dilemmas that Bourdieu's Historical Sociology raises. Nor does a recognized authority in this field, Craig Calhoun.

The American sociologist, in an essay from some time ago, reconnects Bourdieu to this approach in the following way, by also taking up the definition of the close relationship between sociology and history reported by us *above* and from which Bourdieu's observations develop: "to bring out the core of Bourdieu's analytic perspective it is helpful to see him as a historical sociologist. I obviously don't mean he inhabited a subdisciplinary specialty. Nor is the point just that Bourdieu's concepts are useful to those doing historical analysis, though this is certainly true. I do not mean simply that several of his studies were based on historical research, though many were. I mean much more basically that social transformations – and their limits and unintended consequences – were core foci of his sociological project. Bourdieu was not always explicit about the historical specificity of his work especially in his early studies. This resulted in ambiguity about when his analytic concepts were meant to be universal, general to modernity or states or capitalism, or specific to a particular context. [...]. Nonetheless, I suggest, grasping the way in which historical transformations shaped his approach does much to clarify it. As he said, 'one of my constant struggles, particularly through *Actes de la recherche en sciences sociales,* has been to promote the development of a unified social science in which history would become a historical sociology of the past and sociology would become a social history of the present'" (Calhoun 2013, 36–7).

After taking into consideration the contribution of two of the greatest historical sociologists of our time, we offer further elements to elaborate the topic of this paragraph, thanks to the pages of a book-interview by Bourdieu with the historian Chartier, from which his vocation as a sociologist attentive to history emerges additionally strengthened.

Let's start with the precious introduction to the Italian edition edited by a well-known Bourdieu scholar, Mirella Giannini, who, as we have already pointed out in the introductory notes to this contribution, highlights how Bourdieu's biography reflects a historical approach: "Bourdieu places himself in history, where his personal history acts in the great processes that characterized the second half of the last century, developing his 'point of view' on the society in which he lived. Thus he constructs his biography [...] where he emphasizes that he refers to 'the historical conditions in which his work developed,' so that 'young readers can try to grasp the point of view of the author'" (Giannini 2011, 7). Bourdieu's concepts are historical, diachronic concepts, according to which "history has an important place for Bourdieu because he sees it as 'subjectified' in individuals, in their bodies, in their perceptions and interests, in their inclination to act, to take up challenges, and is 'objectified' in individual practices, in constituted stratifications, in social positions and forms of social and symbolic domination, in the social and institutional space, the arena of struggle and transformations" (18).[6]

A severe criticism of a certain kind of history and of the method it uses (Bourdieu 1995) also emerges, lacking among other things that reflexivity, to which we will refer later, and which would allow, if applied, to become aware of the social determinations with respect to the individual who analyses reality and to the study under examination.

These criticisms are then found in Bourdieu's dialogue with Chartier, which opens precisely with the question of what the relationship of sociology with other disciplines must be, and in particular history "how should we conceive the relationship that sociology has with other disciplines which, like my own discipline of history, find themselves faced with this protean and somewhat disturbing monster?" (Bourdieu and Chartier 2015, 2–3).

We find a series of elements that help to frame Bourdieu's relationship with history also in *An Invitation to Reflexive Sociology* (1992, 89). For example, the notion of field, particularly referring to the turning point of '68, "implies that we transcend the conventional opposition between structure and history, conservation and transformation."

His field theory is the antidote to the fatal separation between history and sociology: "we cannot grasp the dynamics of a field if not by a synchronic analysis of its structure and, simultaneously, we cannot grasp this structure without a historical, that is, genetic analysis of its constitution and of the tensions

---

6   According to Emanuela Susca, Bourdieu's belonging to historical sociology should not be taken as a dogma: "interpreting Bourdieu directly as a 'historical sociologist', as some do, even authoritatively, (Calhoun 2013), requires at least remembering that Bourdieu's method is a scientific practice that is admittedly a 'take-it-all' one, that is, open 'towards the entire field of social sciences as they are widely understood' [...] and that, on the whole, the resulting sociology can be labelled as 'historical' no more than 'political' or 'economic' (and the list could go on). Furthermore, it is true that Bourdieu pays particular attention to history and addresses historians by presenting himself as an empiricist and as a historian himself [...]. But this must be read together with the considerations in the book-dialogue with Chartier that look at sociology and history as distinct and only partially comparable" (Susca 2021, 80).

that exist between positions in it, as well as between this field and other fields, and especially the field of power" (90).

Continuing the controversy with the great historians and the great sociologists, Bourdieu goes as far as to say "what we need, in effect, is a form of structural history that is rarely practiced, which finds in each successive state of the structure under examination both the product of previous struggles to maintain or to transform this structure, and the principle, via the contradictions, the tensions, and the relations of force which constitute it, of subsequent transformations" (91).[7]

In *The Rules of Art*, the reference to history loses, once again, any abstract, analytical, neutral connotation and reveals itself instead as an antidote to the social determinisms that condition the biographical trajectory: "only social history can effectively supply the means to rediscover the historical truth in the objectivized or incorporeal traces of history which present themselves to awareness in the guise of a universal essence. [...] Free thought must be won by a historical anamnesis capable of revealing everything in thought which is the forgotten product of historical work. Becoming resolutely aware of historical determinations, a true reconquest of the self (which is the exact opposite of the magical flight into 'essential thought') offers a possibility of really controlling these determinations. [...]. The effort I have made here to try to advance this knowledge would be justified, to my mind, if I had succeeded in demonstrating (and convincingly) the possibility of a way of thinking about the social conditions of thought which gives thought an opportunity of freedom in relation to those conditions" (Bourdieu 1996, 311–2).

As previously anticipated, the theme of reflexivity also constitutes in itself a theme of discussion and criticism towards historians. Starting from *Sketch for an self-analysis* (Bourdieu 2008), Bourdieu's works are full of this methodological attitude. For example in *Pascalian Meditation* he states that "the most effective reflection is the one that consists in objectifying the subject of objectification. I mean by that the one that dispossesses the knowing subject of the privilege it normally grants itself and that deploys all the available instruments of objectification (statistical surveys, ethnographic observation, historical research, etc.) in order to bring to light the presuppositions it owes to its inclusion in the object of knowledge" (Bourdieu 1999, 10), fundamental to objectify oneself, to ensure mastery of the social conditions of production of

---

7   And further on, he interacts with Elias praising his intentions to combine "the historical psychosociology of an actual grand historical process, the constitution of a state" but distancing himself from the need he felt "to ask who benefits and who suffers from the monopoly of the state over legitimate violence" (Bourdieu 1992, 92–3).

the historical and sociological discourse on the social world, through the historical critique of the tools of thought, the concepts, the techniques; and at the same time to highlight the shortcomings of history ("strangely, historians are not very inclined towards this reflective use of history," Bourdieu 1992, 65: see also Bourdieu 2022).

We conclude this panoply of references between primary and secondary sources on Bourdieu's Historical Sociology, with a lengthy quotation from Gorski, who in 2013 edited a text dedicated to this topic. According to Gorski, Bourdieu's *sui generis* Historical Sociology is characterized by the fact that "Bourdieu uses history in at least two distinct ways in his work: to critique and to explain. The necessity of historical critique derives from the role of naturalization in processes of misrecognition. One of the most common ways in which dominant actors conceal the arbitrary character of their power from themselves and others is by grounding it in nature. The paradigmatic example of this process, argues Bourdieu, is the grounding of masculine domination in sexual difference (Bourdieu 2001). In this and other areas, historicization is a potent means of denaturalization, a way of uncovering the social that is concealed in the natural. Historicization is another means of establishing the epistemological distance toward folk explanations that makes scientific explanations possible. It can also be a form of explanation in and of itself. Bourdieu's most favored form of historical explanation is the conjunctural. I call this mode of explanation conjunctural insofar as it emphasizes interfield interactions that generate unintended consequences. Bourdieu's account of May '68 is an excellent example of a conjunctural explanation: increases in prosperity and fertility after the Second World War led to a rapid expansion of the educational system and the student population and an attendant expansion in the number of positions and faculties. These increases changed the pace of professorial reproduction and the composition of the professoriate and thereby sparked conflicts within the teaching corps; at the same time, changes within the field of material production were creating a homologous set of tensions among manual laborers. In sum, 'morphological transformations' within the cultural and economic fields generated simultaneous crises in each, which led to an amplification and alignment of each crisis, with consequences that no one sought or foresaw. Bourdieu's conjunctural approach can therefore be seen as a means of transcending the old debate between determinism and contingency in history: while the laws or principles governing fields are, indeed, determinate ones, interactions between fields can lead to unexpected or contingent outcomes.

To sum up: Bourdieu's method might be fairly described as dialectical, dialogical, and conjunctural. It is dialectical in the sense that it proceeds by positing a particular ontological level or phenomenological moment of analysis or both and then negating it or them as a means of achieving a higher level of understanding. An analysis that begins from the whole proceeds to the parts; an analysis that begins with the symbolic proceeds to the material; and the outcome is, one hopes, a perspective that transcends these dualisms to some degree. Indeed, it is to be hoped that this dialectical procedure will eventually allow sociology to overcome the conceptual dualisms that guide the procedure: symbolic versus material, individual versus social, necessary versus contingent, and so on. The result will be not a unified field theory but another, deeper set of dualisms, since without dualisms there can be no dialectic and hence no increase in understanding. Bourdieu's method is also dialogical in the sense that it continually seeks to establish or re- establish a position from which we can question and interrogate the commonsensical folk view of the social world that is embedded in everyday practice. To the extent that this effort is successful, its categories will themselves enter into the folk view of the social world, necessitating a renewed epistemological break. For Bourdieu, then, the work of social science is never done. It is never done because there is always more to be learned through a negation of our present stance and because our hard-won scientific understandings are constantly being swallowed up into social practice. Finally, Bourdieu's method is conjunctural in the sense that it emphasizes how the lawful dynamics of one field can generate the reproductive equilibrium in another, and how simultaneous crises in multiple fields can amplify one another, all with outcomes that were not part of any actor's strategy" (353).

2.1.1 Bourdieu and the Debate in Historical Sociology

In what terms can Bourdieu's parabola be intertwined with the debate and evolution of Historical Sociology and with the key words of the latter – social change, space, time, events, contingency, etc.?

We limit ourselves to pointing out a few analogies and intersections, taking into account the fact that the debate on Historical Sociology is too extensive to be summarized in just a few pages.

Undoubtedly, an author like Bourdieu, often wrongly considered able to offer only an effective *pars destruens*, with his critique of the social world, but not equally able to describe and explain social change, is instead, an author who according to much critical literature (Steinmetz 2018; Pitzalis 2021; Calhoun 2013), offers valid tools in this sense. For example, his integrated system of habitus-capital field, of a historical type, provides an articulated and convincing framework of the great social transformations (Bourdieu and Chartier 2015) and he is particularly useful when tackling, albeit with the necessary circumspection and prudence, a great historical theme such as that of the State.[8]

As regards the agency, this is highlighted as strictly linked to the macro dimension precisely by the relational dimension of Bourdeian sociology – the real is relational – and once again by the relational nature of the mediating concepts themselves.

If, on the other hand, we look at Bourdieu's position, with respect to the so-called three waves,[9] according to Santoro (2008), Bourdieu is among the main intellectual sources of Sewell's program, belonging to the third wave. Although the latter, for that matter, does not skimp on criticism towards the French sociologist, in particular concerning the need for a revision of the original notion of habitus to construct a (structural) theory of historical change.

Finally, what seems most relevant to us, in the link between Bourdieu and Historical Sociology, lies in the fluid nature of the disciplinary boundaries between the two areas, in the difficulty in identifying a shared definition for an approach which appears more as a 'non-approach'.

Taking up Steinmetz again, we could conclude that Bourdieu is such a historical sociologist that he directs future research in topics and areas of study which, using his field theory, renew and further internationalize French Historical Sociology. Provided that he is accepted precisely by virtue of his a-systematic nature (Steinmetz 2018).

One last observation that serves to introduce Elias. Obviously, in Bourdieu's reflection, there is no lack of references to the sociologist born in Wroclaw. We will consider those relating to the State in the appropriate section, here we always refer to the text with Chartier which evokes the topic of the historical process and of the relationship between structures and individual psychology. Bourdieu claims to perceive "that of Elias is basically the one I find most sympathetic, because he does actually take as the basis of an evolving social-historical psychology a major real process, which is the constitution of

---

8   In a recently published volume, this prudence is reiterated, bordering on awe: "I never talk about the State because I don't know what it is and, in this sense, I am much more scientific than the others who don't even know that" (Bourdieu 2022, 331).

9   According to Adam *et al.* (2005), there have been 3 waves within which Historical Sociology is organized: the first is represented by classical sociologists. They tackle social change and the birth of modernity; the second one is the Historical Sociology of North American origin which was born to contrast the theory of modernization and Parsons (1960s) and essentially develops in a key of comparative historical sociology; the third is developed by more recent authors (Abbott, Sewell etc.) who were born already in the second wave (remaining a minority) and emerge today and who, after the *cultural turn*, focus on current issues such as those of emotions, events, race, genre, etc.

a state that moves to monopolize first physical violence (I would add symbolic violence), then all forms of authority" (Bourdieu and Chartier 2015, 60). Also, Bourdieu praises Elias for his analysis on the relationship between sport and violence, but at the same time maintains his reservations both on the specific question of the State and on other aspects of Elias's thought, in particular the fact that his theory of civilization risks being easily treated as a general law of history or of subjecting the latter to historical finalism.

In conclusion, we can say that Bourdieu, who rarely praised scholars and authors who have certainly contributed to the construction of his intellectual universe, is instead particularly docile towards a small circle, to which Elias certainly belongs.

2.2   Norbert Elias

As we have seen, Elias shares a similar biographical trajectory with Bourdieu that can help us grasp some historical changes and vice versa. And as has been noted, he certainly did not benefit from having achieved notoriety only in old age, since his work was discovered late, when he was already on the threshold of being seventy years old. There are many reasons for this delay but being in the middle as regards the area of study certainly hurt him: "too sociologist for historians, too historian for sociologists" (Cavalli 2011, 23).

Cavalli also states: "Elias's historical sociology clearly goes in a different direction. Not only is the study of the societies of the past indispensable for understanding the present, but there are some questions that both historians and sociologists must answer, whatever society they are studying. Elias calls these questions 'process universal features' and provides a list (which, as he himself warns, is incomplete and provisional). Every human social group, if it wants to survive as a group, must give itself an identity, that is, it must know what it refers to when it uses the plural personal pronoun 'we'. It must provide for the daily reproduction of the existence of its members, that is, obtain the means of subsistence, must manage conflicts, internal and external, in order to control violence, must see to the accumulation and distribution of the skills and knowledge required for existence in a given natural and social environment that is constantly transforming. It must finally ensure that the individual members know how to channel and control their drives" (23).

Elias' Historical Sociology would be characterized by four guidelines: "*a.* social reality is intrinsically conflictual; *b.* social reality can only be grasped during its unfolding in the light of long-term processes; *c.* only the historical-comparative method can adequately account for long-term processes; *d.* historical-sociological research must produce great syntheses that hold together processes at both micro and macro levels like a plot" (25).

Concluding these remarks, Cavalli says: "what are often kept divided in thought as if they were two different substances or layers of man, his 'individuality' and his 'social determination,' are nothing more than two different functions which human beings have available in their reciprocal relations: they have no consistency when independent from each other" (29).

Another author, Azuelos, moves along a similar line of reflection. With respect to the dilemma of whether Elias is the most historian of sociologists or the most sociologist of historians, he replies that "this question can in fact be posed for this *marginal établi* who enjoyed mixing disciplines during his life" (Azuélos 2009, 1).

A multifaceted author with a multidisciplinary background, this *marginal établi* shares with Bourdieu a keen interest in history and a tendency not to be categorized in a chosen discipline. The process-based and dynamic nature of history, the concept of configuration, the relational approach, constitute the pillars of his thought as a historical sociologist.

In fact, it is Azuelos again who highlights the concept of society in Elias: "society is not a construction of autonomous individuals, players in their own lives, but the social configurations in which interacting individuals are involved are like parallelograms of forces driven by their own dynamics in an almost always unpredictable direction. Elias rejects any single-cause and linear explanation of social development" (3)[10] and the notion of event which also seems to project him with a leading role into the most current debate of Historical Sociology: "for Elias, the event is conceived as a set of relationships, and at every historical turning point, at every phase in which the destiny of a people seems to be at stake, we are faced with a multiplicity of possibilities, every initiative by an individual or by a human group entangled in a network of seemingly autonomous uncertainties and decisions can tilt the configuration in one direction or another, without the players feeling that they have had total control over a flow in which they have been unwittingly dragged along. The resultant of all these forces, which is history itself in the making, is certainly not evident, but the historian is nevertheless able to reconstruct

---

10   Azuelos also highlights certain limitations of Bourdieu's critique of Elias. Quoting a passage from *The Rules of Art* in which the French sociologist criticizes Elias ("here one sees an example of the simplification committed by those who think of the transformations of modern societies as linear and unidimensional processes, such as Norbert Elias's 'process of civilization': they reduce to a unilateral process the complex evolutions that, when dealing with modes of domination, are always ambiguous, doubled-faced, with the regression of a recourse to physical violence being, for example, compensated by a progression in symbolic violence and in all other gentler forms of control", Bourdieu 1996, 98), he objects that the civilization process is not as linear as described by Bourdieu.

a posteriori the logical sequence of human decisions, which always refer to a plot, to a story" (6).

Similarly to what was done for Bourdieu, in the case of Elias it is again useful to alternate the secondary sources with the primary ones to bring out the distinctive traits of his position as a historical sociologist, albeit *sui generis*. It is therefore unavoidable to think of his article *Retreat of Sociologists to the Present* in which he demonstrates a particular sensitivity for historical depth. Indeed, he starts his argument from the tendency of contemporary sociology, after the Second World War, to escape from the past: "concentration on present issues has found a striking expression in an almost explosive profusion of empirical sociological investigations, partly but no means only of the statistical variety" (Elias 1987, 223). Or in *Mozart. Sociology of a genius*, in which by attributing to sociologists the ability and sensitivity to keep micro and macro dimensions together through the concept of configuration, he wants to highlight how the life of the Viennese musician can be better understood "if we consider it as a micro-process at the central turning point of a macro-process" (Elias and Schröter 1993, 53).

According to Brunet and Morell (2001), in fact, the subject matter of Elias' Historical Sociology is not the individuals, presumably free and unique, but the positions that exist independently of them and of the elements that govern their freedom: "Elias does not intend to study one King in particular, but the network of obligations – relationships – in which he finds himself; not the action of a prince, but the network of obligations – relationships – in which he finds himself integrated. For this reason, he analyses the determinations that weigh on different people, the phenomena that no will (not even the King's will) could transform. Contrary to the vision of *homo economicus,* whose main quality is that of being a *self-made man,* here the thesis is defended according to which self-determination is not sustainable, but we must accept that the players can be defined and constituted only in relation to each other, and not in an endogenous manner" (117).

It is therefore evident how the theme of relationality, of the micro-macro bond and therefore of the (historical) process runs through all of Elias's work. An exemplary paradigm of this is certainly the scholar's greatest work, *On the Process of Civilisation* (2000), which must be understood as a contemporary micro and macro process that can be read in both directions, a statement corroborated by what Elias himself affirms in *Essays*, where one of the essays, polemicizing with other authors – a classic of Elias – traces the difficulty of linking macro and micro in a relational approach to the fact that "the whole trend of our reflection, the whole traditions of our conceptualization, is so much attuned to what I call in German *Zustandsreduktion*. There is no corresponding word which I can at the moment find in English. It means the reduction in thought of all things that you observe as being dynamic to something static. Our whole conceptual tradition, particularly our philosophical tradition, pushes our thinking in that direction and makes us feel that one cannot come to grips with observed happenings as flowing events in speaking and thinking" (1998, 142).

Moreover, as underlined by Brunet and Morell, who take up the words of the author, "what we lack are mental models and a global vision with which we can achieve a better harmony between our conception of human beings as individuals and our idea of the human being as a society" (2001, 116). To overcome this false dilemma, it is necessary to coordinate sociology and history.

Finally, to give the idea of how this author can be considered a pivotal author with respect to the path of sociology and of Historical Sociology in particular, Delanty and Isin express themselves as follows: "in this, Elias's 'processual' historical sociology marked a turn from macro-civilizational analysis towards micro issues of everyday life, the consciousness of the self and cultural practices. The work of Norbert Elias brought the classical tradition further into the domain of everyday life, but the more historical sociology moved in this direction, the more it moved into a post-disciplinary context" (Delanty and Isin 2003, 3).

2.2.1   Elias and the Debate in Historical Sociology

As we have already done for Bourdieu, we can briefly try to place Elias in the debate on Historical Sociology. Here, to some extent, some biographical traits of the author emerge to condition this position. We refer to the time lag with Bourdieu, to the belated success, to the fact that Elias did not set up a school, etc. Nevertheless, we can say very briefly that Elias's Historical Sociology is characterized by its ability to keep micro and macro together, by its attention to historical process and in general by the fierce battle against the presentism of contemporary sociology.

Once again picking up a mirror image of what was proposed in the paragraph relating to the relationship between Bourdieu and Historical Sociology, at the end of this paragraph we can once again observe the numerous analogies between Bourdieu and Elias. In particular, Azuelos underlines the similarities on the question of habitus, on the notion of field, on the theme of power etc., while Brunet and Morell note that both authors concur in conceiving sociology as a historical science which deals with a historically given and therefore variable structure of social relations: "having a sense of history, Elias and Bourdieu know that every socio-structural relationship pattern is subject to constant change, and that the subject of sociological thought does not only consist of social structures, but also of their historical movement. Thus, in a radical break with methodological individualism, Elias and Bourdieu focus their attention on the social practices that occur in the complexity of the strategies of the social game. Practices that must be understood as the product of the relationship between the strategic subject and the field in which he/she produces his/her strategy" (Brunet and Morell 2001, 130).

Our two authors do not think of subject and object as rationally and logically distinct, but as hypotheses through which further constructions are possible. This is a research program aimed at the denaturalization of the world: "we cannot ignore that the cognitive structures through which agents take over the social world are essentially products of the internalization of the world's objective structures. The objectivity of the institutional world is an objectivity of production and of construction of human beings in which, moreover, the product acts again on the producer. Therefore, history cannot be foreign to us" (130).

But it is probably on the subject of the State that a mature area of confrontation emerges between the two authors and which at the same time allows us to say a great deal about the development of the topic in Historical Sociology.

3   Part Two. A Critical Comparison in the Light of the Notion of State

The analysis of the State constitutes a key topic of the Historical Sociology approach.

In fact, in the wide variety of authors who are inspired by Historical Sociology there is a substantial agreement about the centrality of the State as the subject of historical and sociological study, although this awareness has been reached not without some difficulties (Abrams 1988).

An author such as Kumar has created a suggestive synthesis of the sociological interest for the State, underlining how there was a *golden age* as regards this topic, starting from a series of noble fathers who dealt with this: "works as Perry Anderson's *Lineages of the Absolutist State* (1974), Charles Tilly's edited volume, *The Formation of National States in Western Europe* (1975), and Gianfranco Poggi's *The Development of the Modern State* (1978). There was also the rediscovery of the historical essays of Otto Hintze (1975), with its Weberian emphasis on the primacy of politics and of conflicts between states. Since then there have been Michael Mann's imposing multi-volume study, *The Sources of Social Power* (1986–93), John A. Hall's *Power and Liberties* (1986), Charles Tilly's *Coercion, Capital and European States, AD 990–1992* (1992), Thomas Ertman's

Birth of the Leviathan (1997), and George Steinmetz's edited volume, *State/ Culture* (1999). Paul Corrigan and Derek Sayer, in *The Great Arch: English State Formation as Cultural Revolution* (1985) took up a challenge from E.P. Thompson (and Antonio Gramsci) in attempting a comprehensive sociological history of the English/ British state. There have been some important recent studies in particular of the fascist state, such as Mabel Berezin's *Making the Fascist Self* (1997) and Michael Mann's *Fascists* (2004). The influences in all these are mixed, but there is no mistaking the imprint of Weber and Hintze alongside newer approaches from cultural sociology, law, and international relations. It is here perhaps that the departure from Marx is at its clearest, given Marxism's notoriously negligent treatment of the modern state and the nature of political power (though the Gramscian modification of this tradition has been highly influential)" (Kumar 2009, 397).

If instead we observe this subject starting from the study of some of its struc-tural characteristics – e.g. bureaucratization, autonomy, sovereignty, etc. –, it is evident that, albeit leading off from Marx and Weber, we soon go beyond these two classical authors, to highlight the richness of the evolutions, the overcom-ing of a monolithic, unitary and substantialist vision of the State and of its subordination to the class relationship – which at the time aroused a debate culminating in the famous text edited by Skocpol *et al.* (Evans, Rueschemeyer, and Skocpol 1985).

Precisely starting from the historical revival of the concept of State, inaugu-rated by the Skocpol *et al.* text, a series of 'noble' positions followed each other, focusing on evolution in comparative terms, or developing an analysis on a global level; or, yet again, analyzing the historical foundations within historical-geographical contexts where the States mainly appear to be imposed and unnatural. The proliferation of new adjectives – postcolonial, post-conflictual, market making etc. – reveals the centrality of the State as well as its relevance as a subject of study from a perspective of comparative systematic analysis. Furthermore, the *cultural turn* in social sciences also influences the re-reading of state action by introducing the variable of culture as central to the action of the State given its eminently political category.

Dufour (2015) recaps what we have reported, summarizing the various lines of work on the topic that have occurred over time – study of the centralization of power, autonomy of the State, the principle of sovereignty, bureaucratiza-tion processes, and finally, the mechanisms of categorization, classification and education as State regulation – starting from the consideration that at the heart of the analysis of the State there is the effort to distinguish "properties, roles and transhistorical characteristics of political organizations, from those

that are instead typical of certain epochs or certain concrete historical contexts" (134).

From these few preliminary notes, it is clear that studying the State within
Historical Sociology allows both to summarize the historical phases of this
approach and to place Elias and Bourdieu in an even more central position in
relation to Historical Sociology, thanks to their *version* of the topic. In fact, the
hope that moves us in this last part of the contribution is that of bringing out
those traits of profound historicity which characterize the two authors through
the analysis of the State, without however hiding some limits as regards their
reflections, which emerge, as some literature has already done, precisely from
the close comparison of their positions. In other words, the analysis of the State
as a historical object allows us to read in the background the value of a historical approach to the State, which an author like Lachmann (2013, 85) considers
absolutely central: "the best historical sociology of the State allows us to see
how the boundaries between state and civil society shift over time and how
groups both finds unity and identity and conceive and reconceive interests. All
of this is contingent and contingency can be seen in cross-country comparison
as well as single country studies. The goal for HS is not just to trace chains that
culminates in new social policies, citizen rights, war and declarations of independence but to see the entire social landscape in which actors are simultaneously within and outside the state and in which the borders between the two
are complex and shifting."

So how do our authors behave with respect to the intrinsically historical
nature of the State? In our opinion, it would be advisable to develop the reasoning by presenting their point of view, starting from the aspects in common and
then highlighting the differences.

First of all, we previously mentioned how, with respect to the topic, there was
an overall positive evaluation by Bourdieu of the work done by Elias, while the
major differences, we will see, seem to emerge around the concept of violence
and its forms.

For example, Dufour cites Elias and Bourdieu a first time, the former for
the sociogenesis of the State, the latter for social regulation, and underlines
the diriment element given by symbolic violence. According to Dufour, Elias
speaks of a monopoly mechanism underlying the development of the modern State; a monopolization of physical and fiscal violence as an increase in
interdependencies (Dufour 2015, 154) and as the outcome of the struggle for
elimination between smaller elements of domination, while Bourdieu comes
into play for the part relating to classification/categorization, making the State

the monopolist of a meta-capital that allows access to progress towards higher degrees of universalization (154).[11]

While in Elias the State is handled in many of his works – from *On the Process of Civilisation* to *Studies on the Germans* – with the specific intention of relating it to psychogenesis and its advent essentially coincides with the acquisition of the dual monopoly of physical violence and taxation, Bourdieu, drawing inspiration from authors such as Corrigan and Sayer – the only historical sociologists to be praised by the French sociologist – develops his analysis of the State as an outcome of both a critical reading and of a personal elaboration, starting from "an in-depth and often critical reading of numerous works of the so-called comparative historical sociology of politics, mainly of Anglo-American inspiration (Perry Anderson, Samuel N. Eisenstadt, Michael Mann, Barrington Moore or Charles Tilly)" (Dùloye 2014, 14) and building his analysis of the State on a reversal of the relationship between physical and symbolic violence.

As we said at the beginning of the paragraph, it is around this specific aspect that the State game is played out by the two authors, through Bourdieu's criticisms of Elias on the one hand, and through the replies of the latter's students towards the French sociologist's positions on the other.

Where for Elias the State constitutes an open, debated and controversial issue, whose centrality for the historical development of the West is reiterated (Delmotte 2012) as at the heart of the ambivalence relating to the dichotomies subject-object, individual-society, freedom determinism, Loyal (2016; 2017), who worked on an in-depth comparison on the relationship between Elias and Bourdieu in relation to the concept of State, states that Elias "is of course justly famous for his discussion of state formation. As Mennell incisively summarizes it, it combines an earlier analysis of state formation with a less discussed and later analysis of nation-building: yet while there is no doubt that the formation

---

11   Morgan *et al.* (2017) thus place Bourdieu in the analysis of a particular area of study on the State, dedicated to *States, Culture, Symbolic Power and Violence* and characterized by the *cultural* turn: "we can also draw on insights from the cultural turns in sociology and history, and the constructivist one in political science, about how cultural schemas influence categories and classifications, including those that demarcate boundaries between state and nonstate realms. Viewing the state as a 'sociocultural phenomenon' highlights that states are not solely constellations of material power, but embody ideas and beliefs about legitimacy, sovereignty, disinterestedness, and coherence. Such an approach also compels us to scrutinize the narratives about the state that officials – and scholars – produce as a set of cultural or ideological products. In his Collège de France lectures on the State, Bourdieu warns against adopting the selflegitimating categories of the state that only deepen its mystifying character" (10).

of we–identities in the course of nation-building is an important facet of state formation processes, it is subsidiary to the central feature of the formation of a state in the sense in which Weber defined it,that is an organization which successfully upholds a claim to binding rule making over a territory, by virtue of commanding a monopoly of the legitimate use of violence. Establishing such a monopoly involves, on the one hand, securing and extending the boundaries of a territory, to a considerable extent by means of the use of violence against external opponents; and on the other, it involves the internal pacification of the territory. Elias's thesis (to quote it again) is that internal pacification also, in the long term comes to be embodied in a more pacific habitus: if in this or that region, the power of central authority grows, if over a larger or smaller area the people are forced to leave at peace with each other, the molding of effects and the standards of emotion management are very gradually changed as well" (Loyal 2016, 2).

Therefore, for Elias the State becomes a pacification factor which at the same time influences individual conducts, orienting them towards a more peaceful and docile habitus. As already said, the State allows a bifocal view on macro and micro processes.

This is not the place to closely analyze Bourdieu's conception of the State, which in recent years has increasingly engaged its interpreters, but certainly for Bourdieu the State is assumed above all as symbolic power and symbolic violence: "the state, Bourdieu tells us, is the sector of the field of power, or bureaucratic field, that is defined by a possession of the monopoly of legitimate physical *and* symbolic violence. [...] This increased emphasis on symbolic forms and culture in maintaining and reproducing the social order does not, Bourdieu believes, mean relapsing into an idealism, rather it entails what he calls an, 'expanded materialism,' or a 'materialist theory of the symbolic,' where symbolic and material forms of domination co-exist" (3).

Furthermore, two other elements intervene to qualify this category: "the state exists within us. The state, for Bourdieu is not a monolithic, abstract, detached entity engaged in large-scale substantial acts as is commonly assumed – passing legislation, governing, or producing legitimizing discourses to serve dominant class interests [...] the state operates in and through us, state thinking penetrates the minutest aspects of our everyday lives from filling in a bureaucratic form, carrying an identity card, signing a birth certificate, to shaping our thinking and thought: it is the public at the heart of what we consider the private: 'the state structures the social order itself – timetables, budget periods, calendars, our whole social life is structured by the state – and, by the same token, so is our thought' [...]. The state, then, is everywhere exercising an unconscious effect of symbolic imposition: objectively in things, the division in disciplines, age-groups, official statistics, census categories, the curriculum, in national borders; and in mental structures, with the dispositions to classify and act in certain ways [...]. According to Bourdieu, the state is not akin to an object, it is not a bloc but a field of forces, a sector of the field of power which may be called the 'administrative' field, 'bureaucratic field' or 'field of public office.' The state is not a thing or something you lay your hands on, but a reality that exists in its effects and the collective beliefs which underpin these effects. The state exists differently to how people believe it exists: it is not an entity but an administrative or bureaucratic field, part of the field of power, a space structured according to oppositions linked to specific forms of capital tied to different social interests. In addition to claiming the state has a monopoly over the legitimate physical and symbolic violence and regarding the state as a 'bureaucratic' or 'administrative field,' Bourdieu argues that it is the 'central bank of symbolic capital,' the place where a monopoly of legitimate symbolic violence has been established" (4).

The second aspect that Loyal insists on concerns the formation of the State: "according to Bourdieu, the genesis of the state was a recursive phenomenon following the concentration of various capitals – physical, economic, and cultural around the king, and the development of a number of autonomous social fields, including the cultural, economic and juridical field. But this concentration presupposed and depended upon the prior primitive accumulation of symbolic capital" (5).

It is evident that there is some consonance in the concept of State between the two authors, mainly linked to overcoming the subject-object or micro-macro dichotomy, but, above all thanks to Bourdieu's de(merit), what emerges are the latter's criticisms towards Elias and therefore there are more factors of divergence than of similarity. The controversy thus starts from the difference in the focus on the concept of violence to then spread to accuse – [.] Elias – of the risk of running into a form of historical *telos*. According to Dùloye, in *On the State* Bourdieu "although emphasizing the esteem he has for the author of 'The Court Society,' strongly reproaches him for having neglected part of the Weberian legacy which, however, he lays claim to, forgetting 'the symbolic dimension of state power.' Ultimately, by retaining only the double process of monopolization of physical violence and taxation, N. Elias would forget what is essential in the eyes of P. Bourdieu: the concentration of a symbolic capital of authority in the hands of the State that conditions the other processes of concentration evoked by N. Elias. In fact, 'the State is the par excellence legitimizing condition that consecrates, solemnises, ratifies, records' (231). During the subsequent conference cited here, that of 24th January 1991, the sociologist further accentuates his criticism: drawing close C. Tilly and N. Elias, he unites them in the same criticism of economism which tends to reduce 'the State to an organ of coercion and to make it a reflection of economic power'" (Dùloye 2014, 16).

This attitude reveals how "in the end, despite the twenty references to N. Elias in the index of *Sur l'État*, Bourdieu dedicates only a marginal place to the study of the transformations of the 'psychic economy' of individuals which accompany the sociogenesis of the State and which are at the center of Elias's approach, albeit discussed, to the civilization process. By limiting too much Elias' contribution to a reading in terms of military coercion [...], the interpretation proposed by P. Bourdieu does not sufficiently grasp the interest of the paths developed by N. Elias to understand this 'sort of miracle of symbolic efficiency' which translates into the fact that 'the State inculcates similar cognitive structures in all agents subject to its jurisdiction'" (16).

Dúloye's conclusion is that "in his desire to affirm the symbolic efficacy of the State and its claim to be a 'place of management of the universal,' P. Bourdieu [...] forgets that the categories promoted by the State, that the beliefs it intends to spread to strengthen its legitimacy, that the rituals that symbolically attest to its majesty, are not imposed in a simple manner, even less so unequivocally, on the citizens, who have become, in the words of the author, simple 'Leibniz's monads' [...]. In short, it is not so much the capacity of the State to institute the social sphere that must be analyzed, but that of the social players to co-produce the conditions of their voluntary submission, but also to lay claim to their capacity to resist the state order" (17).

Loyal moves along the same critical line and according to him Bourdieu's criticisms of Elias only partially hit the mark. In addition to the aforementioned criticism of having forgotten the symbolic dimension of state power, Bourdieu distances himself from Elias on two other aspects. In primis "he argues that Elias's definition of the monopoly mechanism is tautological since it ignores the means or assets available to a king which lead to his triumph in the competition with its rivals, what Elias calls *the law of monopoly* [...]. Elias, like Weber, ignores the fact that a small group of individuals – the state nobility – secures a monopoly over the monopoly." Against this critic Bourdieu claims that the innovative aspects of Elias "is in the elements of the analysis he makes of the transition from a private monopoly (what I call the dynastic state) to the public monopoly of the state (Bourdieu 2014). [...]. Although he explicitly acknowledges using Elias's genetic theory of the state and his transition from the dynastic state to the bureaucratic state, it is clear that he draws on much more: i) Elias's view that the state 'is a legitimate protection racket'; ii) that the state was Janus-faced, so that together with monopolization of the means of violence and taxation there comes increasing peace, even for the most disadvantaged groups; iii) processes of differentiation, lengthening chains of dependence and interdependence lead to relations of asymmetrical dependency and legitimation; iv) that the king operates a policy of divide and conquer through what Elias calls the 'royal mechanism'; v) the more power becomes concentrated, the more difficult it becomes for the ruler to control it, and his dependency on others increases; vi); that taxes are bound up in a reciprocal virtuous cycle with warfare" (Loyal 2016, 4).

One can agree with Bourdieu about the criticism he raises towards Elias regarding the fact that the latter "ignores the 'monopoly of monopoly' held by small groups, [because] Elias jumps too quickly at looking at the process of 'functional democratisation' where the distribution of power becomes increasingly dispersed over the social figuration as a whole." But this, according to Loyal, must be read in Elias as a perspective to be understood in a long-term historical logic. On the contrary "his argument that Elias's theory of the monopoly mechanism is ultimately tautological is misjudged. Elias spends considerable time providing a rich empirical description of the dynamics and assets underpinning monopolization, in term of questions of land, military campaigns and money resources. In addition, Bourdieu is right to argue that Elias does not examine the symbolic forms or ideological factors underpinning state legitimation, not in *The Civilizing Process* (2000) at least" (4).

Therefore, having highlighted these aspects, Loyal can with good reason underline the merits of Elias and the demerits of Bourdieu: "but there are several respects in which Elias's account of state and state formation remains ahead of Bourdieu's own account and could usefully supplement it. Firstly, Elias is more cautious about applying terms such as political, economic or ideological (symbolic) in a causal sense, not only since these terms cannot be applied to feudal undifferentiated social relations, as Bourdieu recognizes, but also because they are abstractions which look at the same nexus of social relations from different points of view. An economic sphere or field has a symbolic and political aspect as Elias recognizes. By contrast, Bourdieu's discussion of economic, cultural, political fields etc. can sometimes map onto what Elias calls 'spherical thinking' [...].

Second, Elias tends to be more reflexive than Bourdieu in terms of his use of 'processual concepts' that take account of, and try to capture, various social balances and power ratios pertaining to figurations. Elias rarely talks about monopolization *per se* but rather *high degrees* of monopolization of violence and taxation. The emphasis is on shifts in power balances between groups, not on absolutes. Although Bourdieu, at one point for example, uses the term 'statization', or acknowledges the existence of 'relatively' public monopolies [...], his discussion of the move from the personal rule of dynastic kings to the impersonal rule of the bureaucratic state, or public to private he predominantly uses hard-edged contrasts and binaries, deriving ultimately from structuralism. Binaries are of course useful in creating contrasts within social forms, and they are the stock in trade of sociology – *Gemeinschaft-Gesellschaft*, status-contract, military-industrial, feudalism-capitalism etc. But they are less effective, however, in capturing empirical continuities and contradictory multi-polar tendencies and ambivalences.

Third, Elias's approach is in some ways more systematic and methodologically comparative in respect of looking at France, Germany and England. Bourdieu, also looks at these countries as well as Japan and China, in his lectures contained in *On the State*, but more impressionistically, and with less comparative rigor. Bourdieu's primary scientific methodological heuristic is the 'model' which has strong affinities with Weber's ideal types. And though Bourdieu continually reminds us to avoid confusing the 'reality of the model' with the model of reality, the use of models also suffers from the same drawbacks as Weber's ideal types – when empirical processes do not correspond the model is nevertheless retained and rationalized as an ideal type" (4).[12]

A further aspect in which Elias's theory of state formation supersedes Bourdieu's is in terms of another contextual variable – Elias's stronger focus on class: "Elias's book *The Civilizing Process* is subtitled: *'Changes in the Behaviour of the Secular Upper-Class in the West'* and is centrally concerned with the conflict and contestation between the descending nobility and rising bourgeoisie. These groups, within a system of multi-polar tensions, are dependent on the central authority of the king, who plays them off one another to maintain his position of power, often by giving positions of power to individuals from the rising bourgeoisie, a new elite of magistrates and officials, who constituted the *noblesse de robe*, at the expense of the declining nobility. Elias was conscious of class fractions, for example the division in the bourgeoisie between administrators who generally supported the *ancien regime* and wished to acquire the rights and entitlements of the nobility, and the enterprising merchant part of the bourgeoisie who were more in favor of challenging the social formation. But he was also aware of the ambivalence of interests between many of these conflictual groupings challenging the monarch also sometimes meant challenging the whole social order and therefore one's intermediary position

---

12   Furthermore Bourdieu "remains trapped in a nationalist form of sociology, because it is
      recognized the problem of using Prussia and France, peculiarly centered state, as their
      model of the state. Such a state may, however, historically be more of an exception rather
      than rule in terms of its centralization, reach ad penetration of its population" (Loyal
      2017, 123–4).

within it. In such an explanation, Elias does not need to revert to concepts such as acquiring consent or symbolic violence in order to account for why groups acted as they did in relation to a powerful king. It is the overall structure of the configuration and the interests of the groups within it that compels them to act in certain ways. This is neither a question of the nobility being free or forced but a question of the degrees of compulsion operating upon them in a given conjuncture of interdependencies. [...]. This polymorphous and ambiguous analysis of conflict is for the most part absent from Bourdieu's analysis which focuses largely on a binary or tripartite conflict between the dominant, dominated fractions of the dominant, and dominated, or conflicts between the king, his brothers and the bureaucracy" (Loyal 2016, 7).

That said, Bourdieu's contribution remains undeniable: "he provides a dynamic and creative theory of the state, offering a needed corrective to standard views which neglect the role of cultural forms and social classifications and their role in maintaining and reproducing forms of power and domination. Bourdieu's concepts have been fashioned from empirical work and their usefulness is tied to their power of generating insightful substantive analyses. The emphasis on the state's power of nomination, classification, and official validation, in constructing both groups and modes of identification, sanctioning and defining social practices, and the cleavages that exists in the state itself, as a field of power operating in terms of 'antagonistic co-operation' between a left and the right hand, are all fundamental concepts for understanding the modern state" (8).[13]

Beyond Bourdieu's differences, limits and idiosyncrasies, it is undeniable that the analysis of the State conducted by the two authors is essential to study this category from a historical point of view and that this analysis constitutes an actual research program.[14] With this, ideally closing the circle with respect

---

13   Loyal himself in a note underlines the convergences we have already disclosed: "more generally, there are numerous other parallels in their work, both use the notion of habitus and field, seek to transcend the agency-structure divide, and both see state formation as inextricably tied to changes in personality structure and both, following Durkheim, argue that as societies advance they differentiate into separate spheres. They also share a broadly similar world-social democratic view. Though some of the differences in terms of physical violence and symbolic violence can also be accounted for by the paradigmatic crises situations they both respond to – the aftermath of the violence of the First World War and Algeria respectively" (Loyal 2016, 3).

14   Arnoltz (2018, 578) says that "Bourdieu's engagement with the state contains an interesting and innovative research program that should inspire further research [...] and offers methodological and epistemological guidance for studying an object that in large part is an symbolic construct, as well as a research program that offers a number of re-conceptualizations for going beyond common-sense understanding of the state."

to what we said at the beginning, we can state that their perspectives can be placed in an ideal dialogical relationship with many authors, coming from other disciplines and who have made the State the main object of their scientific investigation. Just to name a few, also present in this volume, we think of Mann (2008) with his conception of infrastructural power, or Steinmetz (1999), the first to detect the link between the State and Cultural Studies, to make the State a cultural idea or an ideological form.

4   Conclusions

In these pages we have developed a comparison, on the one hand, between two *sui generis* authors such as Bourdieu and Elias and, on the other, with an equally unique approach, that of Historical Sociology, trying to demonstrate how dialectic between authors and approach provides us with valuable reading keys to improve the understanding of both.

In the last part instead, we focused our attention on the way in which the aforementioned authors have offered a perspective, at times original, of a classic topic for Historical Sociology such as that of the origin and development of the State.

Having reached the end of reflections that can only be provisional and open, we can try to mention, without dwelling on this too much, the reasons why the virtuous connections between Bourdieu and Elias on the one hand and Historical Sociology on the other are numerous and unpublished.

Bourdieu and Elias are authors who are positioned on a ridge, from which they look at different but nevertheless neighboring thematic horizons and areas of study, trying, where possible, to go beyond sclerotic and sometimes simply expedient dualisms. They belong to their time, with a biographical trajectory that they have been able to interpret thoughtfully – I am thinking of Bourdieu from the Bèarn – or to sublimate thematically – I am thinking of the traumatic experiences Elias lived in relation to his family during Nazism; they are authors who, albeit to varying degrees, have been able to analyze power and violence and deal with History and its events without easy shortcuts, interpreting the latter as a typically human affair, without pretence and sugar-coating. They made bold methodological choices, against the tide, and were therefore,

---

Arnoltz's conclusion is that Bourdieu's approach allows both to understand how the historical story of the State is far from being over, its role in transnational relations which mark a new phase of its history, and to explain the processes of de-monopolization of State power.

for this reason and much more, authors that cannot easily be classified, capable of arousing admiration but also distrust and ferocious criticism from the scientific and academic establishment with which they exchanged views.

For these reasons their natural place lies in an intrinsically interdisciplinary approach (Smith 2014, 2079) as Historical Sociology, whose definition is more easily grasped *ex negativo*, by falsification rather than by verification, more by saying what it *is not* rather than *what it is*. Furthermore, because of the manner they have been able to live their own historicity, we can say that they have been able to interpret Historical Sociology more as an open sociological style and not as a subdiscipline better than others. As Kumar wrote at the time, "there should not be a separate, potentially ghettoizable, sub-field called 'historical sociology' comparable to 'family sociology' or the 'sociology of education.' Those areas have their subject – the family, the educational system. What is the 'subject' of historical sociology? Is it not rather simply an approach, a way of doing sociology?" (391) This version, which the authors in question have helped to corroborate, constitutes the sense and measure of the approach, the constitutive style and the limit, and imposes and requires us to accept the condition of impermanence, criticism and openness to discussion, as Lawson *et al* actually said very well: "Historical sociology, therefore, has necessarily porous borders – it is the prototypical open society" (Hobson, Lawson and Rosenberg 2010, 3359).

Of course, there is no shortage of problems. There remains the question of an approach that is hard to define, if not indeed as *ex negativo*. As Ghisleni (1998) argues, the problem of Historical Sociology is that in relation to its growth there has been no similar care in defining its boundaries and in identifying substantive methodologies. Furthermore, it would be subject to a singular paradox that revolves around the notion of time: in a nutshell every sociological research is research which takes into consideration the notion of time and therefore Historical Sociology finds itself having to continually define its area of investigation and its boundaries of action. Problems also remain concerning the real possibility that disciplining the two forms of knowledge is nothing more than a way through which they keep their distance from each other.

The fact remains that illuminating Bourdieu and Elias through Historical Sociology and vice versa constitutes an intellectual challenge to be undertaken; it reveals in the authors analyzed a sensitivity for history which requires providing depth to the present by overcoming a nostalgic (therefore amateurish) or purely historicist attitude. Bourdieu and Elias were theorists of the historical-social *possible* and therefore we can conclude that studying Historical Sociology and these authors helps to transform Nietzsche's *es war* from a burden on the present and the future into an (indeed) Weber-type open challenge for the possible.

References

Abrams, Philip. 1988. "Notes on the Difficulty of Studying the State." *Journal of Historical Sociology* 1 (1): 58–89.

Adams, Julia, Elisabeth S. Clemens, and Ann Shola Orloff. 2005. *Remaking Modernity: Politics, History and Sociology.* Durham: Duke University Press.

Arnholz, Jens. 2018. "Tensions, Actors, and Inventions: Bourdieu's Sociology of the State as an Unfinished but Promising Research Program." In *The Oxford Handbook of Pierre Bourdieu,* edited by Thomas Medvetz and Jeffrey J. Sallaz, 577–600. New York: Oxford University Press.

Azuélos, Daniel. 2009. "Norbert Elias entre sociologie et histoire. Norbert Elias, 'un marginal établi?'" *Individu et Nation.* Centre Interlangues "Texte Image Langage" (EA 4182): Université de Bourgogne.

Bourdieu, Pierre. 1992. *An Invitation to Reflexive Sociology.* Cambridge: Polity Press.

Bourdieu, Pierre. 1995. "Sur le rapports entre la sociologie et l'histoire en Allemagne et en France." *Actes de la recherche en sciences sociales,* 106–7 (March): 108–22.

Bourdieu, Pierre. 1996. *The rules of art. Genesis and structure of the literary field.* Cambridge: Polity Press.

Bourdieu, Pierre. 1999. *Pascalian Meditations.* Stanford: University Press.

Bourdieu, Pierre. 2001. *Masculine Domination.* Stanford: University Press.

Bourdieu, Pierre. 2002. *Si le monde social m'est supportable, c'est parce que je peux m'indigner.* Avignon: Editions de l'Aube.

Bourdieu, Pierre. 2008. *Sketch for a Self-Analysis.* Chicago: The University of Chicago Press.

Bourdieu, Pierre. 2014. *On the State: Lectures at the College de France 1989–1992,* edited by Patrick Champagne, Remi Lenoir, Franck Poupeau, and Marie-Christine Riviere. Cambridge: Polity Press.

Bourdieu, Pierre. 2022. *L'Intérêt au désintéressement. Cours au Collège de France (1987–1989).* Paris: Seuil.

Bourdieu, Pierre, and Roger Chartier. 2015. *The Sociologist and the Historian.* Cambridge: Polity Press.

Bowen, Paulle, Bart van Heerikhuizen, and Mustafa Emirbayer. 2012. "Elias and Bourdieu." *Journal of Classical Sociology* 12 (1): 69–93.

Brunet, Ignasi, and Antonio Morell. 2001. "Sociología e historia: Norbert Elias y Pierre Bourclieu." *Sociológica,* no. 4: 109–30.

Calhoun, Craig. 2013. "For the Social History of the Present: Bourdieu as Historical Sociologist." In *Bourdieu and Historical Analysis*, edited by Philip S. Gorski, 36–66. Durham-London: Duke University Press.

Cavalli, Alessandro. 2011. "Il percorso di Norbert Elias tra sociologia e storia." *CAMBIO – Rivista sulle trasformazioni sociali* I, no. 1 (June): 23–30.

Delanty, Gerard, and Engin F. Isin, eds. 2003. *Handbook of Historical Sociology*. London: Sage Publications.

Delmotte, Florence. 2012. "La sociologie historique de Norbert Elias." *Cahiers philosophiques*, 128 (1): 42–58.

Dùloye, Yves. 2014. "La sociologie historique de l'Etat de Pierre Bourdieu au prisme de la sociologie historique compare: de quelques paradoxes et decalages." *Swiss Political Science Review* 20 (1): 14–8.

Dufour, Frédérick Guillaume. 2015. *La sociologie historique: traditions, trajectoires et débats*. Québec: Presses de l'Université du Québec.

Elias, Norbert. 1987. "The Retreat of Sociologists into the Present." *Theory, Culture and Society* 4 (2–3): 223–49.

Elias, Norbert. 1998. "An Interview in Amsterdam." In *The Norbert Elias Reader*, edited by Johan Goudsblom e Stephen Mennell, 141–51. New York: John Wiley and Sons Ltd.

Elias, Norbert. 2000. *The Civilizing Process: Sociogenetic and Psychogenetic Investigations*. Malden, MA: Basil Blackwell.

Elias, Norbert, and Michael Schröter. 1993. *Mozart: Portrait of a Genius*. Translated from German by Edmund Jephcott of *Mozart: Zur Soziologie eines Genies*. Cambridge: Polity Press.

Evans, Peter B., Dietrich Rueschemeyer, and Theda Skocpol, eds. 1985. *Bringing the State back in*. Cambridge: University Press.

Ghisleni, Maurizio. 1998. "Sociologia storica e cultura materiale." In *Verso una sociologia riflessiva. Ricerca qualitativa e cultura*, edited by Alberto Melucci, 197–218. Bologna: il Mulino.

Giannini, Mirella. 2011. Introduction to the Italian edition of *Il sociologo e lo storico*, by R. Chartier and P. Bourdieu. Bari: Dedalo.

Hobson, John M., George Lawson, and Justin Rosenberg. 2010. "Historical Sociology." In *The International Studies Encyclopedia*, edited by Robert A. Denemark, 3357–75. Malden: Wiley-Blackwell.

Kumar, Krishan. 2009. "Historical Sociology." In *The New Blackwell Companion to Social Theory*, edited by Bryan S. Turner, 391–408. New York: John Wiley & Sons.

Lachmann, Richard. 2013. *What is Historical Sociology?* Cambridge: Polity Press.

Loyal, Steven. 2016. "Bourdieu on the state: An Eliasian Critique in Human Figurations." *Social Character, Historical Processes* 5, no. 2 (July).

Loyal, Steven. 2017. *Bourdieu's Theory of the State. A Critical Introduction*. London: Palgrave Macmillan.

Mann, Michael. 2008. "Infrastructural Power Revisited." *Studies in Comparative International Development* 23 (3–4): 355–65.

Morgan, Kimberly J., and Ann Shola Orloff, eds. 2017. *The Many Hands of the State.* New York: Cambridge University Press.

Paci, Massimo. 2019. *Sociologia storica e spiegazione causale.* Roma: Ediesse.

Pitzalis, Marco. 2021. "Rupture and crisis. Reading Bourdieu through crisis, reading crisis through Bourdieu." *Rassegna Italiana di Sociologia* 1: 269–73. DOI: 10.1423/100631.

Salento, Angelo. 2010. "Un ospite di scarso riguardo. Bourdieu in Italia." In *Bourdieu dopo Bourdieu,* edited by Gabriella Paolucci, 281–316. Torino: Utet.

Santoro, Marco. 2008. Introduction to the italian edition of *Logics of History,* by H. William Jr. Sewell, VII–XXIV. Milano: Bruno Mondadori.

Sewell, H. William Jr. 2005. *Logics of History.* Chicago: The University of Chicago Press.

Smith, Dennis. 2014. "The return of historical sociology." *The Sociological Review,* no. 62: 206–16.

Steinmetz, George. ed. 1999. *State/Culture: State formation after the cultural turn.* New York: Cornell University Press.

Steinmetz, George. 2011. "Bourdieu, Historicity, and Historical Sociology." *Cultural Sociology* (March).

Steinmetz, George. 2018. "Bourdieusian Field Theory and the Reorientation of Historical Sociology." In *The Oxford Handbook of Pierre Bourdieu,* edited by Thomas Medvetz and Jeffrey J. Sallaz, 601–28. New York: Oxford University Press.

Susca, Emanuela. 2021. "Tempo e temporalità in Pierre Bourdieu." In *La sociologia storica contemporanea,* edited by Andrea Borghini, Vincenzo Romania and Luca Corchia, 63–90. *Quaderni di Teoria Sociale* XXI (2).

Tabboni, Simonetta. 1993. *Norbert Elias. Un ritratto intellettuale.* Bologna: il Mulino.

CHAPTER 8

On *Habitus*, Historical Processes and Art Experience

Some Remarks on Pierre Bourdieu's Early Reflections on the Genealogy of the Judgment of Taste

Elena Gremigni

1 Introduction

Pierre Bourdieu believed that the separation between sociology and history widely observed in academia had no epistemological foundation and produced negative effects on scientific research by concealing the profound genesis of social phenomena (Bourdieu and Wacquant 1992a). It is no coincidence then that his primary concepts (*"habitus,"* "field," "capital") were used to highlight the historical processes from which they themselves originated (Wacquant 2006; Steinmetz 2011; Pitzalis and Weininger 2022). His very own research topics were constructed and investigated from a historical perspective in order to show how social structures are a result of the crystallization of past experiences that continue to manifest themselves in the present.

In the context of what Bourdieu himself defined as genetic structuralism, his studies on the genealogy of factors that guide people's choices in the use of cultural products (Bourdieu et al. 1970 [1965]; Bourdieu, Darbel and Schnapper 1969 [1966]; Bourdieu 1979) are remarkably interesting. In particular, his research on photography (Bourdieu et al. 1970 [1965]) and art museum audiences (Bourdieu, Darbel and Schnapper 1969 [1966]) identified the mechanisms behind the social reproduction of taste and pointed out a correlation between cultural consumption and the overall volume and composition of capital owned by users (economic, cultural, social, and symbolic capital), laying the foundation for what would later become the well-known theory of "distinction."

The research on this topic constitutes an important element in understanding the development of Bourdieu's idea of *habitus*, a concept that was also explicitly studied in connection with art fruition in the afterword of the French edition of an art history book by Panofsky (Bourdieu 1967). In his research on the use of artistic and cultural products, the sociologist revealed the groundlessness of the ideology that associated judgment of taste with an immediate or innate natural disposition, identifying its roots in personal, family and class trajectories instead (Bourdieu 1979). In this sense, he hereby highlighted the historical origins of taste categories that tend to perpetuate themselves, because cultural institutions foster social reproduction without putting the necessary strategies in place to promote changes in the original *habitus*.

This study intends to make a contribution to the analysis of Bourdieu's early reflections on the genealogy of the judgment of taste and their connection with the construct of *habitus*. Towards this end, a synthetic history of *habitus* is presented in the first section, which departs from a study of the origins of the concept and continues forward with a discussion of the principal authors who have defined it (Sapiro 2015), in order to demonstrate how the concept has moved from the philosophical to the sociological sphere and on to other fields. In the second section, with the aim of highlighting its historical dimension, Bourdieu's complex definition of this construct is displayed by tracing some particularly significant passages in his work through a methodology based on the so-called "clue paradigm" (Ginzburg 1986 [1979]). The third section instead attempts to demonstrate how Bourdieu's research on art fruition contributed to and permitted his focus on the key role played by this concept in understanding the genesis of human behavior. In this sense, these reflections on the historical significance of *habitus* as a concept raise further questions, to be discussed in the conclusions, regarding the limits of freedom of social agents.

The forms of determinism that seem to emerge from Bourdieu's reflections on *habitus* have, on the one hand, been stigmatized by some critics as the clues to a theory that appears to imply political conservatism, and on the other hand, have been viewed as a pervasive legacy of structuralism and Marxism in particular. The sociologist himself repeatedly responded to such charges by trying to demonstrate the existence of spaces of free action even in situations that tends to perpetuate social reproduction. However, some problematic issues raised by the question of the historicity of *habitus* are not completely resolved. What is at stake, as a matter of fact, is the possibility itself of hypothesizing a transformation of social reality in a context that is still predominantly deterministic.

2   A Look at the Origin and Spread of the Concept of *Habitus*

Habitus is a polysemic construct that has remote origins and has long been used as a conceptual tool in the field of philosophy. The term is the Latin translation of the word *hexis* (having, being in possession of), a noun that comes from the verb *echo* (to hold, keep, have). Plato (1997 [4th cent. BC]) had already used this word to indicate the possession of knowledge (*Theae.*, 197b) or intellect (*Crat.*, 414b), but it was Aristotle (1995 [4th cent. BC]) who defined the concept in a more complete way. In his *Metaphysics*, *habitus* is used to indicate "a disposition according to which that which is disposed is either well or ill disposed, and either in itself or with reference to something else" (*Met.*, V, 20, 1022b, 10). More generally, the *hexis* for Aristotle represented a way of being (intellectual, ethical, corporeal) or a center in which the different experiences that constitute a "second nature" can settle (Sgarbi 2011). As an acquired condition, it indicates a passive state as opposed to the active dimension of the *energheia*, but the *hexis* is also meant as the ability to originate behavioral models that guide future actions. While the *hexis* in the theoretical field is mainly formed through teaching, practical *habitus*, like moral virtues, are acquired through habits (*Eth. Nicom.*, II, 1, 1103a, 15–20). In this sense, the *hexis* presents a connection with the *ethos*, a custom through which a moral character is developed and that brings a practical habit to completion, which Aristotle considered to be similar to nature. Since *hexis* not only originates from a natural basis, but also results from a prolonged exercise over time, it transforms what originally required conscious effort into a spontaneous disposition. Moreover, it differs from the *diathesis*, a simple arrangement of short duration, as it is more stable and durable than the latter and consequently more difficult to remove (*Cat.*, I.8, 8b, 25–28; 9a, 15).

During the Medieval period, the concept of *habitus* largely spread thanks to an attentive reader of Aristotle: Thomas Aquinas. In his *Summa Theologiae* (1981 [1265–1272]) the *habitus* is intended as a permanent and stable quality that distinguishes a particular person's being. It is placed between pure potency and the pure act (*"habitus quodammodo est medium inter potentiam puram et purum actum"*) and must be known through the very act itself (*"necesse est quod per actum suum cognoscatur"*) (*Sum. Theol.*, I, q. 87, a. 2). Thomas Aquinas also specified different forms of *habitus* (*habitus activus*, *habitus corporis*, etc.). Among them, the *habitus operativus* assumes a particularly relevant function, due to the fact that virtue, in the Christian sense, is defined as an operational habit oriented towards the good.

The construct of *habitus* and the related concept of habit were employed on multiple occasions during the Modern period as well, particularly in contrast to Cartesian theories. Gottfried Wilhelm Leibniz, in *Quid sit idea* (1875 [1678]), wrote about *habitudines* to indicate acquired expressive structures that conform to what they express (*"habitudines habitudinibus respondent"*). An important role was also assumed by the concept of habit in David Hume's work *An Inquiry concerning Human Understanding* (1999 [1748–1758]), where it was understood as a principle of human nature. It is the habit that generates a belief that transforms a sequence of events "*hoc post hoc*" into a logical and necessary connection "*hoc propter hoc*." In this way, Hume denied the ontological value of the principle of cause and effect and of inductive inference, undermining one of the fundamental principles of the traditional scientific method and fueling the debate around possible new epistemological perspectives.

In *Enzyklopädie der philosophischen Wissenschaften im Grundisse* (1979 [1817–1830]), Georg Wilhelm Friedrich Hegel – in addition to dedicating ample space to the concept of *ethos* as *Aufhebung* of the external normativity of law and of the inner normativity of morality – analyzed the concept of habit (*Gewohnheit*) in the Science of Spirit.

In the first section of the Subjective Spirit (Anthropology, sentient soul), habit was considered "a second nature," or "an immediate being of the soul [...] created by the soul, impressing and moulding the corporeality which enters into the modes of feeling as such and into the representations and volitions so far as they have taken corporeal form" (Hegel 2007 [1830], § 410). "Hardening" (*Abhärtung*) and "satisfaction" (*Befriedigung*) are two types of habit that make impulses and feelings indifferent. Aptitude or skill (*Geschicklichkeit*) is instead a habit that functions as a memory of practices that transform corporeal determinations into an instrument of spirit. Since it is a constitutive element of all human activities, including thinking, habit was defined by Hegel to be "indispensable for the *existence* of all spirituality in the individual subject" (*ibidem*).

In contemporary philosophy the construct of *habitus* was mentioned in the works of several authors, John Dewey among them. In *Human Nature and Conduct: An Introduction to Social Psychology* (2011 [1922]) Dewey attributed particular importance to the concept of habit, which he did not intend as an acquired structure that determines specific answers, but rather as a disposition learned through experience that orients future actions. Since habit concerns both the ethical and intellectual spheres in their higher forms – intelligence itself is considered a mental habit – it is not surprising to find this concept in Dewey's pedagogical works, such as *Experience and Education* (2015 [1938]). As he wrote in *Democracy and Education* (2016 [1916]), educational processes have the purpose of forming mental habits that allow the individual to interact positively with the environment.

The concept of *habitus* also played a central role in the field of phenomenology. Although Edmund Husserl did not develop explicit methodological reflections on *habitus*, he used many terms that can be traced back to the semantic context of this concept, such as *Habitualität, das Habituelle, Gewohnheit, Habe, Besitz, Sitte, Tradition* and *habitus* itself (Moran 2014). Among the works published during his lifetime, the concept of *habitus* appeared in the *Méditations cartésiennes* (1950 [1931]) and later in *Erfahrung und Urteil* (1999 [1938]).

However, an analysis of habituality emerged above all in his posthumous works, in *Zur Phänomenologie der Intersubjektivität* (1973) and *Ideen II* (1952) in particular. Husserl utilized the concept of habit to define stable properties of the subject (Ego/Ich) that constitute the precipitation of experiences which occur throughout life. These concerned different types of behavior that are both instinctive (emotions, desires, feelings) and rational and which involve the body (bodily *habitus*) and the mind (*Denkgewohnheiten*/habits of thought). Habit is therefore connected with both the capacities to exercise basic skills such as reading, writing, playing a musical instrument etc., and with the expertise necessary to manage higher activities related to knowledge or relationships with other people which imply the acquisition and use of ethical values. Every Ego is a pole of acts and habits and the aim of the transcendental *epoché* is to put the natural attitude between parentheses and suspend judgment in order to allow the pure experience of phenomena to emerge.

In French philosophy the construct of *habitus* was revised by Maurice Merleau-Ponty, who was an attentive and original reader of Husserl. In the *Phénoménologie de la perception* (1945) the concept of *habitude* was used in opposition to behaviorism in order to overcome the idea of a simple automatism between stimulus and response. Not only is *habitude* a passive acquisition of past experiences, it is also an active disposition placed in the body, a memory of the body that allowed Merleau-Ponty to avoid reducing the ego to both the idealism of consciousness and the simple naturalism of the organic body (Magrì 2015).

With the development and consolidation of sociology and anthropology, the construct of *habitus* spread into the social sciences, even before the diffusion of the phenomenological approach, and became a particularly useful conceptual device for understanding the historical origins of collective behavior.

Max Weber borrowed this concept from Thomas Aquinas, in its positive meaning in relation to the virtuous conduct of life above all. It is no coincidence then that the term can be traced to his writings on religion starting from *Die Protestantische Ethik und der Geist des Kapitalismus* (1986 [1904–1905]), where Weber described the *habitus* of the Puritans ("Gesamthabitus des Puritaners"). The term was also employed in the introduction to *Die Wirtschaftsethik der Weltreligionen* (1986 [1916–1919]), which mentioned the affective *habitus* (*Gefühlshabitus*) evoked by religious or magical acts, and in the essay *Hinduismus und Buddhismus* (1986 [1916–1917]), which defined Nirvana as a habit that occurs when any connection with the world is broken. In his posthumous work *Wirtschaft und Gesellschaft* (1976 [1921]) too, the term was used in the section dedicated to the sociology of religion, and again on the issue of religious rituals and ways of life.

During the same period, in his lectures for academic year 1904–1905 addressed to the candidates of the *Agrégation*, published posthumously in *L'Évolution pédagogique en France* (1938), Émile Durkheim also reflected on the concept of *habitus* he had encountered in Scholastic philosophy. According to Durkheim, the enduring disposition of perceiving, thinking and acting is the result of a form of education that shapes the interiority of the subject, like Christianity which acts on people in their fundamental essence as an inclination of the soul. In this sense education should not aim to acquire an extensive amount of knowledge, but rather to form an inner and deep state ("état intérieur et profond"), a sort of polarity of the soul ("polarité de l'âme"), that can orient it throughout life, not only in the field of learning, but also in the ethical and social spheres. When culture contributes to the integral formation of people, it is therefore a *habitus*.

The social nature of *habitus* was examined in depth by Marcel Mauss – Durkheim's nephew and collaborator – in *Les techniques du corps* (1950 [1936]), a communication presented to the Société de Psychologie in 1934 and later published in the *Journal de Psychologie*. Mauss highlighted the role of the training of bodies, especially in the process of internalizing rules and practices of behavior. The bodies, as points of conjunction between nature and culture, the individual and society, would therefore embody the distinctive features of a particular social group in the form of *habitus*.

Alfred Schütz, Husserl's student, introduced the concept of *habitus* instead into the sociological context through the perspective of phenomenology. In *Der sinnhafte Aufbau der sozialen Welt* (1974 [1932]), habit was associated with the practice of "typification," that is the conceptual elaboration that allows people to experience reality by identifying empirical types (Moran 2011). Furthermore, Schütz translated the term *Habitualität*, used by Husserl, with the expression "habitual knowledge," a concept widely analyzed in his posthumous work, *The Structures of the Life-World* (1973), published and completed by Thomas Luckmann, which contributed to its spread in the context of ethnomethodology.

Another of Husserl's students, Norbert Elias, used the construct of *habitus* to indicate the oft unconscious incorporation of emotions and dispositions that a person acquires through real social practices. According to Elias, there is a correspondence between "psychogenesis" and "sociogenesis" and consequently what appear to be simple individual decisions are actually produced by the social transformations of an entire society. In *Über den Prozess der Zivilisation* (1987 [1939]), the evolution of Western people's *habitus* was analyzed in an attempt to explain the different customs and traditions of France and Germany. After the spread of this concept, as a result of Pierre Bourdieu's publications, Elias dealt with *habitus* again in his essay *Wandlungen der Wir-Ich Balance* (1987), where he expressly discussed the social *habitus* of individuals derived from different proximal and distal stratifications. In *Studien über die Deutschen* (1989), the sociologist analyzed one of these components, the national *habitus*, and identified the weaknesses of bourgeois culture and the permanence of warlike values as factors that might have determined the crisis of the Weimar republic and the rise of Nazism to the power.

Reflections on the construct of *habitus*, however, were not limited merely to the spheres of philosophy and the social sciences. Another scholar forced into exile by Nazi persecutions, Erwin Panofsky, who was a student of Heinrich Rickert, contributed to spreading this construct in the field of iconology, a subject of which he is considered the founder (Elsner and Lorenz 2012), starting from the study of Thomas Aquinas as well as using some concepts specific to Husserl's phenomenology (Hart 1993). In *Gothic Architecture and Scholasticism*, Panofsky emphasized the importance of *habitus* at work in every civilization and highlighted in particular how "mental habits induced by Early and High Scholasticism may have affected the formation of Early and High Gothic architecture" (Panofsky 1976 [1951], 27).

It was precisely this attention to overcoming an individualistic conception of artistic creation by underlining the collective components of the work of art through the mediation of *habitus* that aroused the keen interest of Pierre Bourdieu (Bourdieu 1967).

3   *Habitus* and History in Bourdieu's Sociological Theory

Pierre Bourdieu knew very well the complex and articulated history of the concept of *habitus* (Bourdieu 1985, 2002), and in a certain sense, his own personal history, which led him from philosophical studies to sociology, bore some similarity to the historical path of this construct, which has assumed a central role in the social sciences and in the work of the French scholar himself.

Significant traces of numerous and attentive readings have been found and highlighted in his theory by the many researchers who have analyzed the use and evolution of this concept in his work (Héran 1987; Jenkins 1992; Mounier 2001; Krais and Gebauer 2002; Marsiglia 2002; Ravaioli 2002; Lau 2004; Lizardo 2004; Sapiro 2004, 2010 and 2015; Wacquant 2006 and 2016; Grange 2009; Paolucci 2011; Susca 2011; Baldacci 2017; Aiello 2022). Beyond references to the Aristotelian definitions and the subsequent philosophical re-elaborations of the concept in the modern age, with specific reference to Leibniz and Hegel, Bourdieu's numerous reflections made particular mention of *L'Évolution pédagogique en France* by Durkheim, *Les techniques du corps* by Mauss, the essay of both on the methods of *habitus* transmission (Durkheim and Mauss 1903), the concept of habit analyzed by Dewey in *Human Nature and Conduct*, Husserl's phenomenology and Merleau-Ponty's theory of perception. Despite being rather critical of the phenomenological perspective because of its naive attribution of authenticity to a subject's original experience (Throop and Murphy 2002), Bourdieu took up the notion of "corporeal scheme" by Merleau-Ponty (Hanks 2005), in association with Mauss's reflections from an anthropological point of view, in order to define the first aspect of *habitus* on which he began to reflect (Sapiro 2010). The construct of *habitus*, in fact, has multiple meanings in Bourdieu's work.

In his *Questions de sociologie* (1980a), departing from Aristotelian conceptions, he attributed three characteristics to *habitus*: *ethos*, *eidos* and *hexis*. First, he underlined the link between *ethos* and *habitus*, affirming that the latter encompassed the notion of *ethos* that the sociologist used

> in opposition to *ethic*, to designate an objectively systematic set of dispositions with an ethical dimension, a set of practical principles (an ethic being an intentionally coherent system of explicit principles).
>
> BOURDIEU 1993 [1980a], 86

As *eidos*, the *habitus* is "a system of logical schemes" (*ibidem*), a system of forms and categories that are not universal and necessary, as Kant believed, but historically determined. In this sense *habitus* is:

> a system of internalized embodied schemes which, having been constituted in the course of collective history, are acquired in the course of individual history and function in their *practical* state, *for practice* (and not for the sake of pure knowledge).
>
> BOURDIEU 1984 [1979], 467

It was precisely the bodily dimension of *habitus* that Bourdieu emphasized on several occasions, observing how Aristotle himself considered *hexis* to be a bodily disposition. Indeed, Bourdieu recalled how the word *habitus* implies that "which has become durably incorporated in the body in the form of permanent disposition" (*ibidem*), a "bodily *hexis*" which, according to the sociologist, has eminently social origins.

While using different words to underline different aspects of the concept, Bourdieu more frequently adopted the term *habitus* in order to avoid both the issue of associating separate faculties with what is a single disposition and of falling into the age-old problem of the Cartesian dualism between *res cogitans* and *res extensa*.

> The practical principles of classification which constitute the *habitus* are *inseparably* logical and axiological, theoretical and practical. Because practical logic is turned towards practice, it inevitably implements values. [...] Moreover, all the principles of choice are 'embodied', turned into postures, dispositions of the body. Values are postures, gestures, ways of standing, walking, speaking. The strength of the *ethos* is that it is a morality made flesh.
>
> BOURDIEU 1993 [1980a], 86

The construct of *habitus* was therefore used to overcome any form of antinomy between subject and object founded on a substantialist epistemology that is widely spread even in the traditionally theoretical perspectives of sociology. In fact, Bourdieu realized the heuristic potential of this concept for resolving the complementary issues that emerged from constructivist and structuralist approaches. On the one hand, constructivism went too far in its subjectivism by attributing an exaggerated importance to the micro-social dimension and the autonomy of social agents, while on the other, structuralism exaggerated its objectivism by highlighting the role of the macrosocial dimension while neglecting the actions of single individuals who seem to submit passively to the necessity of the social world. With his "structuralist constructivism," Bourdieu proposed a synthetic and monistic perspective that places "objective relations which exist 'independently of individual consciousness and will', as Marx said" (Bourdieu and Wacquant 1992b [1992a], 97), at the heart of social research instead of substances. Twisting Hegel's famous formula, the sociologist stated: "the real is the relational" (*ibidem*). The *habitus* then, in this sense, constitutes a center of relationships that represents a synthesis between subject and object, the individual and the social, interiority and exteriority, as well as the material and the spiritual, activity and passivity, and freedom and necessity, because it is the product of the social reality that is incorporated ("structured structure") and guides practices and perceptions of practices ("structuring structure") without presupposing a conscious intentionality. As Bourdieu wrote, *habitus* are:

> systems of durable, transposable *dispositions*, structured structures predisposed to function as structuring structures, that is, as principles of the generation and structuring of practices and representations which can be objectively 'regulated' and 'regular' without in any way being the

product of obedience to rules, objectively adapted to their goals without presupposing a conscious aiming at ends or an express mastery of
the operations necessary to attain them and, being all this, collectively
orchestrated without being the product of the orchestrating action of a
conductor.

BOURDIEU 2013 [1972], 72

The *habitus* is therefore both *modus operandi* and *opus operatum* and is closely
connected to the dimension of temporality, as a practical disposition oriented
towards the future and as an incorporated past. On the one hand, it allows a
social agent to act effectively and immediately within the "field"[1] while respect-
ing its rules,

the *habitus* is this kind of practical sense for what is to be done in a given
situation – what is called in sport a 'feel' for the game, that is, the art of
anticipating the future of the game which is inscribed in the present state
of play.

BOURDIEU 1998 [1994], 25

On the other hand, the actions, which will themselves become history, are
made possible by the assimilation of rules and schemes that have been learned
through socialization processes that have remote origins: "the *habitus*, the
product of history, produces individual and collective practices, and hence history, in accordance with the schemes engendered by history" (Bourdieu 2013
[1972], 82).

In this sense the *habitus* produces history starting from history. It is the
action of history that operates through social agents unaware of being in some
way the product not only of their own individual past, but also of the collective past. Therefore, according to Bourdieu, it is a construct that could be very
useful for historians who often use generic and misleading expressions like the
'mentality' of an era instead (Bourdieu and Chartier 2010 [1988]).

---

1 As the sociologist stated, "a field may be defined as a network, or a configuration, of objective relations between positions. These positions are objectively defined, in their existence
and in the determinations they impose upon their occupants, agents or institutions, by their
present and potential situation (*situs*) in the structure of the distribution of species of power
(or capital) whose possession commands access to the specific profits that are at stake in the
field, as well as by their objective relation to other positions (domination, subordination,
homology, etc.)" (Bourdieu and Wacquant 1992b [1992a], 97).

Quoting a passage taken from *L'Évolution pédagogique en France* by Durkheim, the sociologist defined *habitus* as an embedded and forgotten story that becomes "unconscious" (Bourdieu 1980b). In opposition to the rational choice theory, Bourdieu's sociology of practice thus highlights the complexity of social factors that often intervene, unconsciously and without any planning, on individual action through the mediation of *habitus* (Bourdieu 1997).

These durable dispositions do not depend mechanically on external structures and are not immutable. Bourdieu underlined this aspect by comparing his theory of *habitus* with the concept of habit defined by Dewey to highlight the active and creative relationship of a social agent with the world (Bourdieu and Wacquant 1992b [1992a], 12). In a response to critics – Alain Caillé first and foremost (Caillé 1986) – who saw a risk of determinism in the relationship between the individual and society, the sociologist wrote:

> *habitus* is not the fate that some people read into it. Being the product of history, it is an *open system of dispositions* that is constantly subjected to experiences, and therefore constantly affected by them in a way that either reinforces or modifies its structures. It is durable but not eternal!
>
> BOURDIEU and WACQUANT 1992b [1992a], 133

Nevertheless, Bourdieu also observed how "most people are statistically bound to encounter circumstances that tend to agree with those that originally fashioned their *habitus*" (*ibidem*). Social agents are therefore conditioned by past experience, "are the *product of history*, of the history of the whole social field and of the accumulated experience of a path within the specific subfield" (136). In other words, they do not have absolute freedom, but rather have a "conditioned" and "conditional" freedom, limited by the internalization of durable social dispositions:

> the *habitus* is an endless capacity to engender products – thoughts, perceptions, expressions, actions – whose limits are set by the historically and socially situated conditions of its production, the conditioned and conditional freedom it secures is as remote from a creation of unpredictable novelty as it is from a simple mechanical reproduction of the initial conditionings.
>
> BOURDIEU 2013 [1972], 95

The sociologist's task is to bring this forgotten story to light "which history itself produces by realizing the objective structures that it generates in the quasi-natures of *habitus*" (Bourdieu 1990 [1980b], 56). As Bourdieu observed:

At bottom, determinisms operate to their full only by the help of unconsciousness, with the complicity of the unconscious. For determinism
to exert itself unchecked, dispositions must be abandoned to their free
play. This means that agents become something like 'subjects' only to
the extent that they consciously master the relation they entertain with
their dispositions. They can deliberately let them 'act' or they can on the
contrary inhibit them by virtue of consciousness. Or, following a strategy that seventeenth-century philosophers advised, they can pit one disposition against another: Leibniz argued that one cannot fight passion
with reason, as Descartes claimed, but only with "slanted wills" (*volontés
obliques*), i.e., with the help of other passions. But this work of management of one's dispositions, of *habitus* as the unchosen principle of all
'choices', is possible only with the support of explicit clarification. Failing
an analysis of such subtle determinations that work themselves out
through dispositions, one becomes accessory to the unconsciousness of
the action of dispositions, which is itself the accomplice of determinism.

> BOURDIEU and WACQUANT 1992b [1992a], 136–7

It is only through the exercise of an "epistemic reflexivity" that both the naive
doxa and the *doxa* of educated common sense can be overcome, that it is possible to identify and understand the complex historical-social stratifications
that are embedded in the individual and guide his choices.

4 The Genealogy of the Concept of Class *Habitus* and Its Connection with Art Production and Fruition

Since his early anthropological research, Bourdieu was particularly interested
in examining the genealogy and the functions of *habitus*. Before he even used
the term he began to reflect upon the structures historically internalized by
some social groups in his studies on Algeria and the Kabyle society, and on
particular forms of traditional *ethos* that were lagging behind those emerging
from the modern economy of the western world (Bourdieu 1958). This lag of
habitus, or *hysteresis*, as Bourdieu would later define it, produced an inability
to adapt to the changed structural conditions which entailed the marginalization of the involved individuals.

While studying the phenomenon of celibacy in Béarn, Bourdieu used the
term *habitus* for the first time in order to explain the difficulties of peasants
to find a place within the marriage market (Bourdieu 1962). Explicitly citing
the reflections of Mauss, who had used this concept in the study of body

techniques, he observed how it was precisely the bodily *habitus* of the peasants, derived from hard work in the fields, that made them unsuitable to the rhythms of modern dances and which relegated them to the role of spectators during what were the almost only opportunities for them to meet members of the opposite sex.

These early studies were still influenced by a predominantly structuralist paradigm, as the author himself would later state (Bourdieu 2004) and as has been pointed out (Marsiglia 2002). Bourdieu's reflections on social *habitus* and on the historical origins of these embodied, durable dispositions were enriched with more articulated and original ideas and observations when the sociologist began to study the means of producing and enjoying art, intended both in its highest sense, as free activity that produces unique objects that are part of the cultural heritage, and in the broader meaning of *téchne*, technique, or manual ability manifested in the production of commonly used items (Hooker, Paterson and Stirton 2001).

Research on the spread of photography, *Un art moyen. Essais sur les usages sociaux de la photographie* (Bourdieu et al. 1970 [1965]), fostered by the production of simple tools at prices affordable to almost everyone, not only gave Bourdieu the opportunity to further study the utilization mechanisms of this "middle-brow art"[2] that he himself practiced, but also to lay the foundations of the theory of *habitus* that would later allow him to overcome the alternative between structuralism and constructivism (Bourdieu 2004). In the introduction to his research conducted in the first half of the sixties, the sociologist defined class *habitus*[3] – "that is, the individual *habitus* in so far as it expresses or reflects the class (or group)" (Bourdieu 1990 [1980b], 60)[4] – as a "founded

---

2   Photography is called a "middle-brow art" because it is placed "within the hierarchy of legitimacies, half-way between 'vulgar' practices, apparently abandoned to the anarchy of tastes and noble cultural practices, subject to strict rules" (Bourdieu 1998b [1965], 97).

3   Bourdieu, drawing inspiration from Weber's reflections on the subject, developed a multidimensional theory of class that took economic, relational and symbolic aspects into account and aimed to identify their positioning in the social space. As Emanuela Susca observed, the sociologist considered class to be "a meeting place between objective realities, which exist and exercise an unquestionable influence on individuals and groups, and subjective representations, which in turn have the power to act on reality transforming it" (Susca 2011, 41). On the concept of class in Bourdieu's work see: Boschetti 1985; Wilkes 1990; Swartz 1997; La Monica 2018. Among the essays that have analyzed class *habitus* in Bourdieu's works see: Brubaker 1985; Weininger 2002; Bennett 2007; Coulangeon 2011; Wacquant 2012.

4   As Bourdieu pointed out, "the singular *habitus* of members of the same class are united in a relationship of homology, that is, of diversity within homogeneity reflecting the diversity within homogeneity characteristic of their social conditions of production. Each individual system of dispositions is a structural variant of the others, expressing the singularity of its position within the class and its trajectory" (Bourdieu 1990 [1980b], 60).

illusion" of the creation of unpredictable novelties, a source of thoughts that actually originate within objectively defined conditions. The act of photographing involves not only aesthetic but also ethical choices and both refer to the *habitus* of the group to which they belong. As Bourdieu wrote:

> if, in the abstract, the nature and development of photographic technology tend to make everything objectively 'photographable,' it is still true that, from among the theoretically infinite number of photographs which are technically possible, each group chooses a finite and well-defined range of subjects, genres and compositions.
>
> BOURDIEU 1998a [1965], 6

Therefore the choice of the object itself does not arise from individual improvisation, but from internalized dispositions, peculiar to the different groups or classes, which make these practices conventional.

> In fact, while everything would lead one to expect that this activity, which has no traditions and makes no demands, would be delivered over to the anarchy of individual improvisation, it appears that there is nothing more regulated and conventional than photographic practice and amateur photographs. (7)

Quoting Nietzsche, Bourdieu recalled the solemn and ritual character of the art that is present, albeit in other forms, in amateur photography as well.

> In Nietzsche's words, "The artist chooses his subjects. It is his way of praising." Because it is a "choice that praises," because it strives to capture, that is, to solemnize and to immortalize, photography cannot be delivered over to the randomness of the individual imagination and, via the mediation of the *ethos*, the internalization of objective and common regularities, the group places this practice under its collective rule, so that the most trivial photograph expresses, apart from the explicit intentions of the photographer, the system of schemes of perception, thought and appreciation common to a whole group. (6)

His research on the practice of photography particularly underlined how the *habitus* of the urban popular class – during the period in question the rural world did not appear to be interested in this activity so closely associated with the urban dwellers' way of life – led the members of this group to give greater importance to the social function of the photos without paying particular

attention to their purely aesthetic dimension. The photos were a tool for preserving *souvenirs* of people, things or events "socially designated as important"
(8) and the interest was therefore oriented on the content, on the function performed, rather than on the formal aspects. It was an aesthetic "which makes the
signifier completely subordinate to the signified" (Bourdieu 1998b [1965], 86).

Anticipating some of the observations he would later develop more fully in
La distinction (Bourdieu 1979), Bourdieu observed how

> the feature common to all the popular arts is their subordination of artis-
> tic activity to socially regulated functions while the elaboration of 'pure'
> forms, generally considered the most noble, presupposes the disappear-
> ance of all functional characteristics and all reference to practical or eth-
> ical goals.
>
> BOURDIEU 1998b [1965], 86

The petty bourgeoisie, on the other hand, by adopting a strategy of "distinction" with respect to the popular classes, attempted to ennoble photography
by creating photo-clubs with the aim of mastering the techniques capable of
bringing out the aesthetic quality of photos.

According to Bourdieu, the aesthetic judgments of the popular classes
were decidedly at odds with the theories ultimately derived from Kantian
philosophy:

> Kant, in order to apprehend in its pure state the irreducible specificity
> of aesthetic judgement, strove to distinguish "that which pleases" from
> "that which gratifies" and, more generally, to separate "disinterestedness,"
> the sole guarantee of the specifically aesthetic quality of contemplation,
> from the "interest of the senses" which defines "the agreeable," and from
> "the interest of Reason" which defines "the Good." By contrast, working-
> class people, who expect every image explicitly to fulfil a function, if only
> that of a sign, refer, often explicitly, to norms of morality or agreeableness
> in all their judgements. Whether praising or blaming, their appreciation
> refers to a system of norms whose principle is always ethical. (85–6)

As has been observed (Bennett 2007), Bourdieu seemed to overlook the developments of the post-Kantian aesthetic on the relationships between cultural
capital, social inequality and cultural consumption. However, criticism of
Kant's philosophy offered him the opportunity to show the fallacy of a widespread aesthetic *doxa*.

Before elaborating a complete response to Kant's *Kritik der Urteilskraft* (1978 [1790]) through the complex and articulated research that would, not by chance, be called *A Social Critique of the Judgment of Taste* (Bourdieu 1979), Bourdieu questioned the universality of pure aesthetic judgment based on formal aspects. The Kantian definition of beauty as "purposiveness without a purpose" (*"Zweckmäßigkeit ohne Zweck,"* I, § 15) was just as socially conditioned as what Kant referred to as "barbaric taste." Bourdieu attempted to highlight the different histories incorporated in the different class *habitus* that produced antithetical aesthetics:

> It is no accident that, when one sets about reconstructing its logic, the 'popular aesthetic' appears to be the negative opposite of the Kantian aesthetic, and that the popular *ethos* implicitly answers each proposition of the "Analytic of the Beautiful" with a thesis contradicting it.
>
> BOURDIEU 1998b [1965], 85

The 'pure' art and the 'pure' gaze are inventions that hide the historical genesis of this kind of aesthetics, the social conditions free from external determinations (Bourdieu 1987; Bourdieu 1992). Those who are dominated, on the contrary, tend to be hostile to the *art pour l'art* because their *habitus* is strongly conditioned by the pragmatic urgencies of everyday life (Bourdieu 1979).

Bourdieu then criticized the assumption that artistic products have intrinsic substantial qualities that originate from creativity or 'genius' and affirmed that the definition of meaning and value of artworks were derived from hierarchies established within the aesthetic field (Dunn 1998). This does not mean he intended to deny aesthetics, but rather that he intended to contrast what in *Les règles de l'art* he defined as *"double dehistoricization,* of both the work and the gaze at the work" (Bourdieu 1995 [1992], 285) through analysis of the "Historical Categories of Artistic Perception" (295). Instead, according to Bourdieu, the aesthetic categories, which are a constituent part of *habitus*, are not given *a priori* but are historically produced and reproduced. Research should reconstruct the history of social conditions of the production and use of art that settled in the different *habitus* of class.

This is what Bourdieu attempted to do in an extensive empirical research project carried out by administering questionnaires to the users of the most important European museums: *L'amour de l'art, les musées et leur public* (Bourdieu, Darbel and Schnapper 1969 [1966]).[5] This pioneering analytical

---

5 As Bourdieu recalled, Paul Lazarsfeld identified a misprint in the statistical elaborations of the research, though he did praise the quality of work, albeit privately, as having no equal in the United States (Bourdieu 2004).

study, financed in large part by the Study and Research Service of the French Ministry of Cultural Affairs, showed that use practices and aesthetic judgments varied greatly on the basis of people's position in the social field, which in turn was determined by the overall volume and composition of capital they held.

Through this research, Bourdieu demonstrated the existence of a clear correlation between higher educational achievement[6] and a greater level of attendance at cultural sites; which led him to the conclusion that "museum visiting increases very strongly with increasing level of education, and is almost exclusively the domain of the cultivated classes" (Bourdieu, Darbel, and Schnapper 1991 [1969] 14).

An analysis of the relationship between economic and cultural capital owned by museum visitors allowed the sociologist to identify several "sub-categories," which laid the foundations for that class and class-fraction theory he would later develop more fully in *La distinction* (1979), by defining the social space produced by the "chiasmus structure" delineated by the possession of these capitals to a greater or lesser extent. As Bourdieu observed:

> education has a specific and determining influence which cannot simply be made up for by belonging to the highest social classes or by the general influence of peer groups. If certain individuals classified as craftworkers and tradespeople have, at all levels of education, a higher visiting rate than other categories, this is because to a large extent they belong to a completely atypical sub-category, both by a higher than average level of education for the category, both by opinions closer to those of the upper classes than to those of the other middle classes.
>
> BOURDIEU, DARBEL and SCHNAPPER 1991 [1969], 18

A visitors' profession therefore does not seem to exert a specific influence and it is instead family or higher education that creates a class or class-fraction *habitus* which then fosters museum attendance.

Cultural needs and aesthetic judgments are not innate, but derive from a durable system of internalized social dispositions that guide the choices of individuals. The class or class-fraction *habitus* can make the visitation of

---

6 In order to better understand the level of education of visitors, Bourdieu included a question in a survey related to the knowledge of Latin. This does not mean he intended to attribute "a mysterious cultural effect [...] to classical studies," but only intended to identify "a sign of cultivated background, since it is known that a tendency towards a more classical education is always increasingly frequent, all other things being equal, the higher the social class" (Bourdieu, Darbel and Schnapper 1991 [1969], 20).

cultural sites extraneous or encourage them. But the ways of enjoying art also depend on *habitus*. Bourdieu identified how time dedicated to museum visits, that is "the time needed for him or her to 'exhaust' the meanings proposed to him or her" (38) was a useful indication of the attitude towards deciphering and appreciating the meanings of the work.

From his research it emerged that popular classes spent less time visiting museums than the middle and the upper classes. Bourdieu explained these data by identifying a crucial issue not only for overcoming the traditional metaphysics of art, but also for the construction of that relational perspective that characterizes his sociological thinking: "Considered as symbolic goods, works of art only exist for those who have the means of appropriating them, that is, of deciphering them" (39). Popular class members who visit museums, spend less time inside because they do not have the adequate *eidos* or "interpretative schemata" (*ibidem*) to understand the meaning of some works of art that require a preliminary comprehension of the code adopted by the artist. As Bourdieu wrote:

> When the message exceeds the limits of the observer's apprehension, he or she does not grasp the 'intention' and loses interest in what he or she sees as a riot of colours without rhyme or reason, a play of useless patches of colour. In other words, faced with a message which is too rich, or as information theory says, 'overwhelming', the visitors feels 'drowned' and does not linger. (38–9)

Only those who have an adequate artistic capital possess "the condition of deciphering the works of art supplied to a given society at a given time" (39). Bourdieu defined artistic competence:

> prior knowledge of the specifically artistic principles of division which allow a representation to be situated, by classification of the *stylistic* indices it encompasses, amongst the possibilities of representation which constitute the artistic universe. (40)

Adopting Panofsky's lesson, Bourdieu believed that every epoch defined its own artistic code as a "historically constituted system founded in social reality" (41). Moreover, "the work of art is in a way created twice over, by the artist and by the spectator, or, rather, by the society to which the spectator belongs" (42). It is for this reason that the understanding of an artistic product requires a double process of historical investigation: on the one hand, it is necessary to know the historical context that produced the artist's *habitus* and the code he or she used, while on the other, it is necessary to understand the origin of the socialization processes that generated a spectator's *habitus* and his or her ability to decipher artistic codes. As Bourdieu observed:

> the legibility of work of art for a particular individual is a function of the distance between the more or less complex and sophisticated code demanded by the work and the individual's competence, defined by the degree to which the social code, itself more or less complex and sophisticated, is mastered. (42–3)

It follows that

> when the code of the work exceeds the code of the spectator in its sophistication and complexity, the latter cannot master a message which seems to him or her devoid of all necessity. (43)

In the conclusions of his research, Bourdieu condemned "the myth of an innate taste" (109), typical of bourgeois society that tended to conceal social conditions, and invited us to investigate the historical conditions that had produced it. It is precisely because taste is not a gift of nature, but a "second nature" (110), that a *habitus* can be shaped and modified. According to Bourdieu, the circle of social reproduction of taste can be broken by a "pedagogic authority" (109) capable of fostering the development of cultural needs and a love of art.

The influence of Panofsky's essays on the reflections about museum visitors is evident not only for the presence of implicit references, but also for the numerous explicit quotations of the art historian's writings in the text. Bourdieu was particularly interested in iconology because it involved overcoming the simple iconographic description of the subjects represented through an attentive reconstruction of the historical and cultural context that attributed particular symbolic meanings to the artwork. It was not by chance the sociologist decided to translate the volume *Gothic Architecture and Scholasticism* into French and wrote an afterword to the text praising the method of iconological interpretation (Bourdieu 1967). In this very essay, Bourdieu expressed his appreciation for the art critic's mention of *habitus* to show the intrinsic link between the categories of scholastic philosophy and those of Gothic architecture which represented the same *modus operandi*. Beate Kreis and Gunter Gebauer believe that on this occasion the sociologist defined the "structuring structure" of *habitus*, after having described its dimension of incorporated history or presence of the past in the present in his studies on Algeria (Kreis and Gebauer 2002). However, this dichotomy – which may be useful for highlighting two fundamental elements of this concept – has been questioned by those who believe these aspects were contemporarily present in Bourdieu's reflections and does not seem to take the role of his research on art into account, which also contributed to defining the complexity of his theory of *habitus* and helped bring the sociologist closer to Panofsky's studies.

The construct of *habitus* used by the art critic was actually different from that Bourdieu developed starting in the second half of the 1960s (Hanks 2005). Panofsky wrote about mental habits that do not extend to the embodied experience, while Bourdieu rejected this purely mentalist viewpoint by attributing a fundamental role to the body as the location of *habitus* (Bourdieu 1972).

Nevertheless, Bourdieu and Panofsky both employed the concept of *habitus* as a useful tool for countering the persistent, widespread, and almost mystical perspective of those critics who exalted the role of a few superior men in artistic creation, neglecting the role of their social group. As Bourdieu wrote:

> To contrast individuality with community so as to better safeguard the rights of creative individuality and the mystery of individual creation is to forgo discovering community at the very heart of individuality in the form of culture – in the subjective sense of *cultivation* or *Building* – or, to speak the language used by Panofsky, in the form of the *habitus* through which the creator partakes of his community and time and that guides and directs, unbeknownst to him, his apparently most unique creative acts.
>
> BOURDIEU 2005 [1967], 226

However, the *habitus* is not only an *opus operatum*, but an *opus operandi* above all that can be revealed through the *opus operatum*. Bourdieu also attributed the merit of having highlighted the active dimension of *habitus* to Panofsky:

> Panofsky shows that culture is not just a common code, or even common repertoire of answers to common problems, or a set of particular and particularized forms of thought but rather a whole body of fundamental schemes, assimilated beforehand, that generate, according to an art of invention similar to that of musical writing, an infinite number of particular schemes, directly applied to particular situations. (233)

In this sense, according to Bourdieu, the *habitus* can be assimilated to the "generative grammar" of Noam Chomsky "as a system of internalized schemes that have the capacity to generate all the thoughts, perceptions, and actions characteristic of culture, and nothing else" (*ibidem*). The *habitus* is therefore a grammar that generates behaviors that become comprehensible the more one knows about the historical series of past conditions. Even a break, innovation or 'revolution' in the stylistic paradigms produced by some artists can be explained by investigating the social-class origin and the individual trajectories produced by cultural education and social relations. Thus "a sort of finality that will only be revealed *post festum*" (238) may emerge.

These last reflections, which intend to enhance the heuristic potentialities of Panofsky's iconology from an epistemological point of view, almost seem to allude to a deterministic theory of human action that Bourdieu always tried to avoid. "Conditioned" and "conditional" freedom indeed risks dissolving in the historical reconstruction of the series of conditions to which the social agent has been subjected: where an individual sees free choice, the sociologist traces constraints and limitations that guide their practices.

The question of the relationship between freedom and necessity was at the very heart of Leibniz's studies, as he tried to respond to Spinoza's philosophical system that denied the existence of free will. Bourdieu, who knew and loved both authors,[7] understood that the construct of *habitus* could allow us to resolve this and other unresolved dualisms in the human sciences, but was aware of the complexity of the problem. Precisely for this reason he returned several times to reflect on this key concept of his sociology, in order to more fully define a theoretical model capable of understanding, on the one hand, the prevalent mechanisms of social reproduction that seem to 'trap' individuals, and on the other, the phenomena of change and social transformation of which these same individuals can become architects, by operating a form of "epistemic reflexivity."

5   Conclusion

The reconstruction of the history of *habitus qua* construct, partial though it may be, demonstrates how this concept has been used by many scholars, belonging to different eras and fields of knowledge, as an important resource for defining the relationship between an individual and the social space in which he or she acts.

---

7   On the influence of Spinoza's theories on Bourdieu see: Lazzeri 2008 and Sévérac 2012. With regard to the French sociologist's references to Leibniz's philosophy, see Robbins 2006.

The *habitus* however is not just a conceptual tool whose transformations can be described over time. It is a construct that also has its own intrinsic historicity, in that it is a durable disposition that originates from past experiences.

Bourdieu devoted many reflections to *habitus*, enriching it with further meaning over time and attributing a central role within his sociological theory to it as a function of mediation between objective social structures and the practices of social agents. This "history made into a body" (Bourdieu 1990 [1982], 191) that sediments within individuals and orients their practices is both an individual and a collective story, which is of substantial interest because it allows us to understand *habitus* as an "embodied class" (Bourdieu 1984 [1979], 437).

The first studies on the production and consumption of artistic practices carried out by Bourdieu in the Sixties revealed a stratification of conditions in the *habitus* of social agents which depended on the class or class-fractions to which they belonged. Behind the choice of a subject to photograph or the fruition of some artwork were judgments of taste that unconsciously originated from the position occupied in the social space, which in turn was a function of the quantity and composition of capital they held.

The study of aesthetics and art criticism therefore constituted an opportunity for Bourdieu to deal with the big issue of social inequalities. The different classification categories within the arts characteristic of the different classes or class-fractions – more refined and 'pure' for the dominant, more general and linked to concrete functions for the dominated – are only ostensibly marginal sociological questions because they are testimony to the existence of enormous inequalities in access to cultural resources as well as economic ones. It is no coincidence that Bourdieu fully elaborated his theory of social class within his most famous work dedicated to the fruition of cultural heritage and the consumption of commodities, *La distinction* (Susca 2011). The sociologist had the merit of demonstrating through empirical data that culture is eminently a question of social class. In this sense the most complete answer to existing differences neither consists in rehabilitating minor forms of culture or those considered inferior, and even less, in ratifying an elitist vision of culture intended as the privilege of a select few. If it is true that it is only the outcome of struggles in the field that establish which artworks and cultural products are worthy of becoming fetishes, acquiring a sort of universal 'aura', then ethics and politics must still be "aimed at universalizing the conditions of access to what the present offers us as most universal" (Bourdieu and Wacquant 1992b [1992a], 88).

An analysis of the historically constituted social stratifications that are to be found in the *habitus* allowed Bourdieu to elaborate a materialist theory of

knowledge that overcame the ideology of virtues or individual gifts by attributing cultural choices to their conditions produced by the concrete resources
available. At the same time the materialism implied by the notion of *habitus*,
according to the sociologist himself (Bourdieu 1972; Bourdieu and Wacquant
1992a), was inspired by the young Karl Marx's reflections on the subject.[8] As
the philosopher proposed a theory of praxis in the *Thesen über Feuerbach* (1998
[1845]), against Feuerbach's naturalist-oriented materialism, that provided the
possibility that people could modify reality through their own action, Bourdieu
believed, in much the same way, that the history that leads to the formation
of *habitus* does not imply a passive dependence on the social structures that
produced it. The *habitus* is rather an art "in the strongest sense of practical
mastery" (Bourdieu and Wacquant 1992b [1992a], 122), and in particular an
ars inveniendi (*ibidem*) that a social agent exercises within the field. However,
an individual's freedom and creativity are, at the same time, quite limited. As
Bourdieu himself observed, "to speak of *habitus* is to assert that the individual,
and even the personal, the subjective, is social, collective," and therefore that
"the human mind is *socially* bounded, socially structured" (126).

From a gnoseological point of view, this theoretical perspective offers the
possibility of interpreting and even predicting individual behaviors on the
basis of a careful analysis of the social history that produced a specific *habitus*.
However, to affirm, as Bourdieu did, that knowing a certain professor's history
and position in the academic field makes it possible to imagine what they will
do in a certain situation, for example in May of 1968 (136), basically means falling into a form, at least partially, of ontological determinism that the sociologist intended to reject. The *ex post* reconstruction of a series of conditions that
led to certain choices in some particular junctures cannot actually have any
scientific basis and risks becoming a simple description of a random sequence
of events, if the real existence of a cause and effect relationship acting *ex ante*
is not supposed.

According to Bourdieu, knowledge of the conditions that affect individual
action can allow us "to step back and gain distance from disposition" (*ibidem*).
However, it is not easy to convert this gaze and acquire this awareness. Even
though Bourdieu highlighted the difficulties in environmental adaptation
of those who, like him, possessed a "divided *habitus*" (Bourdieu and Sayad,
1964; Bourdieu 2004) – that is a *habitus* in which the conditions of very different classes and social experiences coexist – this situation seems to foster
an awareness of values, logical classifications and historically acquired bodily

---

8   Regarding the relations between Marx and Bourdieu see: Santoro 2010; Paolucci (ed.) 2018.

dispositions that guide the practices of individuals. In reading Bourdieu's texts, however, the doubt arises that even the few social agents capable of consciously reflecting on their own *habitus* eventually come to this form of epistemic reflexivity precisely because of the particular social conditioning they received.

Bourdieu was aware that an excessively deterministic view of reality risks sanctioning the theoretical impossibility of overcoming social inequalities and for this very reason felt the need to safeguard the freedom of action to modify one's own existence through the concept of *habitus*, in the field of a social science that must also assume a political role. As Spinoza's philosophy teaches, on the other hand, ontological determinism (Spinoza 2002 [1677]) does not exclude that one may aspire to pursue profound political and social transformations (Spinoza 2002 [1670]). It is a matter of accepting the idea that agents of change are determinant and determined at the same time.

References

Aiello, Miriam. 2022. *Mente e habitus. Fondamenti filosofici e approdi cognitivi della teoria della pratica di Bourdieu.* Roma: Castelvecchi.

Aquinas, Thomas. 1981 [1265–1272]. *Summa Theologiae.* Latin Text and English Translation, Introductions, Notes, Appendices and Glossaries. Cambridge, New York: Blackfriars, MacGraw-Hill book.

Aristotle. 1995 [4th cent. BC]. *The Complete Works of Aristotle. The Revised Oxford Translation.* Edited by James Barnes. 2 vols. Princeton: University Press.

Baldacci, Massimo. 2017. "Bourdieu, l'*habitus* e il problema del sostrato formativo." In *Il mondo dell'uomo, i campi del sapere.* Edited by Emanuele Susca, 199–207. Napoli, Salerno: Orthotes.

Bennett, Tony. 2007. "Habitus Clivé: Aesthetics and Politics in the Work of Pierre Bourdieu." *New Literary History* 38 (1): 201–228.

Boschetti, Anna. 1985. "Classi reali e classi costruite." *Rassegna Italiana di Sociologia* 26 (1): 89–99.

Bourdieu, Pierre. 1958. *Sociologie de l'Algérie.* Paris: PUF.

Bourdieu, Pierre. 1962. "Célibat et condition paysanne." *Études rurales* 5–6: 32–135. Doi: 10.3406/rural.1962.1011.

Bourdieu, Pierre. 1967. "Postface." In *Architecture gotique et pensée scolastique.* Edited by Erwin Panofsky. Paris: Les Éditions de Minuit.

Bourdieu, Pierre. 1972. *Esquisse d'une théorie de la pratique, précédé de trois étude d'ethnologie kabyle.* Paris: Éditions du Seuil.

Bourdieu, Pierre. 1979. *La distinction. Critique sociale du jugement.* Paris: Les Éditions de Minuit.

Bourdieu, Pierre. 1980a. *Questions de sociologie.* Paris: Les Édition de Minuit.

Bourdieu, Pierre. 1980b. *Le sens pratique.* Paris: Les Éditions de Minuit.

Bourdieu, Pierre. 1982. *Leçon sur la leçon.* Paris: Les Éditions de Minuit.

Bourdieu, Pierre. 1984 [1979]. *Distinction. A Social Critique of the Judgement of Taste.* Translated by Richard Nice. Cambridge (Massachusetts): Harvard University Press.

Bourdieu, Pierre. 1985. "The Genesis of the Concepts of Habitus and Field." *Socio-criticism* 2 (2): 11–24.

Bourdieu, Pierre. 1987. "The Historical Genesis of a Pure Aesthetic." *The Journal of Aesthetics and Art Criticism,* n.s., 46: 201–210.

Bourdieu, Pierre. 1990 [1980b]. *The Logic of Practice.* Translated by Richard Nice. Stanford, CA: Stanford University Press.

Bourdieu, Pierre. 1990 [1982]. "A Lecture on the Lecture." In *In Other Words. Essays Towards a Reflexive Sociology.* Translated by Matthew Adamson. Standford, CA: University Press.

Bourdieu, Pierre. 1992. Les règles de l'art. Genèse et structure du champ littéraire. Paris: Éditions du Seuil.

Bourdieu, Pierre. 1993 [1980a]. *Sociology in Questions.* Transalted by Richard Nice. London, Thousand Oaks, New Delhi: Sage Publications.

Bourdieu, Pierre. 1994. *Raisons pratiques. Sur la théorie de l'action.* Paris: Éditions du Seuil.

Bourdieu, Pierre. 1995 [1992]. *The Rules of Art. Genesis and Structure of the Literary Field.* Translated by Susan Emanuel. Stanford: University Press.

Bourdieu, Pierre. 1997. *Méditations pascaliennes. Eléments pour une philosophie néga-tive.* Paris: Éditions du Seuil.

Bourdieu, Pierre. 1998 [1994]. *Practical Reason. On the Theory of Action.* Translated by Richard Nice. Stanford: Stanford University Press.

Bourdieu, Pierre. 1998a [1965]. "Introduction." In *Photography: A Middle-brow Art.* Edited by Pierre Bourdieu, Luc Boltanski, Robert Castel, Jean-Claude Chamboredom, and Dominique Schnapper, 1–10. Translated by Shaun Whiteside. Cambridge: Polity Press.

Bourdieu, Pierre. 1998b [1965]. "The Social Definition of Photography." In *Photography: A Middle-brow Art.* Edited by Pierre Bourdieu, Luc Boltanski, Robert Castel, Jean-Claude Chamboredom, and Dominique Schnapper, 73–98. Translated by Shaun Whiteside. Cambridge: Polity Press.

Bourdieu, Pierre. 2002. "Habitus." In *Habitus: A Sense of Place* Edited by Jean Hillier and Emma Rooksby, 27–34. Aldershot, Burlington, Singapore, Sidney: Ashgate.

Bourdieu, Pierre. 2004. *Esquisse pour une auto-analyse.* Paris: Éditions Raisons d'Agir.

Bourdieu, Pierre. 2005 [1967]. "Postface to Erwin Panofsky. Gothic Architecture and Scholasticism." In *The Premodern Condition: Medievalism and the Making of Theory.* Edited by Bruce Holsinger, 221–242. Chicago: University of Chicago Press.

Bourdieu, Pierre. 2013 [1972]. *Outline of a Theory of Practice.* Translated by Richard Nice. Cambridge: University Press.

Bourdieu, Pierre, Luc Boltanski, Robert Castel, Jean-Claude Chamboredom, Gérard Lagneau, and Dominique Schnapper. 1970 [1965]. *Un art moyen. Essais sur les usages sociaux de la photographie.* Nouvelle édition revue et augmentée. Paris: Les Éditions de Minuit.

Bourdieu, Pierre, Luc Boltanski, Robert Castel, Jean-Claude Chamboredom, and Dominique Schnapper. 1998 [1965]. *Photography: A Middle-brow Art.* Translated by Shaun Whiteside. Cambridge: Polity Press.

Bourdieu, Pierre, and Roger Chartier. 2010 [1988]. *Le sociologue et l'historien.* Marseille: Éditions Agone et Raisons d'Agir.

Bourdieu, Pierre, Alain Darbel, and Dominique Schnapper. 1969 [1966]. *L'amour de l'art, les musées et leur public.* Nouvelle édition revue et augmentée. Paris: Les Éditions de Minuit.

Bourdieu, Pierre, Alain Darbel, and Dominique Schnapper. 1991 [1969]. Translated by Caroline Beattie and Nick Merriman. *The Love of Art. European Art Museums and Their Public.* Cambridge: Polity Press.

Bourdieu, Pierre, and Abdelmalek Sayad. 1964. *Le Déracinement. La crise de l'agriculture traditionnelle en Algérie.* Paris: Les Éditions de Minuit.

Bourdieu, Pierre, and Loïc J.D. Wacquant. 1992a. *Réponses. Pour une anthropologie réflexive*, Paris: Éditions du Seuil.

Bourdieu, Pierre, and Loïc J.D. Wacquant. 1992b. *An Invitation to Reflexive Sociology.* Cambridge: Polity Press.

Brubaker, Rogers. 1985. "Rethinking Classical Theory: The Sociological Vision of Pierre Bourdieu." *Theory and Society* 14 (6): 745–775.

Caillé, Alain. 1986. *Splendeurs et misères des sciences sociales. Esquisses d'une mythologie.* Genève, Paris: Librairie Droz.

Coulangeon, Philippe. 2011. *Les métamorphoses de la distinction. Inégalités culturelles dans la France d'aujourd'hui.* Paris: Grasset & Fasquelle.

Dewey, John. 2016 [1916]. *Democracy and Education: An Introduction to the Philosophy of Education.* New York: Macmillian.

Dewey, John. 2011 [1922]. *Human Nature and Conduct: An Introduction to Social Psychology.* Lexington: Filiquarian Publishing.

Dewey, John. 2015 [1938]. *Experience and Education.* New York: Free press.

Dunn, Allen. 1998. "Who Needs a Sociology of the Aesthetic? Freedom and Value in Pierre Bourdieu's Rules of Art." *boundary 2* 25 (1): 87–110.

Durkheim, Émile. 1938. *L'Évolution pédagogique en France.* Paris: PUF.

Durkheim, Émile, and Marcel Mauss. 1903. "De quelques formes de classification. Contribution à l'étude des représentations collectives." *Année sociologique* 6: 1–72.

Elias, Norbert. 1987 [1939]. *Über den Prozess der Zivilisation. Soziogenetische und psychogenetische Untersuchungen.* Frankfurt am Main: Suhrkamp Verlag, 2 vols.

Elias, Norbert. 1987. "Wandlungen der Wir-Ich Balance." In *Die Gesellschaft der Individuen,* 207–315. Frankfurt am Main: Suhrkamp Verlag.

Elias, Norbert. 1989. *Studien über die Deutschen. Machtkämpfe und Habitusentwicklung im 19. und 20. Jahrhundert.* Frankfurt am Main: Suhrkamp Verlag.

Elsner, Jas, and Katharina Lorenz. 2012. "The Genesis of Iconology." *Critical Inquiry* 38 (3): 483–512.

Ginzburg, Carlo. 1986 [1979]. "Spie. Radici di un paradigma indiziario." In *Miti, emblemi, spie. Morfologia e storia,* 158–209. Torino: Einaudi.

Grange, Juliette. 2009. "L'habitus, de la philosophie à la sociologie et retour." In *Pierre Bourdieu, un philosophe en sociologie.* Edited by Marie-Anne Lescourret. Paris: PUF.

Hanks, William F. 2005. "Pierre Bourdieu and the Practices of Language." *Annual Review of Anthropology* 34: 67–83.

Hart, Joan. 1993. "Erwin Panofsky and Karl Mannheim: A Dialogue on Interpretation." *Critical Inquiry* 19 (3): 534–566.

Hegel, Georg, Wilhelm Friedrich. 1979 [1817–1830]. *Enzyklopädie der philosophischen Wissenschaften im Grundrisse.* In *Werke in 20 Bänden.* Band 8. Frankfurt am Main: Suhrkamp Verlag.

Hegel, Georg, Wilhelm Friedrich. 2007 [1830]. *Hegel's Philosophy of Mind . Translated from 1830 Edition, together with the Zusätze by* William Wallace and A.V. Miller, with Revisions and Commentary by M.J. Inwood. Oxford: Oxford University Press.

Héran, François. 1987. "La seconde nature de l'habitus. Tradition philosophique et sens commun dans le langage sociologique." *Revue française de sociologie* 28 (3): 385–416. Doi: 10.2307/3321720.

Hooker, Richard, Dominic Paterson, and Paul Stirton. 2001. "Bourdieu and the Art Historians." *The Sociological Review* 49 (1): 212–228. Doi: 10.1111/j.1467-954X.2001.tb03543.x.

Hume, David. 1999 [1748–1758]. *An Enquiry concerning Human Understanding.* Oxford: Oxford University Press.

Husserl, Edmund. 1950 [1931]. *Cartesianische Meditationen und Pariser Vorträge.* Edited by Stephan Strasser. The Hague: Martinus Nijhoff.

Husserl, Edmund. 1999 [1938]. *Erfahrung und Urteil. Untersuchungen zur Genealogie der Logik.* Edited by Ludwig Landgrebe. Hamburg: Felix Meiner.

Husserl, Edmund. 1952. *Ideen zu einer reinen Phänomenologie und phänomenologischen Philosophie. Zweites Buch: Phänomenologische Untersuchungen zur Konstitution.* Edited by Marly Biemel. Den Haag: Martinus Nijhoff.

Husserl, Edmund. 1973. *Zur Phänomenologie der Intersubjektivität. 1905–1935.* 3 vols. Edited by Iso Kern. Den Haag: Martinus Nijhoff.

Jenkins, Richard. 1992. *Pierre Bourdieu.* London, New York: Routledge.

Kant, Immanuel. 1978 [1790]. *Kritik der Urteilskraft.* In *Werkausgabe in 12 Bänden.* Edited by Wilhelm Weischedel. Band 10. Frankfurt am Main: Suhrkamp Verlag.

Krais, Beate, and Gunter Gebauer. 2002. *Habitus.* Bielefeld: Transcript.

La Monica, Alessandro. 2018. "Classes sociales. Percorsi di ricerca nella sociologia dopo Bourdieu." In *Contesti di crisi. Nuove forme della disuguaglianza e ricerca sociologica.* Edited by Andrea Salvini, 187–225. Pisa: University Press.

Lau, Raymond W.K. 2004. "Habitus and the Practical Logic of Practice: An Interpretation." *Sociology* 38: 369–387.

Lazzeri, Christian. 2008. "Reconnaissance spinoziste et sociologie critique. Spinoza et Bourdieu." In *Spinoza et les sciences sociales. De la puissance de la multitude à l'économie des affects.* Edited by Yves Citton and Frédéric Lordon, 354–398. Paris: Éditions Amsterdam.

Leibniz, Gottfried Wilhelm von. 1875 [1678]. "Quid sit idea." In *Die philosophischen Schriften von Gottfried Wilhelm Leibniz.* Band 7. Edited by Carl Immanuel Gerhardt, 263–264. Berlin: Weidmann.

Lizardo, Omar. 2004. "The Cognitive Origins of Bourdieu's Habitus." *Journal for the Theory of Social Behaviour* 34 (4): 375–401.

Magrì, Elisa. 2015. "L'auto-riferimento del corpo vivo. Sull'abitudine in Hegel e Merleau-Ponty." In *Hegel e la fenomenologia trascendentale.* Edited by Danilo Manca, Elisa Magrì and Alfredo Ferrarin, 81–100. Pisa: ETS.

Marsiglia, Giorgio. 2002. *Pierre Bourdieu. Una teoria del mondo sociale.* Padova: Cedam.

Marx, Karl. 1998 [1845]. "Thesen über Feuerbach." In *Karl Marx/Friedrich Engels Gesamtausgabe (MEGA).* Band 4, no. 3. Edited by Internationalen Marx-Engels Stiftung, 19–21. Berlin: Akademie Verlag.

Mauss, Marcel. 1950 [1936]. "Les techniques du corps." In *Sociologie et Anthropologie*, 363–386. Paris: PUF.

Merleau-Ponty, Maurice. 1945. *Phénoménologie de la perception.* Paris: Gallimard.

Moran, Dermot. 2011. "Edmund Husserl's Phenomenology of Habituality and Habitus." *Journal of the British Society for Phenomenology* 42 (1): 53–77.

Moran, Dermot. 2014. "The Ego as Substrate of Habitualities. Edmund Husserl's Phenomenology of the Habitual Self." *Phenomenology and Mind* 6: 24–39. Doi: 10.13128/Phe_Mi-19549.

Mounier, Pierre. 2001. *Pierre Bourdieu, une introduction.* Paris: La Découverte.

Panofsky, Erwin. 1976 [1951]. *Gothic Architecture and Scholasticism.* New York, London and Scarborough, Ontario: New American Library.

Paolucci, Gabriella. 2011. *Introduzione a Bourdieu.* Roma-Bari: Laterza.

Paolucci, Gabriella. ed. 2018. *Bourdieu e Marx. Pratiche della critica.* Milano: Mimesis.

Pitzalis, Marco and Elliot B. Weininger. 2022. "Rupture and crisis in Bourdieusian sociology. Introduction." *Rassegna Italiana di Sociologia* 63 (2): 281–297. Doi: 10.1423/
104929

Plato. 1997 [4th cent. BC]. *Complete Works.* Edited, with Introduction and Notes, by
John M. Cooper, and Douglas S. Hutchinson, Indianapolis, Cambridge: Hackett
Publishing Company.

Ravaioli, Paola. 2002. "Tra oggettivismo e soggettivismo. Problemi ed evoluzione della
teoria sociale di Bourdieu." *Rassegna italiana di sociologia* 43 (3): 459–485.

Robbins, Derek. 2006. *On Bourdieu, Education and Society.* Oxford: The Bardwell Press.

Santoro, Marco. 2010. "Con Marx, senza Marx. Sul capitale di Bourdieu." In *Bourdieu
dopo Bourdieu.* Edited by Gabriella Paolucci, 145–172. Torino: UTET.

Sapiro, Gisèle. 2004. "Une liberté contrainte. La formation de la théorie de l'*habitus*,
suivi d'un entretien avec Pierre Bourdieu." In *Pierre Bourdieu, sociologue.* Edited by
Louis Pinto, Gisèle Sapiro and Patrick Champagne, 49–91. Paris: Fayard.

Sapiro, Gisèle. 2010. "Una libertà vincolata. La formazione della teoria dell'"habitus.""
In *Bourdieu dopo Bourdieu.* Edited by Gabriella Paolucci, 85–108. Torino, UTET.

Sapiro, Gisèle. 2015. "Habitus: History of a Concept." In *International Encyclopedia of
the Social & Behavioral Sciences.* Edited by James D. Wright, 484–489. 2nd edition,
vol. 10. Oxford: Elsevier.

Schütz, Alfred. 1974 [1932]. *Der sinnhafte Aufbau der sozialen Welt. Eine Einleitung in die
verstehende Soziologie.* Frankfurt am Main: Suhrkamp Verlag.

Schütz, Alfred., and Thomas Luckmann. 1973. *The Structures of the Life-World.* Evanston,
IL: Northwestern University Press.

Sévérac, Pascal. 2012. "Le Spinoza de Bourdieu." In *Lectures contemporaines de Spinoza.*
Edited by Claude Cohen-Boulakia, Mireille Delbraccio and Pierre-François Moreau,
47–62. Paris: Presses de l'Université Paris-Sorbonne.

Sgarbi, Marco. 2011. *"Aristotele e il problema della soggettività." Trans/Form/Ação*
34: 105–116.

Spinoza, Baruch. 2002 [1670]. "Theological-Political Treatise." In *Complete Works.*
Edited by Michael L. Morgan, 383–583. Indianapolis, Cambridge: Hackett Publishing
Company, Inc.

Spinoza, Baruch. 2002 [1677]. "Ethics." In *Complete Works.* Translations by Samuel
Shirley. Edited, with Introduction and Notes, by Michael L. Morgan, 213–382.
Indianapolis, Cambridge: Hackett Publishing Company, Inc.

Steinmetz, George. 2011. "Bourdieu, Historicity, and Historical Sociology." *Cultural sociology* 5 (1): 45–66. Doi: 10.1177/1749975510389912.

Susca, Emanuela. 2011. *Pierre Bourdieu: il lavoro della conoscenza.* Milano: FrancoAngeli.

Swartz, David. 1997. *Culture and Power. The Sociology of Pierre Bourdieu.* Chicago-
London: University of Chicago.

Throop, C. Jason, and Keith M. Murphy. 2002. "Bourdieu and Phenomenology: A Critical Assessment." *Anthropological Theory* 2 (2): 185–207.

Wacquant, Loïc J.D. 2006. "Pierre Bourdieu." In *Key Contemporary Thinkers*. Edited by Rob Stones, 261–277. London, New York: Macmillan.

Wacquant, Loïc J.D. 2012. "Potere simbolico e costituzione dei gruppi: come Bourdieu ha riformulato la questione delle classi." *Polis* 26 (3): 370–400.

Wacquant, Loïc J.D. 2016. "A Concise Genealogy and Anatomy of Habitus." *The Sociological Review* 64 (1): 64–72.

Weber, Max. 1986 [1904–1905]. "Die protestantische Ethik und der Geist des Kapitalismus." In *Gesammelte Aufsätze zur Religionssoziologie*. Band 1. Tübingen: Mohr (Siebeck).

Weber, Max. 1986 [1916–1917]. "Hinduismus und Buddhismus." In *Gesammelte Aufsätze zur Religionssoziologie*. Band 2. Tübingen: Mohr (Siebeck).

Weber, Max. 1986 [1916–1919]. Die Wirtschaftsethik der Weltreligionen. In *Gesammelte Aufsätze zur Religionssoziologie*. Band 1. Tübingen: Mohr (Siebeck).

Weber, Max. 1976 [1921]. *Wirtschaft und Gesellschaft*. Tubingen: Mohr (Siebeck).

Weininger, Elliot B. 2002. "Class and Causation in Bourdieu." In *Bringing Capitalism Back for Critique by Social Theory*. Edited by Jennifer M. Lehmann, 49–114. Bingley: Emerald Group Publishing Limited (*Current Perspectives in Social Theory*, vol. 21).

Wilkes, Chris. 1990. "Bourdieu's Class." In *An Introduction to the Work of Pierre Bourdieu. The Practice of Theory*. Edited by Richard Harker, Cheleen Mahar and Chris Wilkes, 109–131. London: Macmillan.

CHAPTER 9

Michael Mann's History of Social Power

Eleonora Piromalli

Michael Mann, born in 1942 in Great Britain and living in Los Angeles since 1987, belongs with Norbert Elias, Barrington Moore Jr., Charles Tilly, Perry Anderson and Theda Skocpol to that tradition of historical macrosociology whose methodological origins are to be found in classical European socio-logical thought.[1] Mann is the author of one of the most innovative models in contemporary power research and historical sociology, the IEMP model. This approach finds its closest inspiration in Max Weber: through an analysis adopt-ing the ideal-type as its fundamental paradigm, it combines history, theoretical sociology and the reference to empirical data. Mann develops and employs the IEMP model in his work *The Sources of Social Power* (Mann 1986; 1993; 2012; 2013), a monumental oeuvre in four volumes in which he retraces the history of human societies by examining, from the Neolithic to the present day, the forms and variations of social power.

The power relations that have succeeded one another throughout human history can best be studied, according to Mann, by analyzing them through four ideal-types: ideological, economic, military, and political power («IEMP» as their acronym, Mann 1986, 2). These ideal-types are always intertwined in social reality and constitute the "organizational tools" (5) that human beings, in forming networks of collective action to fulfill their purposes, have adopted since the dawn of civilization. The four sources of social power interrelate through the individual and collective action of subjects, as well as interacting with more contingent and historically diversified variables. In this way, they produce the concrete relations of power, social stratifications, institutions and "crystallizations"[2] recognizable in the different phases of human history. Considered as ideal-types, they are the fundamental analytical keys through which it is possible to study the history of power.

In this essay, I summarize the main lines of Mann's historical sociology, with particular focus on his work on social power. First of all (1), I examine Mann's

---

1   The first two paragraphs of this essay constitute an abridged translation of the first and the second chapter of Piromalli (2016).

2   With regard to "crystallizations," a concept specific to the theory of the state elaborated by Michael Mann, see below, § 4.

organizational conception of power and his approach to historical macroso-ciology. Secondly (2), I analyze the four sources of social power (ideological, economic, political, and military power) and the different forms of organiza-tional power Mann identifies: infrastructural and despotic power, collective and distributive power, intensive and extensive power, authoritative and dif-fused power. Finally (3), in a necessarily synthetic way, I go through the histor-ical reconstructions presented in *The Sources of Social Power*, so as to give an overview of the practical application of the IEMP model.

1   Michael Mann's Organizational Conception of Power

In *The Sources of Social Power* Mann aims at demonstrating that, by means of the IEMP model, sensible generalizations on the changing patterns of power relations through history can be made. The four sources of social power con-stitute, at the maximum depth of analysis and systematization we can reach, the ideal-types through which it becomes possible to shed some light on the tendencies, regularities and developmental patterns of human history, with regards to the relations of social power.

Society, writes Mann, "is a network of social interaction at the boundaries of which is a certain level of interaction cleavage between it and its environ-ment" (13). Societies, he says, are made up of the intersection and overlapping of a plurality of *power networks* with different boundaries. These networks are generated by social actors, who interact to pursue their own ends. Interwoven with each other, the power networks give rise to particular concentrations of social interaction, always open to the possibility of new overlaps and inter-sections with spatially adjacent networks (2). A society, therefore, is consti-tuted by networks of power that, in intertwining with each other, give rise to more intense and stable complexes of interaction than those present in the surrounding environment.

For Mann, "power is the ability to pursue and attain goals through mastery of one's environment" (6). This is not, he maintains, the only possible or cor-rect conceptualization of power; it is, however, the most appropriate general description of *power understood in an organizational sense*. Mann does not intend, as he explicitly states, to enter into conceptual disputes about "power itself," its essence and "faces" (6).[3] Rather, he focuses on power as a *means of collective organization* that human beings use to coordinate their action and/or

---

3   A good example of this type of research is Lukes 1974.

achieve their goals. The human species is characterized by an intrinsic dynamism, which differentiates it from animals and makes it capable of history (4).
The sources of social power are the *organizational means* that human beings
use collectively to pursue their ends. What the original human goals actually
are, for Mann, is irrelevant for determining how the sources of power mutually interact throughout history. It is unlikely, for example, that military power
represents an original and primary aim of human beings, especially in relation
to the immense proportions it has reached today; however, it constitutes an
effective *means* of pursuing other needs, primary or derived. The question of
what the original human aims are is devoid of empirical relevance, since we
can only observe the historical actualization of human ends in general (6).

The reference to the empirical level is also key to understand why the
sources of power theorized by Mann are exactly the four that he enumerates.
The human capacity to recognize causal sequences in history is limited, and
social reality is much "messier" (Mann 1986, 4) and more varied than it can be
ever represented in our theories. Some elements of this reality appear to us
with greater strength and evidence, although they are probably not the only
ones to constitute such reality. These, however, are the only elements that,
to the eyes of the historical sociologist, can be stably discerned throughout
human history, or, in other words, that are observable in every epoch, although
in different conformations. With regard to social power, there are four such elements – ideological, economic, military, and political power (28). Through the
theoretical model based on the four ideal-types, it is possible to make sensible
generalizations about historical events. Those, however, do not present suffi-
cient regularity to speak of historical laws. On the other hand, history neither is
the realm of pure contingency: in many cases, regularities can be detected with
respect to the mutual intersection of different networks of power.

Mann examines empirical data through the eye of a sociologist, trained to
recognize developmental patterns, historical regularities and causal links. He
places his work in the field of historical macrosociology,[4] understood as a specific type of sociological enterprise referring to broad historical periods and
vast geographical areas. Its methodology consists of a continuous comparison
between conceptual insights and empirical data: the development of a general
idea, on the basis of historical documentation, is followed by a more in-depth
comparison with the historical sources, which brings to a fine-tuning of the
theoretical hypothesis, that is then re-examined by reference to the historical
data (Mann 1986, viii). This approach allows Mann to adopt a synthetic and

---

4   Regarding Mann's theory in relation to historical sociology, see Spohn 2009.

critical attitude towards empirical data and their possible interpretations: "we need theories to make sense of, and to systematically organize, our data (and we need good data to evaluate our theories)," he writes in *The British Journal of Sociology* as a reply to Goldthorpe's polemic against macrosociology (Mann 1994, 42; Goldthorpe 1991). Mann's idea is that, in order to obtain "good data," historical sociologists must, to a large extent, make recourse to the work of historians who come into direct contact with the sources; at the same time, however, thanks to their aptitude for general and diachronic theory and their knowledge of the organization of societies, historical sociologists can critically analyze primary data and verify the interpretations provided by historians (Mann 1994, 40–1). In this way, the historical sociologist gains access to new ways of verifying and evaluating empirical data, can develop theories characterized by a broad temporal scope and capable of recognizing historical dialectics and regularities, and can propose reasoned hypotheses on the forms and the changes of human societies in history.

Mann rejects the idea that there would be a pure truth of historical facts, immutable, independent of our perceptions and completely transparent to our gaze. "My own epistemological position," he writes, "is more Kantian" (42): an objective, total and neutral knowledge of empirical facts is not possible; but, on the other hand, denying them any reliability would lead us to an endless relativism. We can only act "as if" what we see corresponds to the truth, while always remaining open to different perspectives. We can only "present the facts as we see them, engage with the contrary facts produced by others and demonstrate to the satisfaction of third parties that our perception generates more explanatory and predictive power" (42).

Of course, it would not be possible to retrace the multi-millennial history of social power by considering, for each era, the events taking place in every single geographical region of the world. For this reason, Mann focuses his attention on what he calls the *leading edge of power*: that is, the place or region in which, in a given historical epoch, power relations are more organizationally advanced, thus devising a higher capacity to integrate social groups and territories (Mann 1986, 31). What Mann focuses on, therefore, is the organizational "infrastructure" of power, in macro-historical and socio-spatial terms: how human beings organize their social action through power relations, and "how geographical and social spaces can actually be conquered and controlled by power organizations" (9).[5]

---

5   On the relationship of Mann's theory with the discipline of historical geography, see Jones 1999 and Harris 1991.

Through his organizational conception of power, Mann aims at reaching a third position between structuralism and the theory of social action. On the one hand, structuralism analyses society in terms of structures and functional levels, but fails to give an adequate explanation of why social reality would be organized precisely in this way. The theory of social action, on the other hand, analyzes in detail the actions and motivations of subjects, but finds it difficult to take into account institutions, as well as the supra-individual consequences of collective action. Mann calls his method "structural symbolic interactionism" (Mann 1986, xi): human beings organize their collective action by generating *networks of interaction* around the four main sources of power; by consolidating these networks through shared and customary practices; and by stabilizing them in institutions and social concretizations. An adequate theory must, therefore, take into account both social action and the organizational and routine structures through which social action is coordinated.

2   The Four Sources of Social Power

In the previous paragraph, I gave an overview of the main theoretical points of Mann's IEMP model; in this section, I expound more in detail the four sources of social power and their characteristics, before presenting Mann's conception of "organizational materialism."

1. *Economic power* derives from the actions of extraction, transformation, distribution and consumption of resources that human beings undertake collectively for the satisfaction of their material needs (Mann 1986, 24). None of these phases, for Mann, holds a theoretically privileged role over the others: Marxists assign primacy to the relations of production, with the motivation that production precedes distribution both logically and historically. For Mann, however, this amounts to not recognizing that every existing social organization represents "a social fact" on a par with the others, and that it can, therefore, exercise a power not dissimilar from their own (24). The concept of social class is part, for Mann, of the sphere of economic power: the economically dominant classes are those that manage to monopolize the control of the economy, or to centralize its advantages disproportionately on themselves (25).

2. *Military power* is essentially "the social organization of concentrated lethal violence" (xiii): through this definition, Mann aims at highlighting the theoretical separation that, differently from Weber, he introduces between military and political power. Military power has emerging properties that substantially differentiate it from political and state power: it is

a concentrated, physical, lethal power, very different from the routinized, mediated and regulated force of political institutions. It, furthermore, tends to autonomize itself from the legitimate control of civil society and presents despotic and arbitrary traits, both in its internal organization and, above all, towards the enemy. There are, of course, cases where political power and military power proceed as one: for example, Nazi Germany, Stalinist Russia, Maoist China, and the Catholic Inquisition. However, argues Mann, the association of political and military power is usually the result of a long escalation that takes place in a limited number of cases (xiii). Moreover, all sources of power can sometimes merge with each other, without this being a reason to abandon the theoretical distinction between them.

3. *Political power* is a centralized, institutionalized, and territorial power, which Mann identifies with the power of the state. The state enjoys a certain amount of autonomy, deriving from its centrality and territoriality. Hence its ability to regulate social relations in the territories of its influence. In addition to domestic politics within a national territory, international diplomacy administered by individual states also falls within political power. The military aspect of geopolitics falls, instead, within military power. In his review of the first volume of *The Sources of Social Power*, Perry Anderson writes that "any exercise of 'political' power manifestly depends on the possession of either ideological or military power, and normally a combination of both force and belief" (Anderson 1986, 1405).[6] Mann agrees that political power can interweave itself with other forms of power: he calls this characteristic of the sources of power "promiscuity." On the empirical level, the ideal-types corresponding to the four sources of power are always intertwined (Mann 1986, 17); "promiscuity," therefore, concerns not only political power but all four forms of social power. Military power, for example, in many cases functions effectively only with the support of political, economic, and/or ideological power, to the point that the form it takes in a certain period does not depend solely on its internal developments. Recognizing the empirical promiscuity of the sources of power, however, does not amount to denying their autonomy and conceptual irreducibility: like military (and ideological, and economic) power, political power has its specific characteristics, not reducible to those of different sources.

4. *Ideological power* concerns cultural elaborations, normative conceptions, aesthetic and ritual practices. It can be transcendent or immanent.

---

6 For similar objections see also Wickham 1988.

Its transcendent form is the most autonomous, as its legitimation is set apart from, and above, secular authority structures. The most immediate example of transcendent ideological power is offered by religions, but also utopian visions of a radically different social order can fall within it. Immanent ideological power, instead, refers to secular and socially existing forms of economic, political, or military power. It intensifies the cohesion and mutual attachment of the actors involved, thus increasing their collective power with regard to certain goals: examples of this are nationalism or imperialism as political ideologies. Ideological power, in order to propagate and exert its effects on society, needs material and organizational infrastructures through which it can be transmitted: communication routes, logistically interconnected groups, networks of proselytism, of cultural diffusion or ideological propaganda (23–4).

Taking an intermediate position between idealism and materialism, Mann thus introduces his conception of "organizational materialism": ideas do not influence society only through their persuasive power; they also need concrete carriers, communication channels, and dissemination networks. The contrast between, on the one hand, "materialist" authors such as Marx, Engels, and their theoretical tradition, and, on the other, "idealist" authors such as Weber, Durkheim, and Parsons, has given rise to an unnecessary dispute, which, for Mann, "has hindered the development of sociological theory" (Mann 1979, 97). There can be no exclusive opposition between "ideas" and "material reality": neither Marx nor Weber ever stated this, although their thinking has frequently been simplified in these terms. In Weber's intention to demonstrate how *ideas* become *real forces* in history, Mann rightly writes, there is as much idealism as materialism, as well as in his general theory (the "iron cage" is but an "ideal" institution taking on material weight: see Mann 1979, 99, 106). For Marx, in turn, the economic base is the combination of both the *practices* and the *ideas* that in each age are relevant to the purpose of material production. Moreover, the superstructure retroacts on the base: ideas, in the form of class consciousness, play a decisive role in generating a revolutionary situation (105–8). The point is not, therefore, to criticize Weber from a materialist perspective or Marx from an idealist one, but to object both to those Marxists "who insist on regarding historical materialism as a distinct historical method that has nothing in common with idealism," and to those idealists who see ideas as "free-floating" (106). In order to have an effect on society, ideas always need to be mediated by institutions or by routinized social practices.

Mann explains historical change through his model of "neo-episodic change": in moments of major social change, new actors, needs or social relations emerge interstitially into existing power structures: new social groups, in other words, manage to develop significant amounts of collective power thanks to the infrastructures and organizational methods initially put in place by the formerly dominant populations. The emergent groups impose themselves as new actors of power, supplanting the ones that have unwittingly contributed to their emergence. In antiquity, this process can be observed in two recurrent occasions: in the frequent case of peripheral, semi-nomadic peoples who increase their collective power by exploiting the techniques and the resources developed by the dominant groups of the core, until conquering them; and in the equally frequent case of local elites who, by privately appropriating the resources entrusted to them by the central authority, end up affirming themselves as autonomous centers of power.

Power relations – besides being constituted by just one of the four sources of social power, or, more frequently, by the interweaving of two to four sources – can take different organizational forms. The first organizational pair Mann considers is the one constituted by *despotic* and *infrastructural* power. Despotic power consists in "the range of actions which the [state] elite is empowered to undertake without routine, institutionalized negotiation with civil society groups" (Mann 1988, 5). It is, therefore, greater in states based on the personalistic and absolute power of the sovereign or groups in command. Infrastructural power is instead "the capacity of the state to actually penetrate civil society, and to implement logistically political decisions throughout the realm" (5).[7] Infrastructural power presupposes a centrally coordinated division of labor between the main activities of the state; the widespread literacy of state agents; the use of a system of currency, uniform weights and measures; rapidity in communications and transport. Despotic power ensures the immediate execution of the sovereign's will within the sphere over which his direct dominion extends. Infrastructural power, instead, allows the sovereign's will to branch out and expand indirectly throughout society. These two forms of power are autonomous on the ideal-typical level, but present themselves as intertwined in social reality, albeit at different relative intensities. In general terms, their relations are summarized by Mann according to the following table (Mann 2008, 357; see also Mann 1993, 60):

---

7   See Soifer 2008 for an inquiry on the possible conceptualizations and ways of measuring the state's infrastructural power.

TABLE 9.1   Two dimensions of state power

		Infrastructural power	
		Low	High
Despotic	*Low*	Feudal	Democratic
power	*High*	Imperial/absolutist	Authoritarian

In order to describe the different organizational forms that the relations of social power can take, Mann theorizes three other pairs in addition to the one constituted by despotic and infrastructural power. As we have seen, Mann identifies power in general with "the ability to pursue and attain goals through mastery of one's environment" (Mann 1986, 6). From this definition, he derives the pair of *distributive* and *collective* power. The first corresponds to the power that a subject A exercises over a subject B. It configures itself as a zero-sum game (6): for B to gain power over A, A must lose a corresponding amount of power, and vice versa. Collective power, on the other hand, refers to a power that can be jointly exercised, by subjects in cooperation with each other, over the natural environment or other human groups. Mann takes up the theorization of this organizational form from Talcott Parsons' article *The Distribution of Power in American Society*. Against the solely distributive approach applied by Wright Mills in *The Power Elite*, Parsons observed that, in order to understand the relations of social power, it is necessary also to consider the collective aspect of power: the distribution of wealth between social classes certainly concerns distributive power, but the mere fact that there is *something* to distribute, is itself the effect of an exercise of power – of *collective power* (see Parsons 1957, 123–43).

The third couple of organizational forms of power presented by Mann is composed of *extensive* and *intensive* power: the former refers to the ability of organizing big numbers of people over large territories, in order to involve them in minimal forms of stable cooperation; intensive power, on the other hand, refers to the ability of creating close organizational bonds in order to obtain from the participants a high level of mobilization or collective commitment. Finally, Mann outlines the couple constituted by *authoritative* and *diffused* power. Authoritative power is exercised through explicit orders and conscious obedience; diffused power, instead, spreads throughout a population in a more spontaneous, unconscious and decentered way. Rather than on precise orders, it is based on voluntary compliance, by subjects, with practices and beliefs perceived as moral, natural, or conducive to the collective interest.

Intensive, extensive, authoritative and diffused power can be represented as in the following table, in relation to practical examples (Mann 1986, 9):

TABLE 9.2   Forms of organizational reach of social power

		Organizational power	
		Authoritative	Diffused
Organizational power	*Intensive*	Army command structure	A general strike
	Extensive	Militaristic empire	Market exchange

3   A History of Social Power

After having expounded, in the previous sections, the main lines of the IEMP model and Mann's approach to historical sociology, in what follows I propose a synthetic overview of the historical reconstructions that Mann presents in *The Sources of Social Power*.

The first volume of *The Sources of Social Power*, as its subheading reads, retraces the history of social power "from the beginning to AD 1760." Mann locates the historical origin of social power proper in the first great civilizations that arose in alluvial floodplains: the Mesopotamian and the Egyptian civilization, Shang China, the Olmec, and the Maya civilization. He identifies two historical regularities, whose functioning he documents in his historical reconstructions and through accurate reference to historical-archeological data: the "dialectic of centralization and decentralization" and the "dynamic of empires of domination and multi-power-actor civilizations." According to the dialectic of centralization and decentralization, the inhabitants of the "core," i.e. the river valley, initially possess an advantage over the populations of the surrounding areas: the greater fertility of their territories allows them to develop more advanced material, cultural, and organizational resources. However, as Mann accurately documents in his reconstructions, the groups of the periphery manage to adapt these resources to their own conditions. Subsequently, they further develop the techniques learned from the core, which, in turn, gets increasingly weakened by internal struggles and the lack of renewal of its consolidated institutions (Mann 1986, 131). The core thus becomes an easy prey of conquest for the now militarily well-organized periphery, capable of exploiting innovative battle techniques. The former periphery thus becomes the new core, but the same dialectic is soon to start again. Together with the dynamic of multi-power-actor civilizations and empires of domination, the dialectic of centralization and decentralization characterizes the whole history of the ancient world.

The dynamic of multi-power-actor civilizations and empires of domination concerns the form taken by the leading edge of power (539). Mesopotamia's multi-power-actor civilization (i.e. a plural and decentralized civilization, constituted by city-states) is the first leading edge of power in the ancient world. A centralized and formerly peripheral empire of domination, the Akkadian one, destroys the Mesopotamian network of city-states, replacing it with its centralized organization. Later, as a result of the Indo-European migrations, the Akkadian empire loses its position of leading edge of power to the multi-power-actor civilizations of Phoenicia and Greece. Greece, in turn, is supplanted by the Roman Empire, a centralized empire of domination. The Roman Empire, finally, is the terrain on which arises the multi-power-actor civilization of feudal Europe, unified by the network of ideological power of Christianity. In short, as documented by Mann throughout the first volume of *The Sources of Social Power*, in ancient times the leading edge of power moved further and further west, alternating between multi-power-actor civilizations and empires of domination. According to Mann, this shift towards west is due both to the greater fertility of the western territories compared to the eastern ones, and to the obstacle constituted, in the east, by the military power of the Islamic peoples and the nomads of the steppes (508–10). In the first volume of *The Sources of Social Power*, in addition to what already mentioned, Mann proposes an original theory of private property and of primitive accumulation (Mann 1986, 82–98), as well as expounding his conception of organizational materialism (310–20).

In 1993 Mann publishes the second volume of *The Sources of Social Power. The Rise of Classes and Nation-States, 1760–1914*. In it, the author develops his theory of the modern state and a theory of the social classes: state and classes respectively constitute the main political and the main economic and social actor of this historical phase. With regards to the state, Mann develops his own approach based on "crystallizations" (Mann 1993, 44–88). A crystallization is the specific form taken by the institutions of a state within a variety of possible configurations, relatively to a series of significant (and theoretically justified) categories: political representation, centrality, type of economy, military power, ideologies reflected and affirmed by the institutions. In the period covered in the second volume of *The Sources of Social Power* (1760–1914), for example, states face two main challenges in terms of political power: the emergence of a national consciousness in their population and the struggles for political representation. In response to these challenges, states provide themselves with representative or non-representative institutions and with centralized, or non-centralized, forms of government. Mann identifies, therefore, the categories of "representation" and "centralization"; with respect to the former, states can assume a monarchic-authoritarian crystallization, like Prussia and the Austro-Hungarian empire, or a democratic-representative one, like Great Britain and the United States. With regard to the latter, they can crystallize themselves as centralized governments, as France, or as federal governments, as the United States. With respect to the crystallization constituted by military power, states can configure themselves as militarist or pacifist (although, in the period considered in the volume, they were all militarist); with regard to economic power, as capitalist or socialist; and, in terms of ideological power, their institutions can reflect and promote a wide variety of ideologies. Modern states are thus defined by Mann as "polymorphic," i.e. characterized, for every epoch, by a plurality of possible crystallizations (Mann 1993, 75–81).

His theory of crystallizations allows Mann to retrace, in both a clear and nuanced way, the macro-processes of social, economic and political change that characterize "the main creative phase of modern Western history" (217), i.e. the industrial revolution in Great Britain, the American Revolution, and the French Revolution. Thanks to the theoretical approach based on crystallizations, Mann also reconstructs the genesis of the three major power actors of this period: classes, nations and the modern state. They are born together, from the social struggles deriving from the fiscal crisis of the state, induced, in turn, by military reasons. Properly modern social struggles explode when individuals become aware of the influence of the territorial state on their lives and on their collective possibility of changing political balances. In developing this consciousness, they come to perceive themselves as a "nation," while the existence of different material interests between the social groups inhabiting what these now conceive as a single national territory comes to the forefront: therefore, social classes aware of their common identity emerge as specific economic-political actors (214–52). States already crystallized in a representative sense (i.e. with representative institutions) are more likely to be able to channel social conflict into these institutions, thereby preventing an escalation of the struggles; monarchic-authoritarian states are more exposed to the possibility of a revolution. All past crystallizations of state institutions influence the events triggered by the emergence of new actors of power, as well as on the form of future crystallizations (86–7).

In the historical phase from 1760 to 1914 the state expands its functions; state political elites increase their cooperation with big capitalism and military elites interested in the development of the armaments industry. Mann's account of organizational power proves to be particularly effective, on the interpretative level, with reference to the clash between social classes taking place in different European countries in this historical phase (628–85). With regard to the outbreak of the First World War, Mann gives a key role not only to the consequences of often erroneous and counterproductive military strategies, but also to the values and ideologies typical of the political and military elites of the time (honor, glory, status, the fear and shame of being considered weak) and to the crystallizations of the states involved. He focuses his analysis on Germany. In this nation, in the years preceding the First World War, an "additive" development of crystallizations takes place (791) that, in the geopolitical equilibrium and ideological context of the time, is decisive for the outbreak of the conflict. All the main actors that make up the German State, in conditions of substantial semi-autonomy, take their crystallization of reference to the extreme: the monarchy multiplies its authoritarian political and geopolitical decisions; the military announces, with indifference to the foreseeable consequences on the political climate, its project of strengthening the ground army and of building a powerful naval fleet; the many nationalist groups voice increasingly rhetorical and aggressive positions; capitalists heighten their territorial conception of economic interests (294–6). All this is both fueled by, and leading to, what Germany perceives as an encirclement by other states; from there, the outbreak of war only needs a pretext.

The third volume of *The Sources of Social Power* does not begin where the second one ended. "In preparing Volume 3" explains Mann, "I decided I had to rectify an omission in Volume 2: the neglect of the global empires created by the most advanced countries" (Mann 2012, vii). Between 1870 and 1890, the most powerful nation-states start their race for colonial empires. This opens a long process that will turn the world into the battleground of competing colonial empires: Spain, Portugal, Holland, Great Britain, France, Russia, Germany, Belgium, the United States, Japan, and Italy. Mann approaches this context through his usual interpretative key based on the four ideal-types of power. All empires are the result of a combination of military and political power, supported by economic and ideological power; the different crystallizations of the colonizing state condition the form of its colonialism, as Mann accurately details in the book (18–57).

Following an in-depth analysis of the First World War, Mann's historical-sociological exploration continues with the examination of three other mainly military-political processes: the Russian revolution, the Chinese revolution, the failed revolutions in Germany and Austria (Mann also expounds his own theory of revolution; see Mann 2012, 130–167).

The multifactorial explanation based on the IEMP model is also applied by Mann to the Great Depression, which was generated by the overlapping of different processes related to economic, political, geopolitical, and ideological factors. After this crisis, capitalism demonstrates its capacity for self-reform through the institutionalization of the welfare state (241–60). Mann highlights how the First World War paved the way for the series of economic, military, and political crises that transformed the leading edge of power in the following years. These crises, associated with different political, economic, and military crystallizations, divide the leading edge of power into three distinct geopolitical blocs: North-Western Europe, Southern and Eastern Europe, and Russia. In the period of the great totalitarianisms, each of these blocks follows its own specific route on the basis of its previous crystallizations. The punitive peace treaties after the First World War fuel again Germany's aggressiveness, creating a framework of geopolitical instability that will be the precondition for the Second World War. This time, Mann's analysis also includes, exceptionally, the subjective factor: the immediate cause of the Second World War, he writes, was Adolf Hitler. This war did not result, as the First World War, from miscalculations favored by widespread ideologies of aggressive nationalism; it was initiated by a single person, armed with an ambitious project of conquest: "For the only time in this book," states Mann, "I attribute enormous causal power to an individual" (345). Of course, this special variable is welded to a set of geopolitical interests pressing towards the outbreak of the conflict. World War II "was a collision between imperialists: the old regime seeing peace and collective security as the better way to preserve empire, and the arrivistes believing they would have to fight to get one" (428).

The subheading of the fourth – and last – volume of *The Sources of Social Power* reads *Globalizations, 1945–2011*. Globalization is not, for Mann, a process led by a single source of social power, nor does it imply a unitary development, capable of giving rise to a single global order or to a single world society. Globalization is the result of the interweaving of different historical-social processes, whereby, with changing speed, intensity and modalities, different territorial areas of the world enter into mutual relations; these, however, are not assimilated or homogenized under a single order (Mann 2013, 10–1). Globalization fragments as much as it unites, preserving – and in many cases sharpening – the peculiarities of the different societies: new conflicts arise around the four sources of power, and, in many regions of the world, ethnic and cultural identities get strongly reaffirmed in opposition to real or perceived attempts at assimilation. Globalization creates a more interconnected world, but not a more harmonious or uniform one. Globalization is therefore, for Mann, "universal but polymorphous" (Mann 2013, 10): it characterizes the whole globe, but leads to differentiated outcomes.

The historical phase to which the fourth volume of *The Sources of Social Power* is dedicated sees the emergence of the United States as the leading edge of power (see also Mann 2001, 467). The historical processes that Mann considers in this volume, always through the IEMP model, are decolonization, the Cold War, the military expansion of the USA in the world, and the complex political and economic dynamics of the Soviet Union, from the post-war period, to the dissolution of the USSR, up to the present day. There are also analyses dedicated to the transformation of the People's Republic of China into an experiment of dynamic fusion between communism and capitalism, with its lights and shadows. Capitalism takes different forms in different parts of the world, from Western neo-liberalism to Chinese state-capitalism, from the oligarchic capitalism dominant in Russia, Africa and Latin America, to the intersections between capitalism and barter still current in many developing countries. In the globalized world, also ideologies take on a plural character: liberal democracy is more widespread than ever, but there are also ideologies strongly opposing it, like militarist imperialism and armed fundamentalism. These, Mann writes, arise as a result of the power imposed by the US in the regions it exploits or ostracizes (Mann 2002). The geopolitical, economic and ideological empire built by the United States is weakening, and it is not easily predictable who will succeed it in world leadership. The next leading edge, Mann hypothesizes, could be a consortium of powers, made up of the United States, the European Union, China, India, and Japan. In the next future, the US will probably lose the center of the stage, but not get off it (Mann 2013, 421).

Modernity "lengthened the life span, brought mass prosperity, deepened citizenship, perfected the arts of killing people and destroying the planet, and expanded international collaborative institutions" (421). A heterogeneous list, in which good and evil are intentionally mixed. Human dynamism is in fact, says Mann in the closing pages of *The Sources of Social Power*, intrinsically dual: positive developments and steps forward go hand in hand with setbacks, risks, and disasters. In this uneven mix, however, a dynamic is recognizable according to which

> out of most disasters came some further attempt at improvement: in the Keynesian aftermath of the Great Depression, in the establishment of international institutions after World War II, including peace in Europe through the European Union; in arms reduction programs after the ending of the cold war, and in the beginning of moves during the Great Recession toward a more multi-centric regulation of global capitalism, most specifically in the growing stature of the G-20 group of countries, which includes all four BRIC countries. (423)

For an empirical sociologist like Mann, of course, this dynamic is of no predictive value. It is only based on what has happened so far and there are no guarantees of its validity for the future: "There is no end of history, no ultimate primacy, no necessary continued progress, for the unintended consequences of human action constantly create new interstitial problems, plural outcomes are always possible, and human beings have the capacity to choose well or badly, for good or ill" (423).

References

Anderson, Perry. 1986. "Those in Authority." *The Times Literary Supplement,* no. 12: 1405–6.

Goldthorpe, John. 1991. "The Uses of History in Sociology: Reflections on Some Recent Tendencies." *The British Journal of Sociology* 42 (2): 211–30.

Harris, Cole. 1991. "Power, Modernity, and Historical Geography." *Annals of the Association of American Geographers* 81 (4): 671–83.

Jones, Rhys. 1999. "Mann and Men in a Medieval State: The Geographies of Power in the Middle Ages." *Transactions of the Institute of British Geographers, New Series* 24 (1): 65–78.

Lukes, Steven. 1974. *Power. A Radical View.* New York: Macmillan.

Mann, Michael. 1979. "Idealism and Materialism in Sociological Theory." In *Critical Sociology. European Perspectives,* edited by J. W. Freiberg, 97–120. New York: Irvington.

Mann, Michael. 1986. *The Sources of Social Power: Volume 1. A History of Power from the Beginning to AD 1760.* New York: Cambridge University Press.

Mann, Michael. 1988. "The Autonomous Power of the State." In *States, War and Capitalism. Studies in Political Sociology,* edited by Michael Mann, 1–32. Oxford: Basil Blackwell.

Mann, Michael. 1993. *The Sources of Social Power: Volume 2. The Rise of Classes and Nation-States, 1760–1914.* New York: Cambridge University Press.

Mann, Michael. 1994. "In Praise of Macro-Sociology: A Reply to Goldthorpe." *The British Journal of Sociology* 45 (1): 37–54.

Mann, Michael. 2001. "Globalization Is (Among Other Things) Trans-National, Inter-National and American." *Science & Society* 65 (4): 464–9.

Mann, Michael. 2002. "Globalization as Violence." Consulted January 23, 2020. http://www.sscnet.ucla.edu/soc/faculty/mann/globasviol%5B1%5D.pdf.

Mann, Michael. 2008. "Infrastructural Power Revisited." *Studies in Comparative International Development* 23 (3–4): 355–65.

Mann, Michael. 2012. *The Sources of Social Power: Volume 3. Global Empires and Revolution, 1890–1945.* New York: Cambridge University Press.

Mann, Michael. 2013. *The Sources of Social Power: Volume 4. Globalizations, 1945–2011.* New York: Cambridge University Press.

Parsons, Talcott. 1957. "The Distribution of Power in American Society." *World Politics* 10 (1): 123–43.

Piromalli, Eleonora. 2016. *Michael Mann: Le fonti del potere sociale*. Milano: Mimesis.

Spohn, Wilfried. 2009. "Historical and Comparative Sociology in a Globalizing World." *Historická sociologie*, no. 1: 9–27.

Wickham, Chris. 1988. "Historical Materialism, Historical Sociology." *New Left Review*, no. 171: 63–80.

CHAPTER 10

The Sociology of Concepts or the Sociology of Judgments?

Schmitt, Benjamin, Weber

Carmelo Lombardo and Lorenzo Sabetta

1   Political Judgments and the Sociology of Concepts

The interrelated themes that run through this essay are connected with some questions arising from the work of classical sociologists and their legacies: how can sociology arrive at making political judgments?[1] Is such an aim attainable at all in the first place? Is it a worthy one? If so, for whom are said judgments valid and why? What kind of specific validity should these judgments aspire to? How can circumstantial judgments, sprung from concrete cultural situations and intended for particular targets, travel across time, giving proof of resilience, if not objectivity? Needless to say, these questions are not comprehensively answered here, but they mark out the range within which our analysis is couched and situated. Our point of departure is to recognize how the possibility of fleshing out political judgments within the field of sociology has been caught (as it often happens in intellectual disputes, especially academic ones) between Scylla and Charybdis, that is, between the dismissal of the possibility itself of advancing whatever political judgments and the conviction that these judgments are not only accessible to sociologists but should also possess normative significance. Advocates of the former perspective would emphasize the altogether contextual character of any political course of action, considering therefore impossible to set forth objective accounts, while advocates of the latter would deem necessary to develop a broadly applicable set of scientific principles that can grapple with every political decision. This thorny opposition, here caricatured as perfectly dichotomic (justificationism v. normativism), is somehow exemplar, calling into question the very separation between two interrelated facets of political judgments. On the one hand, their contingent aspects (e.g., their terminus a quo or initial stage, the fortuitous or pragmatic

---

1   Although this chapter is the result of the joint work of both authors, Carmelo Lombardo is the author of paragraphs 3, 4, and 5, while Lorenzo Sabetta is the author of paragraphs 1 and 2.

conditions of their original application, the idiosyncrasies of their target, etc.);
on the other, their general dimension (that is, their logical form, the hypothetical transcendental validity based on formalized principles). In this sense, political judgments are affected by both the history of concepts (their diachronic
mutations that happen over different epochs) and their concrete usage (the
synchronic contingency of their momentaneous use into certain fields). This
nexus is obviously decisive for the theoretical reconstruction of "the historically contingent, socially conditioned, and occasionally highly conflicting uses
and abuses of concepts by individuals and groups in their particular historical projects" (Pankakoski 2010, 751). It may also reflect, though, case-by-case
analyses aside, on the project of developing a science of society willing to
acknowledge the historical embeddedness of political actions but nonetheless
up to the task of bringing forth objective evaluations, rationally formalized
and perforce, to some extent, abstract. However, this possibility of abstracting
from the concreteness of political situations (the "concrete decision made by
a concrete person in a concrete situation," 754) has been partially ruled out by
the sociology of concepts since its inception, because of its very raison d'être.

In the third of his *Four Chapters on the Concept of Sovereignty* (arguably
the core chapter of the whole volume, both titled in fact *Political Theology*),
Carl Schmitt cryptically identifies a domain that he labels "sociology of concepts" (2006, 45). This puzzling expression – anticipated, a few pages earlier,
by its narrower variation "sociology of juristic concepts" (*soziologie juristischer
Begriffe*, ibid., 37) – apparently points out a niche sociological subfield, but
this is not actually the case. To Schmitt, it is neither a field nor a domain,
but a resource or a tool, and not just any tool, but the foundational methodology of his political theology, whose study concerns the analogies between
the metaphysical-theological image of a definite epoch and the systematic
structure of those concepts used in that given epoch.[2] Such "diagnostic tool"
(Hollerich 2004, 111) is not, strictly speaking, sociological, and Schmitt's use
of the term is (deliberately) quirky. It does not really carry any externalist

---

2   Schmitt's general line of reasoning is widely known and so are his examples – the "fun-
    damentally systematic and methodical analogies" between jurisprudence and theology,
    the state of "exception" and the "miracle," the modern lawgiver and the omnipotent God.
    Needless to say, this summary is cursory and absolutely sketchy (for more nuanced interpre-
    tations, see Herrero 2015; Schupmann 2017; Croce and Salvatore 2020; Sferrazza Papa 2021).
    Meier (2011, 184) would object that this outline is too close to the clichéd "secularization the-
    orem," according to which political theology only "denotes an assertion of conceptual history
    or a hypothesis from the sociology of knowledge, which deals with "structural analogies"
    between disciplines and historical recastings, and whose scope is limited to the entryway
    into "Western rationalism" and the "epoch of the modern state" or to modernity."

undertones: his sociology of concepts is not looking for material determinants of spiritual phenomena, nor is about tracing "a conceptual result back to a sociological carrier," which would be "a sociological problem, but not a problem of the sociology of a concept" (Schmitt 2006, 44); its rationale is not correlating ideas and the vantage point of a specific social class or group. One of Schmitt's basic points, indeed, is that "ideas come from other ideas" (Kahn 2011, 101). In order to construe the conceptual structure in which the organization of society in a given time is entangled, according to him, concepts need to be treated in their own right, not as epiphenomena of something else (individual motivations, materialistic causes, etc.). This is the force of concepts (Cordero 2019, 4–6), the reason why to make sense of how certain political experiences are articulated, they must be enunciated within the prevalent discursive field of their historical moment. To establish "the structural identity of theological and juridical concepts, modes of argumentation and insights" (Schmitt 2008, 42), Schmitt claims that the sociology of concepts must transcend "juridical conceptualization oriented to immediate practical interest. It aims to discover the basic, radically systematic structure and to compare this conceptual structure with the conceptually represented social structure of a certain epoch" (Schmitt 2006, 45). That these analogies are systematic and profound, lying at the root of any given conceptual structure, should not mislead the interpreter. The point is showing how the abstract compound of juristic concepts connects to a tangible complex of power, the usage of concepts in a concrete setting, in a particular time and place, against determinate foes.[3] This last factor cannot be underestimated. The specific climate surrounding a particular concrete case involves also the strategic use of concepts and their built-in conflict potential.[4] Schmitt boldly argues that "every political concept is a polemical concept. It has a political enemy in mind and, with respect to its intellectual rank, intellectual force, and historical significance, it is determined by this enemy" (1930, 5). He stresses the same point (which is also a methodological one, since it stipulates how political concepts should be analyzed in order to foreground their political nature – see Pankakoski 2013, 234) elsewhere:

---

3 Precisely because of the prominence of contextuality and concreteness in Schmitt's approach, it strikes Meierhenrich and Simons (2016, 17) as ironic that his concepts left "indelible impressions" and displayed "ostensible timelessness," making sense of this somehow incongruous dynamic through their aesthetic appeal, epiphanic formulation, and fruitful ambiguity.

4 In the same spirit, Koselleck notes that "in politics, words and their usages are more important than any other weapon" (2004, 54).

First of all, all political concepts, images, and words have a polemical meaning; they refer to a concrete opposition, they are tied to a concrete situation the ultimate consequence of which is a grouping into friends and enemies (manifesting in war or revolution), and they become empty and ghostly abstractions when this situation is forgotten. Words like "state," "republic," "society," and "class," or further, "sovereignty," "Rechtsstaat," "absolutism," "dictatorship," "plan," "neutral or total state" etc. are incomprehensible if one does not know who *in concreto* is to be met, fought, negated, and refuted with such a word.[5]

From this instrumental weaponization of concepts (of necessity either hostility-laden or not properly enucleated) it follows the rejection of any pluralistic stance that might jeopardize the antagonism against enemies necessary for mobilizing political action – and, one could argue, the absoluteness of decisionism starts sliding down the slippery slope from political theology to "political theozoology" (Taubes 2013, 29), as a tragic (though, perhaps, not inescapable) implication of the friend/enemy opposition. But what is at stake here, epistemologically? In a way, the very indifference to this issue characterizes Schmitt's approach to conceptual history and the sociology of concepts, at least in the sense of his lack of interest in some value-neutral research programs or noncommittal inquiries: "he explicitly practiced a form of political writing that aimed at "capturing" or "occupying" concepts. Schmitt thought of concepts as "real carriers of political energy" that could effectively separate friends and enemies" (Müller 2014, 81). Not a transferable method, not even just a means of understanding, his sociology of concepts *itself* can be construed *primarily* as an attack mounted against liberalism and liberal constitutionalism, which allegedly deceive themselves in thinking they have dispensed with any omnipotent God (i.e., any dogmatic and authoritative figure) or assuming, in a delusional way, that all political-ethical problems can be comprehended and unraveled within the frame of a coherent body of law (see Roberts 2015, 468; Bielefeldt 1997). Through a "radical conceptualization"

---

5   We are citing Pankakoski's translation (2010, 753) instead of the original one (Schmitt 2007, 30–1). An analogous emphasis on the concreteness of Schmitt's approach is shared by Vatter (2016, 249): "political theology, with its central concept of sovereignty, is a theory that claims to explain how an abstract complex of norms (jurisprudence) connects to a concrete complex of power (sociology): this is what it means for political theology to be "a sociology of juristic concepts" (...). If the system of norms is not to remain a ghostly abstraction, if this normative system is to become a concrete legal order, then it needs to link up with a real person who must also be a real representative of the entire juridical order."

(*radikale Begrifflichkeit*, Schmitt 2006, 45) these contradictory premises are exposed, and certain values are given precedence over (supposedly illusionary and inconsistent) others – here lies the social dimension of the sociology of concepts.[6] Knowledge is not seen as a legitimate goal per se, independent from its relationship with the political, and Schmitt "resolves Weber's epistemological tension by framing concepts as weapons to be mobilized in specific political conflicts" (Lebow and Lebow 2017, 177): inevitably antagonistic, political concepts should be understood (and marshaled) in terms of who is impacted by them. By the same token, but in an opposite direction, Schmitt's "methodological extremism," "for which the formation of a concept is paradoxically but necessarily dependent upon a contact with a singularity that exceeds or eludes the concept," makes his mode of investigation similar to Benjamin's, as Samuel Weber underscored (1992, 7), creating a family feeling among their analyses of current affairs through theological concepts.

Why Max Weber? Why Walter Benjamin? Why Weber and Benjamin mentioned (and placed) alongside Schmitt? Not that these comparisons would be unprecedented: the interplay of references and allusions among these three towering figures in the history of political thought is subtle and dense, and a number of analyses have tried to elucidate this web of reciprocal influences and links, which are often illuminating and counterintuitive (Ulmen 1985; Heil 1996; Agamben 1999; Bredekamp 1999 and 2016; Lombardo 2006; De Wilde 2008; Engelbrekt 2009; Löwy 2009; McQuillan 2010; Thiem 2013; Tagliacozzo 2014; Raciti 2019). However, the rest of this essay does not engage with the philologically driven debate over alternative sets of critical synopses,[7]

---

6   It has been argued (see Galli 1996) that Schmitt's authentic achievement consisted in radically exposing himself at the outset of the modern age, fashioning therefore a peculiar critique of modernity – as we will see below, this assessment seems to hold true also for Walter Benjamin. Thus, "Schmittian 'concreteness' means bringing thought and political order into contact with contingency, with the contentious instability of reality" (Galli 2020, 124).

7   Nor do we dwell on those anecdotal episodes (though numerous and revealing, particularly in terms of sociology of intellectuals and intellectual relationships) that punctuate this triadic constellation. One cannot help, however, but mention at least two of them: the long-suppressed letter of esteem sent on December 9, 1930, by Benjamin to Schmitt for acknowledging his influence on the *Origin of the German Trauerspiel*, a short note which Taubes considered (2013, 16) a "ticking bomb that comprehensively shatters our preconceptions regarding the intellectual history of the Weimar period," given that "Benjamin's interest in Schmitt's theory of sovereignty has always been judged as scandalous" (Agamben 2005, 53). The other episode took place in 1964, at the Fifteenth Convention of the German Sociological Association, held in Heidelberg in honor of Max Weber's centenary: in front of a hard-to-believe audience (which included Marcuse, Horkheimer, Adorno, Albert, Bendix, Aaron, and Parsons among others) the then 34-year-old Jürgen Habermas claimed "that Carl Schmitt was

in compliance with the tightrope exercise of spotting historical continuities and discontinuities of ideas where they do exist, avoiding identifying them where they do not in fact exist. We rather try to selectively address Weber's and Benjamin's considerations only in terms of their functions in contemporary political sociology, that is, in light of the current condition of sociological theory in the matter of advancing political judgments.[8] Weber and Benjamin (two otherwise different interpreters of political thought, but equally immersed in the conflictual climate of their time) were both absorbed by the polemics and struggles of their age, facing the crisis of political liberalism in pre- and post-Weimar politics and Europe's societal and political modernization. In this view, Weber's and Benjamin's (and Schmitt's for that matter) categories mirror the contingency of their conditional use: both subjects of the sociology of concepts, the paradigms of political judgments they bequeathed are nonetheless different. While Benjamin (at once the most loyal and disloyal interpreter of Schmitt's sociology of concepts) firmly avoided the mundanization (*verweltlichung*) of his political categories, the passage from transcendence to immanence molded Weber's model – we think this hiatus, ceteris paribus, is especially relevant for today's sociology. Significantly, expanding on the same Schmittian passage on the sociology of concepts, the American theologian Adam Kotsko (2013) argued that this "raises an interesting question: namely, is it only in early modernity that such a procedure is possible, i.e., that the theological/metaphysical ideas and juristic concepts reach the level of totality at the same time?" Once again, the relationship between concepts formation and their usage (i.e., between their logical structure and the contingent circumstances that occasioned them, *determining whether or not these two moments should be kept distinct*) seems to be critical when it comes to articulate political judgments without falling either into teleological and contextual justificationism or into universalistic and abstract normativism.

2   Benjamin's Sociology of Concepts, or the Intention "to Interrupt the Course of the World"

Benjamin's vision of revolutionary politics is based on the fertile miscegenation of his messianic Marxism, as is widely acknowledged and discussed in the

---

a legitimate student of Max Weber" and perhaps even his "natural son" (see Engelbrekt 2009, 668), a controversial hyperbole never overlooked by successive commentators.

8   This argumentation is obviously inspired by Robert K. Merton's (1967, 1–37) distinction between "history" and "systematics" of sociological theory (on which see also Jones 1983).

literature, where this oxymoronic couple has been variously considered compatible and reconcilable or incongruous and fictitious. Through the provocative claim that "Marx has secularized the messianic time in the conception of the classless society" (Benjamin 1974, 1231), Benjamin promotes an understanding of Marxism that does not fall under the category of positivism, thus avoiding succumbing to the false allure of progress (Buck-Morss 1989; Gold 2006). In his framework, theology and historical materialism are not supposed to dilute each other or trade off, but rather mutually energize one another. Even though the role of theological language in Benjamin's writing is anything but immediate (see Goldstein 2001), throughout his work theology represents "the scientific mainstay" of any detailed commentary on reality (Benjamin 1999, 460). Rather than analytical methods, however, we are left with metaphorical and impressionistic statements: "my thinking is related to theology as blotting pad is related to ink. It is saturated with it. Were one to go by the blotter, however, nothing of what is written would remain" (471). Its traces may linger unnoticed, imperceptibly written, but to Benjamin theology has not yet finished saying what it has to say: as for Schmitt, the decisive objective is finding out (and bringing into action) the unobserved role of theological influences at the heart of political matters, and not for some uninvolved gnoseological purposes, for otiosely parsing how the mark of what is sacred or metaphysical is inscribed in what is profane – the point is to activate the latter and steer it in a certain direction, unreachable without the spark of theology. Benjamin (1969, 253) felt that this unpalatable, unmodish accomplice (a "hunchbacked dwarf") might enliven again the now-ossified automaton of historical materialism:

> theology for Benjamin is not a goal in itself; its aim is not the ineffable contemplation of eternal verities, nor, even less, reflection on the nature of the divine Being, as might be thought from its etymology: it is in the service of the struggle of oppressed. More precisely, it must serve to re-establish the explosive, messianic, revolutionary force of historical materialism.
>
> LÖWY 2005, 27–8

As pointed out by Rolf Tiedemann (1999, 933–5), Benjamin learned *au contraire* the lesson of the Surrealists (for whom oneiric visionary experiences remain just oneiric and visionary, mythology being mere mythology). They taught him that theological experiences should not be rehabilitated per se, but conveyed into everyday life: hence, the idea of "profane illuminations," in which resides the "true, creative overcoming of religious illumination" (Benjamin 1986, 179). To this end, his critique of the philosophy of progress (i.e., his conception of history in direct opposition to historical progressivism) zeroes in on a synthesis of the present with the past, aiming at assembling, unlocking, and bringing to light a suddenly emergent dialectical image (*dialektische bild*), a flash of lightning that promises to disrupt the continuous flow of events and the determinism of every progressive interpretation of human destiny as well: "its significance is its interruptive force" (Ferris 2008, 121). In this sense, the messianic represents "a humanity that is finally liberated from the naturalized history of Progress" (Marramao 2008, 398), able to fully live in a now-time (*jetztzeit*) that breaks with chronology and whatever experiences of ordinary time, through a revolutionary leap into a condensed and unmechanical time which is indeed "Messianic time, the time of redemption of the world and the demand for the end of history understood as history's stop, rather than its culmination" (Pensky 2004, 193). Messianic time, representing the "true state of exception" that subdues the Antichrist, provides a counterbalancing force against violence intrinsic to history, the only antidote for that enemy whose victory would make unsafe "even the dead" (Benjamin 1969, 255).[9] The theological-political entanglement reaches here its acme, its maximum intensity which is also its greatest promise: this "Messianic cessation (*Stillstellung*) of happening" would open up "a revolutionary chance in the fight for the oppressed past (*unterdrückte Vergangenheit*)" (Benjamin 1969, 263). Not a positive telos, not some evolutionary measures or piecemeal interventions, nothing but the wish "to interrupt the course of the world," that according to Benjamin (1985, 39) was "Baudelaire's deepest wish" and (based on the biblical account of Joshua praying that God helps his people in the battle of Gibeon by stopping the sun) "the wish of Joshua" too.[10] The potentiality "to make the continuum of history

---

9   Derrida's interpretation (1999, 248) is that a Marxist messianicity "refers, in every here-now, to the coming of an eminently real, concrete event, that is, to the most irreducibly heterogeneous otherness. Nothing is more 'realistic' or 'immediate' than this messianic apprehension, straining forward toward the event of him who/that which is coming." On the relationship between Derrida's take on the messianic as *messianicité sans messianisme* and Benjamin's materialist theology, see Khatib 2013.

10   An additional reference of this heliotropic metaphor is one of Karl Kraus' poems, explicitly cited by Benjamin: "Let time stand still! Sun, you come to completion! / Make the end great! Announce eternity! / [...] You golden bell, melt in your own heat, / become a cannon against the cosmic foe!" Expanding on this passage, Vandeputte (2019, 132) observes that Benjamin's resistance against the empty sequentiality of history manifested by a "stream of becoming" is rendered "as a resistance against time – that is to say, against time that manifests itself as a continuous flow. [This] demand for the cessation of the flowing time in which the time that passes is not differentiated from a time that is yet to come; [...] a resistance that is also a repugnance at a flowing time in which every past and future are merely modifications of an ever-same present."

explode" (Benjamin 1969, 261) would realize the encounter between "mundane" struggles for emancipation and "spiritual" promises of redemption.

There are myriad ways of (mis)interpreting Benjamin's fragmentary thought. Our focus here, however, is on his idea that certain deep-seated collective desires have to be connected with buried, yet to be ignited, socially transformative ends (see Cohen 1993, 21). As with Schmitt's sociology of concepts, the uncovered link between theology and politics is the metaphysical linchpin of a radical interpretation of modernity, essential for dismantling its self-understanding. Their conceptual analyses are just as radical, literally: getting to the metapolitical roots of the concepts they analyzed is conducive to undo predominant historical narratives, retrieve the suppressed of history, intensify the consciousness of the present condition (either to fight for the political or to take up the fight of the downtrodden of the past), bridge historical and eschatological awareness (see Lievens, 2016). It is with this in mind that Benjamin, for instance, took up the question of violence (*Gewalt*) and the possibility of its historical overcoming in his 1921 *Critique of Violence*. The "critique" refers to the development of a set of conceptual tools for interpreting and evaluating violence, especially concerning the issue of justified violence in the pursuit of revolutionary struggles. Several overlapping distinctions are set forth: law-positing (*rechtsetzend*) and law-preserving (*rechtserhaltend*) violence; mythical law-positing violence and divine law-destroying violence; power and justice. The *Kritik* (plausibly drafted at the same time as the *Theological-Political Fragment*) is famed to be enigmatic, and we won't add yet another layer of exegetical commentaries to the vast literature already out there. What seems remarkable for our purposes is the historical background of Benjamin's piece – the fall of the Second Reich, the heavy toll of German casualties during WWI, the bloodbath of the Spartacist uprising of 1919, the new front of the Bolshevik Revolution. Facing this tumultuous scenario, Benjamin resolves to articulate an "authentic theology of the role of violence in messianic redemption" (Jacobson 2003, 203), opposing boundless and bloodless destruction that only expiates to the bloody law-making power that demands sacrifices and sets boundaries. There is a pure violence, thus, paralleled to the violence outside of positive law generated by the general strike, unalloyed violence "figured as at once revolutionary and divine" (Butler 2006, 214). This divine violence does not make the world divine but rather allows, in the name of the living, the Profane to gain a fullness independent of the religion of guilt and the religion of capitalism (see Galli 2020, 101); only outside the legal order lies the possibility of a politics of pure means (see Gentili 2019), that no longer justifies any legal order whatsoever.

Violence is but an example. In a consistent manner, Benjamin's analysis of concepts (e.g., temporality, sovereignty, experience, artwork, state of exception among others) practically subscribes to Schmitt's dictum that spiritual and substantial identities are to be found between the metaphysical underpinnings of concepts and the state of consciousness characteristic of certain historical-political realities. Extremes meet, and one is the flip side of the other: although their opposition, content-wise, could not be more marked (suspension of law v. rule of law; real state of exception v. state of exception; Behemoth v. Leviathan; Messiah v. sovereign authority; order disruption v. order preservation; Judaism v. Catholicism), they share the same logic of inquiry for turning the narrative of modernity on its head. Desecularizing its concepts, they deploy theological categories to read the present against the grain, putting into play two worlds and two languages, that of theology and that of politics.[11] The result is drastically contingent and unrepeatable – to use a Weberian vocabulary, it does *not* ask to be surpassed and outdated, and calls for enactors rather than theorists, commentators rather than practitioners. This sociology of concepts, actually, strives against the ongoing process of intellectualization (again, a Weberian category), epitomized by the modern conviction that "there are no mysterious incalculable forces that come into play, but rather that one can, in principle, master all things by calculation" (Weber 1946, 139). Expatiating on Benjamin's essay on *gewalt*, Werner Hamacher has underscored that

> the decision reached by pure, critical violence cannot be made by cognitive means. The decision eludes judgement. [...] The strike is not a matter of theory; it can be the object neither of prognoses nor of programmes; it belongs to the order of events that break through the continuum of history, as they do the commensurability of its cognition.
>
> 1994, 126

This critique of modernity informed by messianic sources is alien to Max Weber, whose model for making political judgments works exactly the other way around: messianic temporality is not the pattern for analyzing historical time, and theological references are instead secularized in order to perform such analysis.[12]

---

11   It may sound paradoxical that theological sources can prompt concreteness, messianic metaphysics triggers terrestrial courses of action, eschatology wards off eschatology: "one can understand this paradox only by stressing that even a metapolitical struggle has to produce its own symbols that give this struggle a certain intensity" (Lievens 2016, 420).

12   Esposito (2015, 25) observes that the idea of "disenchantment" (*Entzauberung*) in Weber's categorial apparatus has a role similar to the one played by the concept of mundanization (*Verweltlichung*) or "becoming-worldly" in the Hegelian system. However, "contrary to Hegel's mundanization, Weber's disenchantment does not dissolve the exteriority of

3   A Different Stance in the Face of Despair

Still on Benjamin's sociology of concepts, another remark should be made on his four-page fragment *Capitalism as Religion*, penned in 1921 (right after the *Theological-Political Fragment* and the *Critique of Violence*), where the argument about the properly religious nature of capitalist systems is advanced. Although directly inspired by Weber's work on the Protestant ethic and starting from similar assumptions, Benjamin critically distances himself from the Weberian outline – indeed, the point of his diagnosis condensed in the expression "Capitalism as Religion" "can be highlighted in contrast with Max Weber's work" (Hamacher 2002, 85). Benjamin intends to furnish "the proof of the religious structure of capitalism," which is conceived "not merely, as Weber believes, as a formation conditioned by religion, but as an essentially religious phenomenon" (Benjamin 1996, 288). Value-freedom (*Wertfreiheit*) is replaced with a vehement anticapitalist critique that uses Weber's research "as ammunition in order to mount a thorough attack on the capitalist system, its values, its practices and its 'religion'" (Löwy 2009, 72). Worries, feelings of depression, and the spiritual hopelessness induced by capitalism – the first "cult that creates guilt, not atonement" (Benjamin 1996, 288) – are delineated, but such delineation is not meant to yield an adequate picture of reality, being intended instead as a polemical weapon against a system inherently skewed to accrue guilt and make it universal. Since this concatenation pivots on a brand-new kind of rationality peculiar to capitalism, a logic of rational causality that attributes guilt and cause, origin and provenance, the Weberian methodological apparatus, itself based on establishing causal relationships, is "structurally capitalistic in its inspiration [and] cannot therefore provide any means of liberation from capitalism and its structure" (Hamacher 2002, 86). Weber's attempt to demonstrate the mutual derivation of modern economic forms and 17th century Protestantism, highlighting the noneconomic roots of the spirit of capitalism, is replaced by Benjamin with a metaphysically-driven effort to find a way out of capitalist culpability and its generalization of despair. Drawing from Gustav Landauer's libertarian socialism, Benjamin recurs to the political-theological concept of *Umkehr* (return/conversion), which means at the same time "interruption of history, *metanoia*, expiation, purification and

---

the outside in the unity of the world; rather, it drags it inside itself like a line of tangency that separates life from itself by stripping it of its naturalness" (35); the Weberian category indicates also the unsolved friction between politics and economics, the process of mechanization through which the fulfillment of vocation (*Beruf*) becomes nothing more than an economic operation.

... revolution" (Löwy 2009, 70).[13] Yet, the authentic fear from which despair emerges is that there is no real way out: "worries are the index of the sense of guilt induced by a despair that is communal, not individual and material, in origin" (Benjamin 1996, 290). Such absence of alternatives warrants a radically alternative viewpoint, best expressed by Adorno (1987, 247) in the concluding aphorism of *Minima Moralia*: not just "reconstruction, mere technique," but a kind of knowledge adequate to "displace and estrange the world, reveal it to be, with its rifts and crevices, as indigent and distorted as it will appear one day in the messianic light" – this should be the compass of "the only philosophy which can be responsibly practiced in the face of despair." Staring into the abyss of historical gloom and present hopelessness, to Benjamin, one cannot but enlist metaphysics and theology in the effort. Critique on the heights of despair does not propose any iterable method but rather its opposite, an intellectual operation actually as contingent as possible that should work like a defibrillator, historical evidence being "seized only as an image which flashes up at the instant when it can be recognized" (Benjamin 1969, 255), with an "instantaneous logic" (Beck 2019, 136). Weber too, however, writes in the face of a looming "polar night of icy darkness and hardness" (1946, 128), though his dismal prognosis is motivated by the lack of political groups capable of measuring up "to the world as it really is," neither prone to "dully accept world and occupation" nor enticed by "mystic flight from reality" (128). Weber, too, lamented the condition of "mechanized ossification" (*mechanisierte Versteinerung*) of the modern world, where commodities, markets, and the bureaucracy are forging a "steel-hard casing" that cannot be dismantled at any time (Weber 2001, 123–4), using a metaphor (*stahlhartes Gehäuse*) that may have been influenced by the image of the "iron cage of despair" devised by the English Puritan poet John Bunyan.[14] Significantly, straight after this tirade of nearly-legendary status Weber almost recants his allusive words, reassessing his overall position:

> Here, however, we have fallen into the realm of value-judgments and judgments rooted in faith, with which this purely historical analysis should not be burdened. The further *task* is a different one: to chart the

---

13 In this view, it holds for Benjamin as well what Cordero (2020, 7) says about Schmitt's sociology of concepts, which "is not primarily interested in the advance of sociological theory and methods but in confronting the sociological blindness produced by a "positivist age" that qualifies as "metaphysical derailments" any concern with the basic conceptual structure which dominates the spiritual organization of society in a given time."

14 But this link is debatable and so is the weight of Parsons' translation: see Tiryakian 1981 and Kent 1983.

significance of ascetic rationalism. The above sketch has only hinted at
its importance.

WEBER 2001, 124

Whereas for Adorno (and Benjamin as well) making oneself responsible in
the face of desperation means acting in light of redemption, Weber envisages
responsibility mainly as being accountable for the effects of one's conduct
and acting accordingly, taking therefore into account "the stupidity of other
men," "the average deficiencies of people," "foreseeable results," "ramifica-
tions," always asking "for consequences" (Weber 1946, 120–1).[15] Weber's "cold
anti-utopianism" (Derman 2012, 120) rebels against embarking on any "paths
toward supposed redemption," and his aversion of faith swindlers "drives
him to fight for the 'disenchantment of the world'" (Kracauer 1995, 135–6). To
him, no intellectual output is more valued in the face of despair than unemo-
tional judgments. Following Hennis' (1991, 53) interpretation, everything that
Weber did, at least since 1893, "was intended to further the 'pitiless sobriety of
judgement.'"

4   Weber as a Sociological Model for Developing Political Judgments

This last expression is adopted by the 29-year-old Weber in a short essay where
he reports on a course held in Berlin by the Protestant Social Congress, distinguishing the nature of his course from two other contemporaneous assemblies,
both organized with the aim of training workers' associations, lecturing them
against social democracy and in defense of the Christian economic order. By
contrast, Weber stresses the academic character of his course that would have
dealt, nonetheless, with the field of political economy, which is inherently
open to different interpretations and actually tackled from diverse angles – a
Weberian problem by definition. What is more needed, then, is

> the full *sobriety* of judgment (*die volle Nüchternheit des Urteils*), which
> follows only from the knowledge of the *economic* determinants of social
> phenomena and the difficulties opposed to socio-politically desirable
> solutions. The furtherance of this insight into the real factors of power,
> instead of the fruitless attempt to suppress the pursuit of empty social

---

15   In this sense, Weberian responsibility is not concerned with the purity of individual acts,
        having instead to answer to a wider collective forum (Bruun 2019, 297; see also Bonolis
        and Sabetta 2019).

activity, is unfortunately the only way of stopping precarious dilettantism, that is, dilettantism that in ignorance of the economic causes of an illness applies quack remedies to the symptoms. These courses should serve this purpose and *no* other, [since one should] *not* place much emphasis on the solutions of the great problems of these times, but rather – and keeping to these limits required a certain resignation – completely focus on highlighting the economic difficulties, promoting that these problems are altogether understood in their entire extent, ensuring that the *right* practical questions are asked.

WEBER 1993, 236, emphasis in original

Hennis remarks that this issue of *rightly* assessing practical problems and gauging their full (though unwelcome) consequences is "not substantially developed in later writings," stated there "once and for all" (236). As exaggerated as it may sound, looking back at Weber's work and reading it through the lens of our contemporary intellectual and social milieu, its heterogeneous contents actually turn out to be bounded together, in fact, by what one can call sociology of judgments. Such discerning ability to understand the links of interdependence existing among socio-historical events permeates the entirety of Weber's opus, marked by the elaboration of judgments (i.e., by establishing the existence of relationships among meaningful cultural phenomena) and analyses of the logical structure underlying the very possibility of elaborating such judgments.[16] However, this does not mean to judge in the moral sense of the term, to advance value-judgments whose motives are rooted in dogma, but rather to follow a "logic of judgment" whose validity is attested by logical operations and empirical controls. While Weber's methodological essays can be read as a detailed description of how this "logic of judgment" should kick in, his political papers (e.g., Weber 1995 and 2010) are often considered occasional and conditional, if not accidental – but then again, are not political developments always inherently contingent? Weber felt always "bound to participate in public affairs" (Honigsheim 2003, 13) and his "work is set deep within the controversies of the time" (Hennis 1991, 27). The largely formalistic character of his theory of politics (see Mommsen 1992, 189), in this light, is not merely the expression of epistemological agnosticism, being consequential to his attempt to keep contingencies and generality separated. Weber's proclivity for theoretical constructs can be interpreted as a willingness to investigate existentially

---

16   Our analysis draws again on Hennis' interpretation (1987), according to which the hallmark of Weber's intellectual personality lies in his "faculty of judgment."

pressing problematics through ideal-typical, pure concepts *applicable otherwise, reclaimable, and differently assembled*: other one-sided viewpoints can be adopted, selecting other sets of relevant elements. Since presuppositionless analyses are logically impossible – "a chaos of 'existential judgments' about countless individual events would be the only result of a serious attempt to analyze reality 'without presuppositions'" (Weber 1949, 78) – and the necessity of *wertbeziehung* is virtually unavoidable, the first step should be the recognition of the entire scope of problems associated to the political course of action under analysis to which many different practical answers can be given (Hennis 1994, 122). In other words, to develop political judgments which are unpassionate and level-headed (*nüchtern*) one must recognize those "'inconvenient' facts" which are unpleasant for her/his party opinions (Weber 1946, 147) – and for every political opinion there are "inconvenient" facts. Ineluctable as organizing principles, for eschewing dilettantism value stands have to be relentlessly trained in viewing the various arguments against their own favored solution: although this requires a certain resignation, herein lies the dividing line between "windbags" and "mature" men (127).[17] Thus, whether the specific case under consideration is a historical fact (e.g., the Battle of Marathon, the unification of Germany, or the cultural development of the Incas and Aztecs), a circumscribed action (like a temperamental young German mother slapping her son) or a present situation still underway (as the political futures of Poland or the condition of constitutional democracy in Russia), the logical structure remains the same, primarily based on "the determination of the 'historical significance' of those facts" (Weber 1949, 166). Acutely aware of his partisanship as for the specific contents addressed (may others come and address them differently), Weber constantly interrogates his own presuppositional orientations and analytic foundations, allowing scholars to distinguish between impersonal logical postulates and claims about actors' fundamental assumptions (see Malczewski 2019).

One can thus separate the incidental dimension of Weber's political papers (e.g., that the substance of his analyses may have been overtaken by events, as Weber himself notes in *Deutschlands künftige Staatsform*) from their general dimension.[18] Characterized by the same logic of judgment spelled out in his

---

17   This framework has understandably fueled a narrative of calm and painstaking "sober heroism" (Gane 1997, 556) surrounding Weber's personality (Turner 1992; Lough 2006), often portrayed as that of "a lonely hero of heavy burden" (Robin 2020).

18   Incidentally, it should be noted that Weber himself did not emphasize the sociological relevance of his political writings, while some commentators (see Beetham 1985; Chazel 2005; Lombardo 2009) have observed how they actually raise questions which are far more significant than the mere resolution of those issues characteristic of Weber's age.

methodological writings (a process of abstraction, comparison, determination of the possibilities, consideration of perverse effects, possible generalization, as well as a parallel distinction among factual sources, conceptual base, and nomological knowledge), Weber's political essays do offer a still-viable model of situated neutrality. This does not simply entail the combination of "both passion and perspective," conviction and responsibility, that in unison exemplifies the genuine politician (Weber 1946, 128). Weber did not acknowledge the presence of such politicians around himself, presaging hard times "no matter which group may triumph" (128); actually, he thought that the dilettantism of the ruling class (Junkers, bureaucratic clerks, cynical politicians without the calling, etc.) would have made history a rubbish heap of wasted opportunities. More ambitiously, then, political judgments should detect those junctures and turning points that constitute decisive possibilities for the future course of history, eventually making a case for them. Always occasioned by a concrete historical definiteness, by linking together chains of consequences and concatenations of circumstances, a political analysis might outstrip its own incidental contingency – not a metaphysical transcendence, but a methodological one.

5   Anything in Common? Coda

In this chapter, we have distinguished between two different orientations (which can also be viewed along a continuum rather than as either/or alternatives) with respect to political evaluations and social theory, differentiating the sociology of concepts, concerned with transcending the categories underlying the political organization of a definite period, from sociology of judgments, interested in analyzing the interdependence ties connecting historical events and socio-political courses of action. We have observed that the quest for analogies between the theological underpinnings of concepts and the complex of power of certain historical-political realities follows, at least in Benjamin and Schmitt, a radical conceptualization. Getting to the metaphysical roots of political and juristic concepts goes together with the effort of overthrowing the discourse that modernity has built – its self-conception should be torn down unveiling the latent interplay between theology and politics. Such (metaphysically-laden) sociology of concepts, through a peculiar theological-political entanglement, deliberately keeps its own pragmatic application together with its metatheoretical dimension. Concepts become armaments or defibrillators, not applicable beyond their transient, original usage: the contingency of their concrete displacements into certain fields is everything. By contrast, we have tried to stress how this separation between what is historically conditioned and what is logically established shapes Weber's model, which is still available for altogether different uses and operationalizations. According to Weber, political decisions cannot be derived from some universal and transcendental principles, but this does not entail that decisions cannot be rationally justified: the acting person and the judgment expressed about that both constitute political-historical evidence, subject to rational interpretation. Weber excludes any transcendent foundation of political thought, which should be always centered upon the determinants of social phenomena and their repercussions: faith in the rightness of one's values may be present no matter what, but since it is hardly the case that "from good comes only good and from evil comes only evil," the right question to ask is about the aftermath and side-effects of what *seems* the most personally appealing solution.

Despite its title, this essay does not have an antinomical structure, and there is no question of ranking frameworks and pigeonholing them, which would be all the more grotesque in the case of Benjamin, who lost the chance of an academic appointment when his *Habilitationsschrift* was turned down by the University of Frankfurt but has been meanwhile fully rehabilitated; his fragmentary corpus continues to speak to us "more impressively" than other well-polished theoretical buildings (Benjamin 1977, 235). Schmitt's writings, too, still find growing appreciation, with the additional challenge of understanding his work in spite (or because) of his association with Nazism.[19] We have not even sought to reaffirm the trite vision of Max Weber's theory as pluralist in delineating a series of incommensurable life-orders strangers to each other, according to which science and politics require different stances toward social reality, one of controlled inquiry, the other of ideological struggle. We have rather focused on the burdensome task of exercising judgments based on specific instances only, tentatively advancing from particular observations to general concepts.

A final remark. The most typical kind of action within communal relationships, according to Weber (1978, 1375), is the consensually oriented action (*Einverständnishandeln*), performed in accordance with other participants in a specific consensual group (*Einverständnisgemeinschaft*). Since these communal relationships (*Vergemeinschaftung*) are stable but without any clearly

---

19   While incarcerated in a civilian detention camp after the end of World War II, Schmitt (2017, 23) directly refers (commenting a radio speech by Karl Mannheim) to the concept of *verstehen* as appropriately applicable to his own case: "'understanding' has been discussed so often and so much among sociologists that it would be good to test this understanding, for once, in a desperate situation, and not only in the atmosphere of 'well-organized sociologists' conferences.'"

stated legislation, the uniformity of behavior rests upon mutual agreement, that is, consent (*Einverständnis*). From the intertwinement of these ideal-typical constructs, following the 1913 essay on the categories of interpretive sociology (the so-called *Kategorienaufsatz*), at least three levels of analysis may be taken into account: social relationships, social relationships determined by an intentional rational order, and social relationships adjusted in compliance with some power structures. In this sense, it comes as no surprise that Jean-Pierre Grossein (2005, 698) has reckoned the concepts of order (*ordnung*) and action (*handlung*) so vital in the Weberian framework that one could rein-terpret the whole history of sociology (and not just Weberian sociology, but sociology as such) against the background of these two concepts.[20] When it comes to political judgments, the special importance attached to communal relationships and their regulation can be translated into the identification of some intersubjective basis (neither objective nor subjective) on which said judgments can be established:

> the power of judgment rests on a potential agreement with others, and the thinking process which is active in judging something is not, like the thought process of pure reasoning, a dialogue between me and myself, but finds itself always and primarily, even if I am quite alone in making up my mind, in an anticipated communication with others with whom I know I must finally come to some agreement. From this potential agree-ment judgment derives its specific validity.
>
> ARENDT 1961, 220

If political action depends upon political judgments, such judgments depend, in turn, upon some commonality, something in common.

References

Adorno, Theodor W. 1987. *Minima Moralia: Reflections from Damaged Life.* New York: Verso.

Agamben, Giorgio. 1999. *Potentialities. Collected Essay in Philosophy.* Stanford, CA: Stanford University Press.

Agamben, Giorgio. 2005. *State of Exception.* Chicago: The University of Chicago Press.

---

20   This perspective seems particularly attuned to the definition of agency recently provided by Reed (2020, 30).

Arendt, Hannah. 1961. *Between Past and Future. Six Exercises in Political Thought.* New York: The Viking Press.

Beck, Humberto. 2019. *The Moment of Rupture: Historical Consciousness in Interwar German Thought.* Philadelphia: University of Pennsylvania Press.

Beetham, David. 1985. *Max Weber and the Theory of Modern Politics.* Cambridge: Polity Press.

Benjamin, Walter. 1969. *Illuminations. Essays and Reflections.* New York: Schocken Books.

Benjamin, Walter. 1974. *Gesammelte Schriften I.* Frankfurt am Main: Suhrkamp Verlag.

Benjamin, Walter. 1977. *The Origin of German Tragic Drama.* London: NLB.

Benjamin, Walter. 1985. "Central Park." *New German Critique,* no. 34 (Winter): 32–58.

Benjamin, Walter. 1986. *Reflections. Essays, Aphorism, Autobiographical Writing.* New York: Schocken Books.

Benjamin, Walter. 1996. *Selected Writings, Volume 1, 1913–1926.* Cambridge, MA: Harvard Belknap.

Benjamin, Walter. 1999. *The Arcades Project.* Cambridge, MA: The Belknap Press of Harvard University.

Bielefeldt, Heiner. 1997. "Carl Schmitt's Critique of Liberalism: Systematic Reconstruction and Countercriticism." *The Canadian Journal of Law and Jurisprudence* 10 (1): 65–75.

Bonolis, Maurizio, and Lorenzo Sabetta. 2019. "Verso una congiunzione funzionale delle due 'etiche' weberiane." *Quaderni di Sociologia* 81 (LXIII): 7–26.

Bredekamp, Horst. 1999. "From Walter Benjamin to Carl Schmitt, via Thomas Hobbes." *Critical Inquiry* 25 (2): 247–66.

Bredekamp, Horst. 2016. "Walter Benjamin's Esteem for Carl Schmitt." In *The Oxford Handbook of Carl Schmitt,* edited by J. Meierhenrich and O. Simons, 679–704. New York: Oxford University Press.

Bruun, Hans H. 2019. "Politics and Ethics, and the Ethic of Politics." In *The Oxford Handbook of Max Weber,* edited by E. Hanke, L. Scaff, and Sam Whimster, 291–311. New York: Oxford University Press.

Buck-Morss, Susan. 1989. *The Dialectics of Seeing. Walter Benjamin and the Arcades Project.* Cambridge, MA: The MIT Press.

Butler, Judith. 2006. "Critique, Coercion, and Sacred Life in Benjamin's 'Critique of Violence.'" In *Political Theologies. Public Religions in a Post-Secular World,* edited by Hent De Vries and Lawrence E. Sullivan, 201–19. New York: Fordham University Press.

Chazel, François. 2005. "Les *Écrits politiques* de Max Weber: un éclairage sociologique sur des problems contemporains." *Revue Française de Sociologie* 46 (4): 841–70.

Cohen, Margaret. 1993. *Profane Illumination: Walter Benjamin and the Paris of Surrealist Revolution.* Berkeley and Los Angeles, CA: University of California Press.

Cordero, Rodrigo. 2019. "Giving society a form: Constituent moments and the force of concepts." *Constellations* 26 (2): 194–207.

Cordero, Rodrigo. 2020. "The Negative Dialectics of Law: Luhmann and the Sociology of Juridical Concepts." *Social & Legal Studies* 29 (1): 3–18.

Croce, Mariano, and Andrea Salvatore. 2020. *L'indecisionista. Carl Schmitt oltre l'eccezione*. Macerata: Quodlibet.

Derman, Joshua. 2012. *Max Weber in Politics and Social Thought: From Charisma to Canonization*. Cambridge: University Press.

Derrida, Jacques. 1999. "Marx & Sons." In *Ghostly Demarcations: A Symposium on Jacques Derrida's Specters of Marx*, edited by Michael Sprinker, 213–69. London: Verso.

De Wilde, Marc. 2008. *Verwantschap in Extremen: Politieke Theologie bij Walter Benjamin en Carl Schmitt*. Amsterdam: University Press.

Engelbrekt, Kjell. 2009. "What Carl Schmitt Picked Up in Weber's Seminar: A Historical Controversy Revisited." *The European Legacy: Toward New Paradigms* 14 (6): 667–84.

Esposito, Roberto. 2015. *Two. The Machine of Political Theology and the Place of Thought*. New York: Fordham University Press.

Ferris, David S. 2008. *The Cambridge Introduction to Walter Benjamin*. New York: Cambridge University Press.

Galli, Carlo. 1996. *Genealogia della politica. Carl Schmitt e la crisi del pensiero politico moderno*. Bologna: Il Mulino.

Galli, Carlo. 2020. *Forme della critica. Saggi di filosofia politica*. Bologna: Il Mulino.

Gane, Nicholas. 1997. "Max Weber on the Ethical Irrationality of Political Leadership." *Sociology* 31 (3): 549–64.

Gentili, Dario. 2019. "The Politics of Pure Means: On Paragraphs 10 and 11 of Walter Benjamin's 'Toward the Critique of Violence.'" *Critical Times* 2 (2): 261–9.

Gold, Joshua R. 2006. "The Dwarf in the Machine: A Theological Figure and Its Sources." *MLN* 121 (5): 1220–36.

Goldstein, Warren S. 2001. "Messianism and Marxism: Walter Benjamin and Ernst Bloch's Dialectical Theories of Secularization." *Critical Sociology* 27 (2): 246–81.

Grossein, Jean-Pierre. 2005. "De l'interprétation de quelques concepts wébériens." *Revue Française de Sociologie* 46 (4): 685–721.

Hamacher, Werner. 1994. "Afformative, Strike: Benjamin's 'Critique of Violence.'" In *Walter Benjamin's Philosophy: Destruction and Experience*, edited by Andrew Benjamin and Peter Osborne, 110–38. London and New York: Routledge.

Hamacher, Werner. 2002 "Guilt History: Benjamin's Sketch 'Capitalism as Religion.'" *Diacritics* 32 (3/4): 81–106.

Heil, Susanne. 1996. *"Gefährliche Beziehungen": Walter Benjamin und Carl Schmitt*. Stuttgart: Metzler.

Hennis, Wilhelm. 1987. *Max Webers Fragestellung. Studien zur Biographie des Werks*. Tübingen: J.C.B. Mohr (Paul Siebeck).

Hennis, Wilhelm. 1991. "The pitiless 'sobriety of judgement': Max Weber between Carl Menger and Gustav von Schmoller – the academic politics of value freedom." *History of the Human Sciences* 4 (1): 27–59.

Hennis, Wilhelm. 1994. "The Meaning of '*Wertfreiheit*' on the Background and Motives of Max Weber's 'Postulate.'" *Sociological Theory* 12 (2): 113–25.

Herrero, Montserrat. 2015. *The Political Discourse of Carl Schmitt. A Mystic of Order.* Lanham: Rowman & Littlefield.

Hollerich, Michael. 2004. "Carl Schmitt." In *The Blackwell Companion to Political Theology,* edited by Peter Scott and William T. Cavanaugh, 107–22. Oxford: Blackwell.

Honigsheim, Paul. 2003. *The Unknown Max Weber.* New Brunswick, NJ: Transaction Publishers.

Jacobson, Eric. 2003. *Metaphysics of the Profane. The Political Theology of Walter Benjamin and Gershom Scholem.* New York: Columbia University Press.

Jones, Robert A. 1983. "On Merton's 'History' and 'Systematics' of Sociological Theory." In *Functions and Uses of Disciplinary History,* edited by Loren Graham, Wolf Lepenies, and Peter Weingart, 121–42. Dordrecht: Reide.

Kahn, Paul W. 2011. *Political Theology: Four New Chapters on the Concept of Sovereignty.* New York: Columbia University Press.

Kent, Stephen A. 1983. "Weber, Goethe, and the Nietzschean Allusion: Capturing the Source of the 'Iron Cage' Metaphor." *Sociological Analysis* 44 (4): 297–319.

Khatib, Sami. 2013. "The Messianic Without Messianism: Walter Benjamin's Materialist Theology." *Anthropology & Materialism,* no. 1: 1–17.

Koselleck, Reinhart. 2004. *Futures Past. On the Semantics of Historical Time.* New York: Columbia University Press.

Kotsko, Adam. 2013. "Schmitt's 'sociology of juristic concepts.'" *An und für sich,* (January 17). https://itself.blog/2013/01/17/schmitts-sociology-of-juristic-concepts/.

Kracauer, Siegfried. 1995. *The Mass Ornament: Weimar Essays,* Cambridge, MA: Harvard University Press.

Lebow, David B., and Richard N. Lebow. 2017. "Weber's Tragic Legacy." In *Max Weber and International Relations,* edited by Richard N. Lebow, 172–99. Cambridge: University Press.

Lievens, Matthias. 2016. "Carl Schmitt's Concept of History." In *The Oxford Handbook of Carl Schmitt,* edited by Jens Meierhenrich and Oliver Simons, 401–25. New York: Oxford University Press.

Lombardo, Carmelo. 2006. "La radice dei concetti. Il fondamento della legge in Walter Benjamin e Carl Schmitt." *Sociologia e ricerca sociale* XXVII (80): 5–28.

Lombardo, Carmelo. 2009. "Can Sociology Develop Political Judgements? Beyond Teleological Contextualism and Deontological Universalism." In *Raymond Boudon: A Life in Sociology. Essays in Honour of Raymond Boudon,* edited by Mohamed Cherkaoui and Peter Hamilton, 11–24. Oxford: Bardwell.

Lough, Joseph W.H. 2006. *Weber and the Persistence of Religion. Social Theory, Capitalism and the Sublime.* London and New York: Routledge.

Löwy, Michael. 2005. *Fire Alarm. Reading Walter Benjamin's "On the Concept of History."* London: Verso.

Löwy, Michael. 2009. "Capitalism as Religion: Walter Benjamin and Max Weber." *Historical Materialism* 17 (1): 60–73.

Malczewski, Eric. 2019. "The Weberian Presuppositional Analytic." *Sociological Theory* 37 (4): 363–80.

Marramao, Giacomo. 2008. "Messianism without delay: On the 'Post-religious' political theology of Walter Benjamin." *Constellations* 15 (3): 397–405.

McQuillan, Colin. 2010. "The Real State of Emergency: Agamben on Benjamin and Schmitt." *Studies in Social and Political Thought* 18: 96–108.

Meier, Heinrich. 2011. *Four Chapters on the Distinction between Political Theology and Political Philosophy*. Chicago and London: The University of Chicago Press.

Meierhenrich, Jens, and Oliver Simons. 2016. "'A Fanatic of Order in an Epoch of Confusing Turmoil': The Political, Legal, and Cultural Thought of Carl Schmitt." In *The Oxford Handbook of Carl Schmitt*, edited by Jens Meierhenrich and Oliver Simons, 3–70. New York: Oxford University Press.

Merton, Robert K. 1967. *On Theoretical Sociology: Five Essays, Old and New*. New York: The Free Press.

Mommsen, Wolfgang J. 1992. *The Political and Social Theory of Max Weber: Collected Essays*. Chicago: The University of Chicago Press.

Müller, Jan-Werner. 2014. "On Conceptual History." In *Rethinking Modern European Intellectual History*, edited by Darrin M. McMahon and Samuel Moyn. New York: Oxford University Press.

Pankakoski, Timo. 2010. "Conflict, Context, Concreteness: Koselleck and Schmitt on Concepts." *Political Theory* 38 (6): 749–79.

Pankakoski, Timo. 2013. "Reoccupying Secularization: Schmitt and Koselleck on Blumenberg's Challenge." *History and Theory* 52 (2) 214–45.

Pensky, Max. 2004. "Method and time: Benjamin's dialectical images." In *The Cambridge Companion to Walter Benjamin*, edited by David S. Ferris, 177–98. Cambridge: University Press.

Raciti, Giuseppe. 2019. "Una lettera di Carl Schmitt a Walter Benjamin." *Cultura tedesca*, no. 57: 305–16.

Reed, Isaac A. 2020. *Power in Modernity. Agency Relations and the Creative Destruction of the King's Two Bodies*. Chicago: The University of Chicago Press.

Roberts, Aaron B. 2015. "Carl Schmitt – Political Theologian?" *The Review of Politics* 77 (3): 449–74.

Robin, Corey. 2020. "The Professor and the Politician." *The New Yorker*, November 12.

Schmitt, Carl. 1930. *Hugo Preuss: Sein Staatsbegriff und seine Stellung in der deutschen Staatslehre*. Tübingen: Mohr.

Schmitt, Carl. 2006. *Political Theology. Four Chapters on the Concept of Sovereignty*. Chicago: The University of Chicago Press.

Schmitt, Carl. 2007. *The Concept of the Political*. Chicago: The University of Chicago Press.

Schmitt, Carl. 2008. *Political Theology II. The Myth of the Closure of any Political Theology*. Cambridge, UK: Polity.

Schmitt, Carl. 2017. *Ex Captivitate Salus. Experiences*, 1945–47. Cambridge, UK: Polity.

Schupmann, Benjamin A. 2017. *Carl Schmitt's State and Constitutional Theory: A Critical Analysis*. New York: Oxford University Press.

Sferrazza Papa, Ernesto C. 2021. "Antropologia filosofica, metafisica degli elementi e filosofia della tecnologia in Carl Schmitt." *Politica & Società* 2/2021: 241–260.

Tagliacozzo, Tamara. 2014. "La 'costellazione' del capitalismo tra Walter Benjamin e Max Weber." In *Il culto del capitale. Walter Benjamin: capitalismo e religione*, edited by Dario Gentili, Mauro Ponzi and Elettra Stimilli, 215–29. Macerata: Quodlibet.

Taubes, Jacob. 2013. *To Carl Schmitt. Letters and Reflections*. New York: Columbia University Press.

Thiem, Annika. 2013. "Theological-Political Ruins: Walter Benjamin, Sovereignty, and the Politics of Skeletal Eschatology." *Law and Critique* 24 (3): 295–315.

Tiedemann, Rolf. 1999. "Dialectics at a Standstill: Approaches to the Passagen-Werk." In *The Arcades Project*, by Walter Benjamin, 930–45. Cambridge, MA: The Belknap Press of Harvard University.

Tiryakian, Edward A. 1981. "The Sociological Import of a Metaphor: Tracking the Source of Max Weber's 'Iron Cage.'" *Sociological Inquiry* 51 (1): 27–33.

Turner, Bryan S. 1992. *Max Weber: From History to Modernity*. London and New York: Routledge.

Ulmen, Gary L. 1985. "The Sociology of the State: Carl Schmitt and Max Weber." *State, Culture and Society* 1 (2): 3–57.

Vandeputte, Tom. 2019. "Resistance." In *Re-: An Errant Glossary*, edited by Christoph F.E. Holzhey and Arnd Wedemeyer, 127–32. Berlin: ICI Berlin Press.

Vatter, Miguel 2016. "The Political Theology of Carl Schmitt." In *The Oxford Handbook of Carl Schmitt*, edited by Jens Meierhenrich and Oliver Simons, 245–68. New York: Oxford University Press.

Weber, Max 1946. *From Max Weber: Essays in Sociology*. New York: Oxford University Press.

Weber, Max. 1949. *The Methodology of the Social Sciences*. Glencoe, IL: The Free Press.

Weber, Max. 1978. *Economy and Society: An Outline of Interpretative Sociology*. Berkeley, CA: University of California Press.

Weber, Max. 1993. "Die Evangelisch-Sozialen Kurse in Berlin im Herbst dieses Jahres." In M. Weber *Landarbeiterfrage, Nationalstaat und Volkswirtschaftspolitik: Schriften und Reden, 1892–1899*, edited by Wolfgang J. Mommsen and Rita Aldenhoff, 233–7. *Max Weber-Gesamtausgabe, I/4-1*. Tübingen: J.C.B. Mohr (Paul Siebeck).

Weber, Max. 1995. *The Russian Revolutions*. Ithaca, NY: Cornell University Press.

Weber, Max. 2001. *The Protestant Ethic and the Spirit of Capitalism*. London and New York: Routledge.

Weber, Max. 2010. *Political Writings*. Cambridge: Cambridge University Press.

Weber, Samuel. 1992. "Taking Exception to Decision: Walter Benjamin and Carl Schmitt." *Diacritics* 22 (3/4): 5–18.

CHAPTER 11

In Search of Dialogue with History

A Political Science Research Perspective

Alfredo Ferrara

The trend toward specialization has led scholars to isolate their own discipline from the others and to avoid interdisciplinary dialogue. Furthermore, important scientific breakthroughs have often been marked by the positioning of the discipline at hand with respect to others, and by the sharing or rejection of paradigms or methodologies originating from them. During the twentieth century political science experienced two great waves that have profoundly marked its history and can be explained precisely on the basis of this criterion. In the first half of the 1950s, American political science underwent, for example, the behavioral revolution, which considered the paradigm established in experimental psychology at the beginning of the twentieth century to be the bearer of "more accurate and controlled methods and techniques of investigation," and looked up on it with "an inferiority complex," (Sola 1996, 62). In the second half of the 1970s, another fundamental breakthrough known as the economic approach to politics took place, which was based on the "progressive extension of theories, models and hypotheses from economics to political science," namely the theories of rational choice and of social or public choice (701).

Political science, in choosing these specific currents of psychology and economics as sister disciplines, has progressively abandoned its dialogue with the discipline of history. Nevertheless, a closer examination of the dialogue between these two disciplines reveals that it is much more pronounced than it might seem. This article offers a preliminary map of this dialogue in three different stages: it first examines the birth of political science in the Anglo-Saxon world and highlights that, precisely in the linguistic context out of which the two aforementioned breakthroughs were born, the discipline emerged in the nineteenth and early twentieth centuries as a derivation from history; in the second part, it analyses the distancing between political science and history that occurred in the decades when behavioralism and the economic approach gained ground, and highlights the presence of scholars and trends that continued to maintain open the dialogue with history; and in the third part, it analyses the renewal of this dialogue that has occurred in the last thirty years, especially through the rise of new institutionalism and historical institutionalism.

1   A Derivation from History

James Farr highlights that the birth of political science in the United States took place between the end of the nineteenth and the beginning of the twentieth centuries as part of a continuum shared with the discipline of history, so as to be called the "historical science of politics"; "its object of inquiry was the state," while "its method was comparative, as well as historical" (Farr 2007, 66).[1] He identifies three phases of the early evolution of political science in the United States, each marked by a distinct relationship to history.

The first stage of American political science, during the nineteenth century, was in fact marked by the analysis of the State: political scientists used to think of themselves as State historians, since the study of the history of the State was seen as an essential tool to analyze contemporary politics, in which the consummation of the State was the keystone. One pioneer of these studies was Francis Lieber, especially with the books *Manual of Political Ethics* (1838) and *Civil Liberty and Self-Government* (1853); other protagonists of this first stage include Theodore Dwight Woolsey (1878) and the non-academic scholar Elisha Mulford (1870). In addition to having a common object of study, this first stage can be distinguished by the scholars' commitment to defining a methodological and epistemological profile that would make the discipline identifiable and give it authority; in this respect too, the dialogue with history was not limited to the consideration of history as an archive of case studies, but was quite decisive. First of all, with respect to methodology, it distinguished itself by the combination of historical and comparative methods: as Farr points out, "the basic injunction of one method of another was to compare the origins, development, or contemporary conditions of forms of the State, in one or more nations, ancient or modern" (Farr 2007, 70); this approach was used to study a variety of topics, such as representative government, constitutional law, bureaucratic administration and party organization. Furthermore, great importance was given to principles, models and laws conceptualized as "normative ideals, practical guides, regulative maxims, and explanatory generalities." In this area too, evidence of kinship between these principles and history are revealed to be threefold: "in history, of history, and unfolding in history" (74). *In* history because they "claimed (normative, practical, regulative, or explanatory) relevance only for a particular context or a specific set of conditions or events"; *of* history because they were based on a theory of history, mainly an evolutionary

---

1   The brief historical overview we propose about the birth of political science in the United States of America is based on a James Farr's essay (2007).

version of it; and finally *unfolding in* history because they developed "over time through the experiences of individuals in particular territories" (77).[2]

The second stage began in the 1880s, which continued to dialogue with history and devote attention to the study of the State, was a phase marked by the centrality of the so-called Teutonic Principle or Teutonism, i.e. the idea that "American ideals and institutions of state," particularly the ideals of representation, federalism, deliberation, democracy, self-government, individualism, and nationalism, "were adaptations of earlier English ones that, in turn, found their lineage in Anglo-Saxon Britain and thereby in the history of the Teutonic tribes of Northern Europe." In adopting this principle, American political scientists thought of their country's institutions as forms of development and actualization of a long-standing heritage. As Farr explains, "the Teutonic principle thus satisfied the highest standards demanded by the historical, comparative method and achieved the highest ambitions of developmental historicism" (79–80). The adoption of the Teutonic Principle can be seen in the works of some of the main protagonists of this second stage such as Herbert B. Adams (1882), Woodrow Wilson (1889) and John W. Burgess (1890, 1895) and, with many variations both for those who adopted it as a criterion for research and for those who rejected it, profoundly oriented the debates taking place between scholars of political science. In these authors' studies we see, for example, a racialization of the Teutonic principle, or the explicit or implicit identification of blood continuity as the source of interrelatedness between the Teutonic tribes of Northern Europe and the United States of America. However, some scholars criticized this approach in various ways arguing that the strength of the American nation lays in its own history and not in any kind of racial continuity (Mulford 1870), denying the historical validity of this thesis and considering it the result of a mythological rather than historical approach (Dunning 1937), or rejecting the practical conclusions of the Teutonic principle, i.e. the affirmation of the idea that one race can be politically superior to another (Willoughby 1900).

According to Farr, the third and final stage of harmony between political science and history in the United States occurred with the foundation of the American Political Science Association (APSA) and its collaboration with the American Historical Association (AHA). The AHA was founded in 1884 and from the very beginning hosted political scientists taking a historical orientation. At the same time, many associations – which, unlike the AHA, had local

---

2   For instance, some fundamental principles for the study of American politics – such as sovereignty, representation, federalism, and individualism – were embryonic in the aftermath of the American Civil War but would develop in the following decade's debate.

structures – began to bring together only political scientists. At the annual meeting of the AHA in 1902, a committee was formed that led to the foundation of the American Political Science Association in December 1903. The association was structured in seven departments focusing on different fields of research, all of them adopting a historical approach, especially the study of comparative legislation, constitutional law, and political theory. The proximity of the two associations can also be seen with regard to the joint organization of 15 of the first 21 APSA annual meetings taking place with the AHA, and the presidential addresses being presented by the two presidents during a joint session. This affinity, during the years when the historical method was dominant in the United States, also became evident institutionally: as Farr writes, "political scientists often came off, without apology, simply as historians of the contemporary state or comparative states, armed with political theory, concerned with providing principles, and obligated to fulfil practical duties like civic education" (Farr 2007, 91).

Through these three stages, political science thus experienced a process of institutionalization and delineation of its field of inquiry, attention being focused on the study of State and formal institutions, and a historical-descriptive approach merging with a normative framework. The study of the past served as an ideal source for the study of politics, and political science established itself as a science to serve the State. Works such as *Congressional Government* and *The State: Elements of Historical and Practical Politics* by the future American president Woodrow Wilson (1885 and 1889), *Political Science, or The State Theoretically and Practically Considered* by Theodore Dwight Woosley (1878) and *An Examination of the Nature of the State* by Westel Woodbury Willoughby (1896) are considered to be representative of nascent American political science and of the current that would be called institutionalism; as we will further discuss, it represented an important background for scholars who, from the 1980s onwards, would restore the dialogue between political science and history.

In the following decades, the affirmation of new methodological and theoretical orientations contributed to the distancing of political science from history, bringing the discipline's embryonic chapter, during which dialogue was central, to an end. A focus on observation and quantitative research would bring it closer to psychology (a process that would culminate in the aforementioned behavioral revolution); and a focus on interest groups would bring it closer to sociology, while the affirmation of pragmatism – orienting it towards problem solving – would bring attention to the future and away from the question of historical legacies. At the same time, the First World War was an important watershed: the alignment of the United States and Germany on opposing sides highlighted the cultural differences between the two countries and undermined the authority of the Teutonic Principle.

A clear indication of the importance American political scientists give to dialogue with history is the speech with which James Bryce, as President of the American Political Scientists, opened the annual APSA meeting in 1908, organized jointly with AHA. The title of the presentation was "The Relations of Political Science to History and to Practice." Bryce's argument began with the epistemological status of political science, in line with the debate going on in those years over the relationship between natural and social sciences: the study of politics, Bryce wrote, cannot be considered as equivalent to the study of natural phenomena because it does not allow the use of quantitative instruments: "emotions, opinions and other factors influencing politics are not the subjects of computation" (Bryce 1909, 3). The dialogue between political science and history – according to Bryce – is based on the fact that "the data of politics are the acts of men [...] as recorded in history," more specifically "they are the parts of history that relate to the structure and government of communities." Thus, if history "takes the form of a record of facts and tendencies as they have occurred or shown themselves in past times," political science "assumes the form of a systematic statement of the most important facts" assembling them "upon the thread of the principles that run through them," i.e. organizing them through principles and general concepts, locating their recurrent tendencies. This is why it can be said, writes Bryce, that "political Science stands midway between history and politics, between the past and the present"; it extracts "its materials from the one and applies them to the other" (3–4).

Bryce's approach is based on an anthropological view that differs greatly from contemporary thinking, namely in the idea that there is a "human nature" whose "tendencies" – "embodied in the institutions men have created" – are "insofar uniform and permanent" (3–4). Data provided by history thus allow us to test theoretical hypotheses on a wider range of subjects, but do not stop there. Bryce, in fact, identifies as the first methodological criterion for scholars of political science the adherence to the facts: "keep close to the facts" (4). When approaching a case study, it is not enough to refer to general, permanent tendencies, because "when it comes to studying" the actions of men "at any given time or in any given place, it becomes necessary to know the surrounding and modifying conditions that affect them." To understand the way in which general, permanent tendencies develop in communities "we need to know the racial characteristics of the people, their religion, occupations, education, social structure and in short, all that may be called their environment," which, Bryce concludes, "we get from history" (6).

In Bryce's speech, the idea of meta-historical content pertaining to a constant human nature coexists with a lack of immediate accessibility of such content. It is possible to analyze it in a scientific way only by deeply investigating a variety of historical cases and experiences; and since this variety is offered by historical disciplines, it is a primary task for political science to pursue its relationship with them.

Thirty-four years after Bryce's speech, another presidential address in another country revealed that, although the embryonic phase of political science was largely over, the historicist approach to political science remained in the Anglo-Saxon world. In 1944, in fact, the annual meeting of the Canadian Political Science Association opened with a speech by Robert A. Mackay, then president of the association, entitled "The nature and Function of Social Sciences." Once Mackay had pointed out the dangers of excessive specialization and compared the epistemological status of the discipline to mathematics and philosophy, he made a brief statement full of epistemological implications: "As social scientists, we labor in the stream of history"; and added that "the significance of many of our [political and social] facts alters with history's changing currents." The example he provides is the concept of freedom, the meaning of which in the Canada of those years was profoundly different from that attributed to it by the *sans-culottes* during the French Revolution. This is why a "photographic description" of social institutions and processes "soon ceases to have validity because society moves on, changing its character and its values" (Mackay 1944, 281–2). The social sciences are thus dependent on history according to Mackay in two respects: firstly, "history is the record of the social experience of men" and the task of the political scientist is "to approach history with the deliberate purpose of finding an answer to a particular question"; secondly, "human society really never is," because "it is always becoming," which is why "without historical perspective, the social scientist misses, or wrongly assesses, the dynamic elements of his field of interest, or misinterprets trends, and his 'science' tends rapidly to become a system of dogmatics, a mere mumbo-jumbo disconnected from social reality" (281–2).

Political science in the United Kingdom also has a historicist lineage. In fact, it began with the identification of an academic, epistemological, and methodological project extending from that of history. Before its institutionalization as independent discipline, the study of politics was in fact practiced within the historical disciplines, which had already been through the process of institutionalization in British universities, and therefore had already mapped out a trajectory that political science and sociology would follow; the first professorship of political science was established as late as 1926 at Cambridge, in the Department of History. As Sandra M. den Otter wrote, "the new political science came out of the historically minded culture of the mid-century" (2007, 40). The contribution of the so-called Whig historicism, a historiographical tradition mainly focused on the study of continuity, development, and free-dom in European political history, was remarkable; it portrayed, for instance, English constitutional history as a progressive victory of freedom over tyranny. According to this research tradition, "successive historical epochs were con-nected by a continuous thread, and by an underlying unity of experience" (eadem). Scholars of the Whig tradition in particular "interpreted historical continuity and development from the perspective of present-day dilemmas, and this presentist orientation led Whig historians to search for the origins of modern freedom and to interpret the distant past as culminating in the present" (41).[3]

2   The Ahistorical Waves and Their Exceptions

As mentioned in the introduction, the behavioral revolution first and then the economic approach to politics traced two epistemological and methodological trajectories that pushed political science away from history. As Robert A. Dahl pointed out, "the behavioral political scientist has found it difficult to make systematic use of what has been"; and in fact, this approach to political science was immediately presented as "ahistorical in nature" (1961a, 771). As David Bian Robertson highlights, in considering "individual decisions (in sufficiently large population samples) as the basic unit of analysis" and identifying the "central research question in terms of obvious and relatively small political changes that occur over a brief period" (1993, 7), behaviorists gave less importance, in their analyses, to historical evidence. Scholars who embraced the economic approach to politics, on the other hand, had a different reason for their shift away from history: what Giorgio Sola called the "formal purity of economic models" they adopted allowed little room for the problem of temporality (1998, 701).

In the 1950s – when the behavioral revolution emerged in Anglo-Saxon political science – the Western world was experiencing a phase of relative

---

3 A remarkable name in this story is John Robert Seeley who at Cambridge made an espe-cially important contribution to the derivation of political science from history. In particular, Seeley saw the former not simply as a subject of study related to the latter, but as a method for approaching historical studies: he considered the inductive study of historical-political affairs to be a prerequisite to identifying past laws endowed with predictive powers (cf. Seeley, 1926 [1896]).

political stability and prosperity; it is no coincidence that this same phase, during which "many political variables (such as institutions) appeared as constants" (Robertson 1993, 2), produced an argument postulating the end of ideology. And yet in the margins of behavioralism, the interest in history did not vanish but took on a peculiar form that Robertson calls "historical behavioralism" (8–13), consisting in the application of behaviorist assumptions to historical data. The possibility of acquiring historically reliable quantitative data contributed to the growth of studies with a clear behaviorist matrix that nevertheless adopted a long-term historical perspective: such studies in fact "share research questions whose answers require historical evidence," which is why a "growing criticism of behavioralism itself began to lay the foundation for the discipline's return to history" (13). Among these, we can mention the studies on changes in electoral behavior and cleavages (Key 1955 and 1966), on critical elections in American history (Burnham 1970), on the transition from oligarchy to pluralism (Dahl 1961b), and on interest groups and their relation to the question of political stability (Truman 1953). The renewed political uncertainty experienced in the Western world at the end of the 1960s transformed what had appeared for over twenty years to be constants into variables, therein reviving interest in history. What Robertson calls a "dissatisfaction with ahistorical behavioralism" (cf. Robertson 1993, 13–5) matured and can be observed in the work of Francis Fox Piven and Richard A. Cloward on the Great Society reforms studied from the perspective of the historical development of American welfare (1971), as well as in that of Theodore J. Lowi on the impact of the New Deal on American political history (1969). In these two studies, historical insight serves as a tool to criticize the inefficiency of American politics during years of profound change. This return to history also benefited from studies focusing on the role of the State – for example in the modernization of the "Third World" (Migdal 1983), on the autonomy it can exercise in capitalist societies (Carnoy 1984), or on the growth of bureaucratic power (Aberbach, Putnam, and Rockman 1981) – as well as on economic policies (O'Connor 1973; Moe 1987).

The epistemological basis for a renewed and radical dialogue with history would emerge only from new institutionalism. But as can easily be observed from this brief overview, the ahistoricity of political science was already beginning to be discussed as a problematic element in the years of behavioralist hegemony. Within this context, two scholars stand out and merit a brief excursus, both because they are in strong countertendency to the ahistorical orientation of political science, and because their studies planted the precious seeds of a new and more fruitful relationship between political science and history, the outcome of which would grow with new institutionalism and historical institutionalism: Barrington Moore and Stein Rokkan.

Moore's work is considered a heritage both by sociology and political science. His *Social Origins of Dictatorship and Democracy* published in 1966 sparked significant debate in the main Anglo-Saxon journals of sociology and political science (cf. Femia 1972, Wiener 1975); adopting a comparative method and a long-term historical perspective, Moore aimed to "understand the role of landed upper classes and peasants" (Moore 1973, xiv) in the modernization processes. He identified "three main historical routes from the pre-industrial to the modern world" (xi–xii): the English, French and American route which, through a bourgeois revolution, led to "modern industrial democracies"; the German and the Japanese route, which took place through a "revolution from above" (xi-xii), produced a capitalist economy and culminated in a fascist regime that guaranteed the interests of landowners and entrepreneurs; and finally, the Russian and Chinese route, which, through a peasant revolution, culminated in industrialization and in a communist regime. This comparative perspective was suggested by Moore as useful for gaining a better understanding of the history of specific countries because it allows to: a) ask "very useful and sometimes new questions," b) provide "a rough negative check on accepted historical explanations," and c) construct "new historical generalizations" (x).

The interest in long-term political processes (democratization, political development, State-building and Nation-building) that concerned Western and Central Europe (see Rokkan 1970 and 1999) has been constant in Stein Rokkan's research. "All Rokkan's works," writes Marco Valbruzzi in an essay analysing the Norwegian political scientist's distinctive relationship with history, "have had history as a protagonist" (Valbruzzi 2018, 71). This approach inscribed the interest in variations in the construction processes of European Nation-States and in their long-term causes into his approach to research in political science, based on the "interweaving of historical-institutional analysis and the comparative method on a cross-national scale" (63). Within the open laboratory of Rokkan's works, this brief excursus highlights two aspects that demonstrate the historicist anomaly he represented. Among the various concepts we owe to Rokkan we find the concept of critical junctures, which first appears in political science in his famous work published with Seymour M. Lipset in 1967. The two political scientists, in developing a hypothesis on the structuring of European party systems, emphasise the importance of certain phenomena and events – in particular the Reformation and Counter-Reformation, the French Revolution, the Industrial Revolution and the Russian Revolution – which produced historical breaks; these historical breaks led to the formation of new cleavages which, translated by new or old political actors, inaugurated political cycles allowing party conflict to assume stable forms. These historical event-processes are classified by the two scholars under the label of critical junctures (Lipset and Rokkan 1967, 47), a concept for which a clear definition is not provided in the 1967 essay, but which would have great relevance in subsequent debates. Connected to the theme of critical junctures is the question of timing, which is omnipresent in Rokkan's analyses. The moment at which a political event or process takes place is a key variable. For example, in his overview of European state-building processes, Rokkan shows that in countries where the process took place before the second industrial revolution, the cleavages that emerged from the second industrial revolution (Land-Industry and then Owner-Worker) immediately became central to political systems, favouring the processes of democratization; whereas when the process of state building took place later – as in the cases of Italy and Germany – the cleavages and conflicts were excessive, producing political instability and delaying the process of democratization (see Valbruzzi 2018, 82–3).

3   A Renewed Dialogue

3.1   *New Institutionalism*
The branch of political science that has most significantly contributed to the renewal of dialogue with history has been new institutionalism (and within this branch, in particular, historical institutionalism), which emerged with an autonomous epistemological profile in the 1980s.[4] In this paragraph and in the following one, we will outline the main features of new institutionalism and historical institutionalism, and highlight the reasons that make renewed dialogue with history useful for political scientists.

The renewed interest in institutions that characterizes new institutionalism originated during the hegemony of behavioralist and economic approach to politics, and immediately revealed a tendency toward historicism. Samuel Huntington's *Political Order in Changing Societies*, published in 1968, placed the issue of institutions at the centre of debates in political science. The American political scholar differentiates between institutions – understood as "stable, valued, recurring patterns of behaviour" – and institutionalization, i.e. "the process by which organizations and procedures acquire value and stability" (Huntington 1973, 12).

---

4   The coordinates of new institutionalism proposed in this essay are based on the works of Robertson (1993), Sola (1996) and Peters (1999).

According to Huntington, this process was part of the modernization process and characterizes the political development of societies in terms of their acquisition of the capacity to build strong – that is adaptable, complex, autonomous and coherent – political institutions and procedures (cf. 13–24). Analyzing a variety of case studies, the American political scientist identified two paths pursued by political development in modern times: on the one hand, that of civil societies, which were able to gain consensus and combine a high degree of political participation with a demand for order guaranteed by the institutional structure, and on the other, that of praetorian societies, in which political participation was not counter-balanced by a high degree of institutionalization (cf. 78–92).[5]

During the late 1970s and early 1980s, the interest in institutions – and especially in the State – became increasingly important within political science. It is significant that the central theme of the American Political Science Association meeting in 1981, introduced by the presidential address given by Charles Lindblom entitled "Another State of Mind," was "Restoring the State" (cf. Robertson 1993, 20–2). In addition, two landmark institutions, under the leadership of two innovative and charismatic scholars, were immediately characterized by a focus on institutions: Cornell University and The University of Chicago. Stephen Skowronek – author of *Building a New American State* (1982) in which he analyses the development of the American state in its multiple articulations between 1877 and 1920 – was a professor at Cornell, while Theda Skocpol – a former student of Barrington Moore and author of *States and Social Revolutions* (1979), a text in line with the work of her mentor *Social Origins of Dictatorship and Democracy* from which it takes the comparative method – taught at The University of Chicago. Skocpol's work focuses on social revolutions, defined as "rapid, basic transformations of a society's state and class structures," "accompanied and in part carried through by class-based revolts from below" (4). The cases examined are those of France, Russia and China. The "three major principles of analysis" at the basis of Skocpol's work consist in the adoption of: a) a "nonvoluntarist, structural perspective" on revolutionary causes and processes; b) a "systematic reference to international structure and world-historical developments"; and c) a conception of State institutions "as administrative and coercive organizations [...] potentially autonomous from (though of course conditioned by) socioeconomic

---

5   In Cold War years, it is peculiar that Huntington placed among civil societies both Western liberal democratic systems and Eastern socialist regimes, while he placed among praetorian societies countries that were then called "Third World," considered to still be at the beginning of the modernization process and therefore, without solid institutions.

interests and structures" (14). The final two principles underline how Skocpol considers a world-historical perspective and the autonomy of institutions as keys to understanding social revolutions: these two aspects would be central in the evolution of historical institutionalism. In the 1980s, Skocpol's scientific activity, often carried out alongside other scholars, focused on the "role of the American state in the development of social and economic policy" (Robertson 1993, 21). Some of the most relevant voices of new institutionalism have been formed under the mentorship of these two great scholars.

The official birth of new institutionalism was the publication in 1984 of an article by James Gardner March and Johan Paul Olsen in the *American Political Science Review* entitled "The new institutionalism: Organizational factors in political life" (March and Olsen 1984); this essay in fact was the first to attribute to this emerging orientation of political science the name of "new institutionalism," and outlined theoretical and methodological guidelines that clearly showed the extent to which political science was moving towards a new and more fruitful dialogue with history. The two scholars identify the theoretical trends that provoked a long disinterest in institutions in the emergence of five visions of politics from the 1950s onwards: contextualism ("inclined to see politics as an integral part of society,") reductionism ("inclined to see political phenomena as the aggregate consequences of individual behavior,") utilitarianism ("inclined to see action as the product of calculated self-interest,") instrumentalism ("inclined to define decision making and the allocation of resources as the central concerns of political life, less attentive to the ways in which political life is organized around the development of meaning through symbols, rituals, and ceremonies") and functionalism, a trend that requires further examination as it was most influential and led to a simplified vision of institutions and to the distancing between political science and history (735).

Within political development studies (among which Huntington's work is no exception) the functionalist approach can be identified in the presence of a specific idea of progress, understood as "the more or less inexorable historical movement toward some more 'advanced' level." Based on this idea, the institution's evolution was thought to take place "through some form of efficient historical process," a historical process that, again, "moves rapidly toward a unique solution." This theoretical approach, although it provided a stimulus to analyze long-term historical processes, removed the truly tragic character of history summarized by March and Olsen in the formula "history cannot be guaranteed to be efficient," i.e. history is not necessarily a perpetual equilibrium builder. Using this framework implies depriving ourselves of the theoretical tools for "focusing on transient phenomena that might be less predictable and more subject to the effects of the details of the processes involved"; political phenomena are in fact often characterized by the "indeterminacy of their out-comes." New institutionalism contrasts this approach with the deemphasizing of "efficient histories in favor of relatively complex processes and historical inefficiency," i.e. of history in its various and contradictory outcomes (737–8). The consideration of political institutions as actors with an autonomous role, on the other hand, resituates history as a central interest of political science: "empirical observations seem to indicate that processes internal to polit-ical institutions, although possibly triggered by external events, affect the flow of history" (739).

The new institutionalism that originated with March and Olsen's article echoed the old institutionalism discussed at the beginning of this essay but did not propose a mere return to it (cf. Peters 1999, 15). There were three aspects that maintained continuity: the (a) centrality of institutional studies in polit-ical science, and their (b) historical and (c) autonomous nature (cf. 3–4). Its innovation was instead the result of the knowledge that political science had gained during the years of behavioralist hegemony: if the old institutionalism had a formalistic approach, new institutionalism attributed epistemological and empirical importance not only to political institutions, but also to social and cultural ones, considering them all subjects that contribute to defining the framework of "conditioning within which political life occurs and unfolds" (Sola 1996, 823), and situating it within the composite relationship between State and society. Moreover, it borrowed from behavioralism the rigor of research questions, the importance of empirical evidence and the attention to alternative explanations. The purpose of this approach was to put collective action back at the center of political science and to think of the relationship between politics and the socio-economic environment as marked by mutual influences.

The dialogue that new institutionalists began with history – both due to their research objects (as was already the case for the historical behavioral-ism) and to the importance given to institutions in their theories – led them to advance the idea that past decisions exercise great influence over present and future politics; in Robertson's words, "past decisions shape the institu-tional constraints and opportunities of later periods, including the present," which is why this approach "requires historical analysis" (Robertson 1993, 19). History was no longer considered to be the starting point for the development of political studies, as it was at the end of the nineteenth century, but as a sister discipline to which political science reached out in an effort to engage with the "conditioning that past institutional arrangements exercise on future ones," and with the "directions and consequences of change" (Sola 1996, 824).

Since the appearance of March and Olsen's article, new institutionalism has gained increasing weight in the debates taking place among scholars of political science, paving the way for different research paths, research questions, and theoretical frameworks. An exhaustive overview of new institutionalism is not feasible in this essay, but in order to provide an overall picture we suggest referring to Guy Peters' overview of new institutionalism traced at the end of the 1990s. Peters identifies four common features of new institutionalism and six different currents that developed different approaches. What new institutionalism shares, making it an authoritative current in contemporary political science, is: (a) the understanding of institutions as "a structural feature of the society and/or polity" that can take on formal or informal traits and that transcend individuals by conferring on politics a collective dimension; (b) the acknowledgement of the "existence of some stability over time," produced precisely by the existence of institutions themselves; (c) the understanding of institutions as something that "must affect individual behaviour," as they impose obligations on members of a polity; (d) the importance given to "some sense of shared values and meaning among the members of the institution" (Peters 1999, 18).

Within this common framework, Peters' six different approaches are the following:

1. Normative Institutionalism – whose main scholars were precisely March and Olsen – which pays great attention to institutional norms "as means of understanding how they function and determine, or at least shape, individual behavior" (19);

2. Rational Choice Institutionalism, which instead proposes a synthesis of the functionalist perspective and the new institutional perspective, considers institutions as "systems of rules and inducements to behavior according to which individuals attempt to maximize their own utilities" and as the outcome and balance of economic and social needs (19);

3. Historical Institutionalism, which focuses on "choices made early in the history of any policy, or indeed of any governmental system," which are fundamental for understanding the subsequent decisions and path of development that the institutional system will acquire (19);

4. Empirical Institutionalism, which focuses on governmental structure, considering it crucial in defining "the way in which policies are processed and the choices made by governments" (19);

5. International Institutionalism, which attributes great theoretical weight to the structure in the analysis of States' and individuals' behavior, stressing "the existence of structured interactions" even outside state-level institutions (20);

6.   Societal Institutionalism, which analyses "the structuring of relation-
     ships between State and society"; Peters remarks how the application of
     "an institutionalist characterization" to this miscellaneous field of stud-
     ies is a slight stretch, that is useful to highlight the similarities to insti-
     tutional theory within a framework in which there are still important
     differences (20).

The rise of new institutionalism has thus triggered a renewed debate over the
nature of historical change: unlike previous political currents that conceived
of political development as cumulative, it considers institutional change to be
a "process of policy succession and learning whose trajectory is undetermined
and hard to predict" (Robertson 1993, 25). As its name makes clear, the historical institutionalism branch has been the current of new institutionalism that
has engaged in this dialogue in the most profound way, which is why, we will
now present it in detail in the following paragraph.

3.2   Historical Institutionalism

As in the case of new institutionalism, historical institutionalism also has a
founding work: many scholars had already anticipated its distinctive issues in
the 1980s, but historical institutionalism would appear in the scholarly community with the publication in 1992 of the collective volume *Structuring politics. Historical Institutionalism in Comparative Politics.* The innovation of this
volume that addressed the interest of political science for history can be better understood by taking a step back and analyzing a fundamental paper by
Dennis Kavanagh published in 1991 in *Political Studies* entitled *Why Political
Science Needs History.* The publication of this article is in fact both an important demonstration of the return of the relationship between the two disciplines to the core of the debate over the role/identity of political science and
at the same time, a state of the art of this debate. Kavanagh (1991, 495) argued
that the advantage of the historical approach to political science was not in the
opportunity to adopt its research methodologies, but to use the "knowledge
of the past" that it provides –"to explain present-day political phenomena or
to test propositions"; specifically, he identified five uses of history that were
most recurring in political science at the beginning of the 1990s: as a source
of material, as an aid for the understanding of the historical context of the
present-day phenomena analyzed; as a body of knowledge within which to test
theories and frameworks; as an aid for the understanding of political concepts,
and as a source of lessons. The dialogue between political science and history
that Kavanagh described as an opportunity took place on a purely empirical
ground. Historical institutionalism, on the other hand, is characterized by the
shift of this dialogue beyond the enclosure of empiricism.

In the introduction to *Structuring Politics* by Steven Steinmo and Kathleen Thelen (Steinmo and Thelen 1992), historical institutionalism is described as a scientific project endowed with its own building blocks that differentiate it from other currents of political science. Once again, the polemical referent in relation to which this independent theoretical profile is outlined is behavioralism: unlike the latter, historical institutionalism is characterized by greater attention to the institutional landscape, aimed at explaining the causes of individual behavior and the permanence of cross-national differences; but, as Steinmo and Thelen point out, historical institutionalism also differs from rational choice theory in its rejection of the conception of social and political actors that reduces them to utility maximisers; it approaches the formation of preferences in a problematic way, questioning the institutional conditioning and the long-term stratifications that influence it.

The distinctive element of historical institutionalism is the "theoretical leverage it has provided for understanding the continuity of policy over time within countries as well as policy variation across countries." In fact, it is on the theoretical ground that new institutionalism engages in a dialogue with history; that is, it is the way it thinks about politics that makes it necessary to practice this dialogue. New institutionalism conceives of social and political actors as both "objects and agents of history"; institutions indeed condition the behavior and preferences of individuals, but are also the product of "deliberate political strategies, of political conflict, and of choice" (10). The effort to combine conditioning and agency also has important empirical consequences: historical institutionalism focuses its attention on intermediate-level institutions – such as parties and structured interest groups – that mediate between individual political behaviors and political effects within macro-level structures.

This theoretical perspective problematizes cross-national differences by searching for their causes and re-evaluates "the contingent nature of political and economic development" (12), which is always the result of the encounter between the dynamics of historically determined conditioning and practices of agency. For this reason, historical institutionalism prefers an inductive approach to a deductive one: the latter is based on a few theoretical assertions, while in the former, the confrontation with empirical material is the basis for the formation of theoretical hypotheses. In this approach there are no variables that *a priori* are essential regardless of the historical and geographical context; each context is contingent precisely because it presents a unique interaction of variables, which calls for an explanation that does not allow for shortcuts.

The fields of inquiry investigated by historical institutionalism in its almost three decades of existence have been manifold and include for example, the following topics: modern State, capitalism, political regimes, welfare systems, social and political conflicts, parties, structured interest groups, sovereignty, international security, international political economy, and the evolution of law on a national and supranational level. For a comprehensive overview, which we will not be able to provide here, see the *Oxford Handbook of Historical Institutionalism* (Fioretos, Falleti, and Sheingate 2016a); instead, it is useful for us to go deeper into the theoretical articulation of the relationship between political science and history that characterizes historical institutionalism.

Paul Pierson in his 2004 book *Politics in Time. History, Institutions and Social Analysis* – a fundamental work that, departing from some pillars of historical institutionalism, extends the capabilities of the dialogue with history to all social sciences – wrote that if in past times political science dialogued with history from an empirical standpoint (i.e. studying past social and political phenomena) or in terms of methodology (looking for illustrative material in history to confirm a theory or for a plurality of cases enabling generalizations), dialoguing from a theoretical standpoint implies starting with the idea that "social life unfolds over time" and that "real social processes have distinctly temporal dimensions" (Pierson 2004, 5); and while historical disciplines adopt a descriptive approach to what unfolds over time, political science that chooses to take seriously the claim that history matters has the task of understanding *why, where, how,* and *for what reason* it matters. "Placing politics in time can greatly enrich our understanding of complex social dynamics" (2); and failure to do so will result in a poorer understanding of social and political phenomena. Orfeo Fioretos, Tulia Falleti and Adam Scheingate in the introduction to the *Oxford Handbook of Historical Institutionalism* (2016b) instead base the foundations of the theoretical approach to such dialogue on what they call the "ontological status of institutions" and the "influence of temporal processes." Institutions are in fact "potential causes behind preferences and patterns of political contestation" (9). The institutional arrangements created in past times influence individual behavior and interests and shape politics in the present; it is therefore necessary to go beyond proximate causes and seek remote ones. In line with this characterisation of historical institutionalism, Peter Hall points out that it considers politics "as a process structured across space and time," i.e. it conceives of "the behavior of political actors and the outcomes of political conflict" as twice conditioned, by variables that change over time and space and by "factors that are relatively stable for discrete periods and often divergent across cases" (Hall 2016, 31–2). If, however, the awareness of the spatial shaping of politics is an issue present in political studies (e.g. those on variety of capitalism or the more recent ones on variety of populism), Hall points out that the awareness of its temporal shaping is an issue that historical institutionalism has put at the centre of the research, specifying that this temporal shaping can be understood in two senses (cf. 38): (a) stressing the uniqueness of specific historical periods, which are thus characterized as epochs endowed with distinctive elements, resulting from the intertwining of specific institutional practices, collective cognitive frameworks and relational networks; accepting this view implies the rejection of a vision of politics according to which some variables operate with continuity regardless of context; b) stressing the differences between historical periods, in which openness to institutional and ideological change may be more or less marked; this view of politics is closely associated with a view of history as a "syncopated process divided into different eras" (38) and rejects a view of history as a continuous and homogeneous stream.

Thus, if politics has "distinctly temporal dimensions," is a "process structured across space and time" and the "ontological status of institutions" is the starting point for political studies, studying and thinking about politics *historically*, yet without embracing a descriptive approach that would turn it *into* history, means engaging in explanations for the recurring causal mechanisms in political phenomena. The most important resource that the historical institutionalism tradition has delivered to political science and the social sciences resides perhaps in the broad conceptual toolbox used or articulated in order to understand these causal mechanisms: in some cases these concepts were born out of previous political science debates or out of other disciplines and then developed in a political way, while in still other cases they have been formulated directly by scholars belonging to historical institutionalism. In line with the project outlined by Steinmo and Thelen in 1992, the aim of historical institutionalism is not to formulate grand theories of politics, but rather to formulate hypotheses on causal links that explain the temporal and spatial variety of political phenomena. Taking note of the extreme partiality of the proposed definitions, we will now briefly present the four most relevant conceptual hypotheses of historical institutionalism (see Fioretos, Falleti and Scheingate 2016b, 10–4):

a)   *critical juncture*, first formulated in the aforementioned work by Rokkan and Lipset in 1967; it identifies historical conditions marked by radical uncertainty and openness to change in which the actors' decisions and the outcome of ongoing conflicts are decisive in shaping the start of a new historical phase with stable characteristics (cf. Capoccia 2016);

b)   *path dependence*, originally formulated in economic sciences in the 1980s through studies on technological innovation and subsequently gaineda political perspective; it identifies the causal mechanism that, starting from a critical juncture, produces continuity and strengthens the outcomes caused by the decisions made (Pierson 2004, 17–53; Page 2006);

c)   *intercurrence*, a notion native to the debate over historical institutional-
     ism (Orren and Skowronek 1994); it identifies the condition of coexist-
     ence and stratification within the same polity of institutions originating
     at different times and responding to different purposes and reasoning;

d)   *gradual institutional change*, which is also native to historical institution-
     alism; it identifies a mechanism of incremental change in institutions
     that does not occur through radical breaks, but rather through gradual
     processes that can be characterized by displacement, layering, drift, con-
     version, and exhaustion (Mahoney and Thelen 2010, 15–8; Streeck and
     Thelen 2005, 19–30); as they are characterized by change and not conti-
     nuity, these processes differ from path dependent ones.

3.3   *Other Paths to Dialogue*

New institutionalism and – to an even greater extent – historical institutionalism have thus conferred a new theoretical value onto the dialogue between
political science and history; nevertheless, not all the attempts of the past few
decades to make political science more historical can be ascribed to these currents. In conclusion, we will highlight two cases that emphasize this variety
of approaches: the use of historical analogies and the emergence of research
groups focused on the relationship between politics and history within the
associations that aggregate political science scholars in various countries.

In the last three decades, historical analogies have been used by political
scientists and scholars of international relations engaged in the analysis of
radically innovative global political phenomena. An example of this trend is
the study of the unipolarity of the world order born out of the collapse of the
Soviet system; such studies propose an analogy between the so-called benevolent American Empire and the Roman Empire or the British Empire (cf. Kagan
1998; Donnelly 2002). Another example is the cyberdomain studies analysing
cybertechnologies, cyberwarfare and cyberdeterrence in light of historical
analogies with previous military technologies, warfare and deterrence strategies (cf. Perkovich and Levite 2017; Goldman and Arquilla 2014; Nye, 2001).

The main theoretical insight into the use of historical analogy in the social
sciences is proposed by Mark Kornprobst in an essay published in *Millennium*
in 2007. Building on the idea that "historical analogies are pillars of scholarly
reasoning on world politics," Kornprobst identifies some epistemological and
methodological criteria that allow us to practice a "reflective use of analogies"
(Kornprobst 2007, 47) and to recognize the unreflective ones (among which he
includes the studies on the benevolent American Empire).

The practice of historical analogy belongs to a rhetorical-pragmatist theoretical perspective, according to which "the purpose of inquiry is the generation of useful knowledge," i.e. "working truth" rather than "objective truth"; this perspective attributes gnoseological usefulness to historical analogies, assigning to "debate and adjudication" (34–5) – rather than a single rigorous methodology – the role of judging the usefulness of a specific analogy. Analogies in fact gain importance in scholarly debate "through the exchange of arguments and assent"; a debate in which scholars with different methodological orientations take part is a resource to best evaluate them. Metaphorically speaking, Kornprobst writes that "jurors that all belong to the same camp can hardly be trusted to arrive at a reasonable verdict" (48).

A historical analogy is based on two building blocks: the tenor and the vehicle. The former is the phenomenon under investigation, the latter "an interpretation of a historical event, series of events or era." Its purpose is to make sense "of the tenor in light of the vehicle by equating the former and the latter in a more or less qualified manner" (31). The risk of producing misleading historical analogies lies precisely in the difference between tenor and vehicle, which could make this practice highly arbitrary. In order to overcome this risk, according to Kronprobst, it is necessary to have a wide repertoire of vehicles – that only historical knowledge can provide – through which to expand the series of possible analogies. Awareness that "historical facts are interpretations" is also fundamental, as no vehicle can be taken for granted, but it is necessary to debate over it and over its interpretations. Furthermore, in a qualified and well-argued analogy "not only the similarities but also the differences" (38–9) between tenor and vehicle are thematized; making use only of the former produces a simple equation which, rather than enrich the understanding of the studied subject, impoverishes it.

The tenor, by virtue of its temporal proximity to the scholar investigating it can be either a completely unknown subject or a subject analyzed through dogmatic or mainstream interpretations; comparing it analogically to a vehicle can serve in the first case to provide a minimum amount of intelligibility, and in the second, to spark debate over it, offering interpretations that differ from the current ones. When this happens, we are faced with a meaningful historical analogy that renews interpretations of the research target and raises new questions about it.

The other phenomenon that attests to the dynamism and variety of the discipline's interest in the historical aspects of social and political phenomena is the foundation – within the associations that bring political scientists together on a national level – of research groups specifically dedicated to the relationship between political science and history. The first case was the *American*

Political Science Association, within which a section called *Politics and History* was founded in 1989, with the aim of "bringing together political scientists interested in historical issues and problems drawing from almost every traditional disciplinary subfield" (APSA 2021). In the following years, this initiative was followed in many other countries where similar study groups have arisen (often adopting the same name, naturally in each case translated into the respective national language). In 1997 in Germany, within the *Deutsche Vereinigung für Politikwissenschaft* (German Association for Political Science), an *Arbeitskreises* (Working group) called *Politik und Geschichte* (Politics and History) was founded aiming to bring together political scientists interested in the study of *Erinnerungspolitik* (Politics of Memory) (DVPW 2021); in 2004, within the *Association Française de Science Politique* (French Political Science Association), the *Groupe de recherche "Histoire/Science politique"* (GRHISPO) (Research group History/Political Science) was founded, claiming "a historicised approach to the problems posed by political social sciences and to the categories of analysis they use" (AFSP 2021); in 2015, Italy had its turn, creating within the *Società Italiana di Scienza Politica* (Italian Society of Political Science) a standing group called *Politica e Storia* (again: Politics and History) aiming to "encourage the development and circulation of historical political science by promoting dialogue between political scientists and historians" (SISP 2021), and taking prevailing interest in changing phenomena within the Italian political system (Almagisti, Bacetti and Graziano, eds. 2018); the following year, a Specialist group was founded within the *Political Studies Association* (UK) called *Politics & History*, which aimed to "promote better dialogue between political scientists and political historians" (PSA 2021). The web pages of these groups present the conference activities they have organized, the writings they have produced and their main research interests. They offer a wide variety of analytical subjects and epistemological and methodological approaches.

4   Conclusion

The dialogue between political science and history, which for many decades was a marginal issue within political science, has blossomed in recent decades, especially, but not only with the rise of new institutionalism and historical institutionalism. In times of radical change and political instability, the practicing of medium- and long-term analyses becomes a necessity for political scholars, and this implies not only a temporal extension of the research objects, but also the improvement of methodological tools and theoretical perspectives that allow them to explore the issues of continuity and discontinuity. Today this dialogue has regained scientific legitimacy and seems to be an open ground; the partial map that we have proposed in this essay presents a political science research perspective in dialogue with history, offers multiple research paths and contains the potential for various kinds of experimentation. We therefore hope that this map will soon become outdated, that it will be a mere snapshot that will become more and more partial of an increasingly wide field of inquiry.

References

Aberbach, Joel D., Robert D. Putnam, and Bert A. Rockman, 1981. *Bureaucrats and Politicians in Western Democracies*. Cambridge, MA: Harvard University Press.

Adams, Herbert Baxter 1882. "The Germanic Origins of New England Towns." *Johns Hopkins University Studies in Historical and Political Science*, no. 2: 5–38.

AFSP (Association Française de Science Politique). 2021. GRHISPO. http://www.afsp.msh-paris.fr/activite/groupe/grhispo/txtgrhispo.html.

Almagisti, Marco, Carlo Bacetti and Paolo Graziano, eds, 2018 Introduzione alla politologia storica. Questioni teoriche e studi di caso. Roma: Carocci.

APSA (American Political Science Association). 2021. *Politics and History (Section 24)*. https://www.apsanet.org/section24.

Bryce, James, 1909. "The Relations of Political Science to History and to Practice." *American Political Science Review* 3.

Burgess, John William 1890. Political Science and Comparative Constitutional Law, 2 vols. Boston: Ginn.

Burgess, John William, 1895. "The Ideal of the American Commonwealth." Political Science Quarterly 10.

Burnham, Walter Dean 1970. *Critical Elections and the Mainsprings of American Politics*. New York: Norton.

Capoccia, Giovanni 2016. "Critical junctures." In *The Oxford Handbook of Historical Institutionalism*, edited by Orfeo Fioretos, Tulia G. Falleti and Adam Sheingate, 89–106. Oxford: University Press.

Carnoy, Martin 1984. *The State and Political Theory*. Princeton, NJ: University Press.

Dahl, Robert A. 1961a. "The behavioral approach to political science: Epitaph for a monument to a successful protest." *American Political Science Review*, no. 55:763–72.

Dahl, Robert A. 1961b. *Who Governs?: Democracy and Power in an American City*. New Haven, CT: Yale University Press.

Den Otter, Sandra M. 2007, "The Origins of a Historical Political Science in Late Victorian and Edwardian Britain." In *Modern political science: Anglo-American exchanges since 1880,* edited by Robert Adcock, Mark Bevir and Shannon C. Stimson, 37–65. Princeton: University Press.

Donnelly, Thomas 2002, "The Past as Prologue: An Imperial Manual." *Foreign Affairs* 81 (4): 165–70.

Dunning, William Archibals, 1937. Truth in History and Other Essays, edited by J. G. de Roulhac Hamilton. New York: Columbia University Press.

DVPW (Deutsche Vereinigung für Politikwissenschaft). 2021. *Über uns: DVPW.* https://www.dvpw.de/gliederung/ak/ak-politik-und-geschichte/ueber-uns.

Farr, James 2007, "The Historical Science(s) of Politics: The Principles, Association, and Fate of an American Discipline." In *Modern political science: Anglo-American exchanges since 1880,* edited by R. Adcock, M. Bevir and S. C. Stimson, 66–96. Princeton: University Press.

Femia, Joseph V. 1972, "Barrington Moore and the Preconditions for Democracy." In *British Journal of Political Science* 2 (1): 21–46. DOI: 10.1017/S0007123400008413.

Fioretos, Orfeo, Tullia G. Falleti and Adam Sheingate, eds. 2016a. *The Oxford Handbook of Historical Institutionalism.* Oxford: University Press.

Fioretos, Orfeo, Tullia G. Falleti and Adam Sheingate. 2016b. "Historical Institutionalism in Political Science." In *The Oxford Handbook of Historical Institutionalism,* edited by Orfeo Fioretos, Tulia G. Falleti, and Adam Sheingate, 3–30. Oxford: University Press.

Goldman, Emily O. and John Arquilla J., eds., 2014. *Cyber Analogies.* Monterey: Naval Postgraduate School.

Hall, Peter A., 2016. "Politics as a Process Structured in Space and Time." In *The Oxford Handbook of Historical Institutionalism,* edited by Orfeo Fioretos, Tulia G. Falleti and Adam Sheingate, 31–50. Oxford: University Press.

Huntington, Samuel P. 1973. *Political Order in Changing Societies.* Clinton: The Colonial Press.

Kagan, Robert 1998. "The Benevolent Empire." *Foreign Policy,* no. 111 (Summer): 24–35.

Kavanagh, Dennis 1991. "Why Political Science Needs History." *Political Studies* XXXIX: 479–95.

Key, Valdimer Orlando 1955. "A theory of critical elections." *Journal of Politics,* no. 17: 3–18.

Key, Valdimer Orlando. 1966. The Responsible Electorate: Rationality in Presidential Voting, 1936–1960. Cambridge, MA: Belknap Press.

Kornprobst, Markus 2007. "Comparing Apples and Oranges? Leading and Misleading Uses of Historical Analogies." *Millennium: Journal of International Studies* 36 (1): 29–49.

Lieber, Francis (1838) 1911. *Manual of Political Ethics.* 2 vols. edited by Thedore D. Woolsey. Philadelphia: J. B. Lippincott.

Lieber, Francis. (1901 [1853]). *Civil Liberty and Self-Government,* 4th ed. 2 vols. Edited by Theodore D. Woolsey. Philadelphia: Lippincott.

Lipset, Seymour Martin and Stein Rokkan, eds. 1967. "Cleavage Structures, Party Systems, and Voter Alignments: An Introduction." In *Party Systems and Voter Alignments: Cross-National Perspectives*, 1–64. Glencoe: Free Press.

Lowi, Theodore J. 1969. *The End of Liberalism: The Second Republic of the United States.* New York: Norton.

MacKay, Robert Alexander 1944. "The Nature and Function of the Social Sciences." *The Canadian Journal of Economics and Political Science / Revue canadienne d'Economique et de Science politique* 10 (3): 277–86.

Mahoney, James and Kathleen Thelen, eds. 2010. "A Theory of Gradual Institutional Change." In *Explaining Institutional Change: Ambiguity, Agency, and Power*, 1–37. New York: Cambridge University Press.

March, James G. and Johan P. Olsen, 1984. "The new institutionalism: Organizational factors in political life." *American Political Science Review* 78 (3): 734–49.

Migdal, Joel S. 1983. "Studying the politics of development and change: The state of the art." In *Political Science: The State of the Discipline*, edited by Ada W. Finifter. Washington, DC: American Political Science Association.

Moe, Terry M. 1987. "Interests, institutions, and positive theory: The politics of the NLRB." *Studies in American Political Development* 2: 236–99.

Moore, Barrington 1973. *Social Origins of Dictatorship and Democracy: Lord and Peasant in the Making of the Modern World.* Harmondsworth: Penguin University Books.

Mulford, Elisha 1870. *The Nation: Foundations of Civil Order and Political Life in the United States.* New York: Hurd and Houghton.

Nye, Joseph 2011. "Nuclear Lessons for Cyber Security?" *Strategic Studies Quarterly*, no. 5 (4).

O'Connor, James 1973. *The Fiscal Crisis of the State.* New York: St. Martin's Press.

Orren, Karen and Stephen Skowronek. 1994. "Beyond the Iconography of Order: Notes for a New Institutionalism." In *The Dynamics of American Politics: Approaches and Interpretations*, edited by Lawrence C. Dodd and Calvin Jillison, 311–30. Boulder: Westview Press.

Page, Scott 2006. "Path Dependence." *Quarterly Journal of Political Science*, no. 1:87–115.

Perkovich, George and Levite Ariel E., eds. 2017. *Understanding Cyber Conflict. Fourteen Analogies.* Washington, DC: Georgetown University Press.

Peters, B. Guy 1999. *Institutional Theory in Political Science The New Institutionalism.* London-New York: Pinter.

Pierson, Paul 2004. *Politics in Time. History, Institutions and Social Analysis.* Princeton: University Press.

Piven, Francis Fox and Richard A. Cloward. 1971. *Regulating the Poor: The Functions of Public Welfare.* New York: Vintage Books.

PSA (Political Studies Association). 2021. *Politics & History.* https://www.psa.ac.uk/specialist-groups/politics-and-history.

Robertson, David Brian 1993. "The Return to History and the New Institutionalism in American Political Science." *Social Science History* 17 (1): 1–36.

Rokkan, Stein 1970. *Citizens, Elections, Parties: Approaches to the Comparative Study of the Process of Development.* Oslo: Universitetsforlaget.

Rokkan, Stein. 1999. *State Formation, Nation-Building, and Mass Politics in Europe. The Theory of Stein Rokkan,* edited by Flora. Oxford: University Press.

Seeley, John Robert (1926 [1896]). *Introduction to Political Science.* London: Macmillan.

SISP (Società Italiana di scienza Politica). 2021. *Standing group "Politica e storia" della Società italiana di Scienza politica.* https://standinggroups.sisp.it/politicaesto ria/descrizione/.

Skocpol, Theda 1979. *States and Social Revolutions: A Comparative Analysis of France, Russia, and China.* Cambridge: University Press.

Skowronek, Stephen 1982. *Building a New American State: The Expansion of National Administrative Capacities, 1877–1920.* New York: Cambridge University Press.

Sola, Giorgio 1996. *Storia della scienza politica. Teorie, ricerche e paradigmi contemporanei.* Roma: Carocci.

Steinmo, Sven, Kathleen Thelen, and Frank Longstreth, eds. 1992. *Structuring politics Historical institutionalism in comparative analysis.* Cambridge: University Press.

Steinmo, Sven and Thelen Kathleen 1992. "Historical institutionalism in comparative politics." In *Structuring politics Historical institutionalism in comparative analysis,* edited by Steinmo Sven, Thelen Kathleen and Longstreth, 1–32. Cambridge: University Press.

Streeck, Wolfgang and Kathleen Thelen, 2005. "Introduction: Institutional Change in Advanced Political Economies." In *Beyond Continuity: Institutional Change in Advanced Political Economies,* edited by Wolfgang Streeck and Kathleen Thelen, 1–39. New York: Oxford University Press.

Truman, David B. 1953. *The Governmental Process: Political Interests and Public Opinion.* New York: Knopf.

Valbruzzi, Marco 2018. "Stein Rokkan: la storia al servizio della scienza." In *Introduzione alla politologia storica. Questioni teoriche e studi di caso,* edited by M. Almagisti, C. Bacetti and P. Graziano, 63–88. Roma: Carocci.

Wiener, Jonathan M 1975. "The Barrington Moore thesis and its critics." In *Theory and Society,* no. 2: 301–30.

Willoughby, Westel Woodbury 1900. *Social Justice: A Critical Essay.* New York: Macmillan.

Willoughby, Westel Woodbury. 1896. *An Examination of the Nature of the State.* New York: Macmillan.

Wilson, Woodrow 1885. *Congressional Government.* Boston: Houghton Mifflin.

Wilson, Woodrow. 1889. *The State: Elements of Historical and Practical Politics.* Boston: D. C. Heath.

Woolsey, Theodore D. 1878. *Political Science, or The State Theoretically and Practically Considered.* 2 vols. New York: Scribner.

Conclusion

Andrea Borghini

At the end of this dense and concise dialogue, which has unfolded through-out the pages of this volume, our hope is that we have amply demonstrated that it makes no sense to ask questions about the usefulness or otherwise of Historical Sociology.

In addition to the voices heard in the text, which, starting from different historical, biographical and disciplinary points of view, have tried to put inter-disciplinarity into "practice", as the beating heart of Historical Sociology, there are many others disseminated along the path of intellectual thought, which took a clear position, at the time, reaffirming the centrality of this approach, perspective or, as we prefer to call it, sociological style. We mention a few, not out of pedantry, but to further support the truthfulness of what we have just stated. David Inglis, in one of his oft-cited contributions, states among other things that "consciousness of historical complexity dispels myths, but weak historical consciousness reproduces them" (2014, 100). The reference to myths can only lead us to Elias who stated that *"scientists are destroyers of myths*. By factual observation, they endeavor to replace myths, religious ideas, meta-physical speculations and all unproven images of natural processes with the-ories – testable, verifiable and correctable by factual observation" (1978, 52–3). We close with a 'classic' such as Durkheim, for whom "history is not only the natural framework of human life, man is a product of history. If one takes him out of history, if one tries to conceive him outside of time, fixed, immobile, one distorts him. This immobile man is not man" (Durkheim quoted in Bellah 1959, 89).

These are only three voices, among many. We are confident, with this vol-ume, to have added others, in order to account for what scientific, intellec-tual and, dare I say, ethical value Historical Sociology represents in the times we are going through. The following expression, evidently attributable to the detractors of the approach, occurs in some of the essays which are scattered throughout the literature on the subject: "historical sociologists are all part of a subdiscipline that is regarded as something of a luxury good – the sociological equivalent of a Panerai watch or a Prada bag" (Adams *et al* 2005, 30).

Through these pages, we hope to have broadly demonstrated that this is not a luxury, but a fundamental cognitive and methodological prerequisite for sociological reflection and practice. And that even if it were a luxury, it would be a luxury that we cannot fail to afford.

References

Adams, Julia, Elisabeth S. Clemens and Ann S. Orloff. 2005. *Remaking Modernity: Politics, History and Sociology.* Durham (NC): Duke University Press.

Durkheim, E. Introduction a la morale, in Revue Philosophique, 1920, p. 89 quoted in Bellah R. N. 1959. "Durkheim and History." *American Sociological Review*, 447–61.

Elias, Norbert. 1978. *What is Sociology?* New York: Columbia University Press.

Inglis, David. 2014. "What is Worth Defending in Sociology Today? Presentism, Historical Vision and the Uses of Sociology." *Cultural Sociology* 8 (1): 99–118.

Name Index

Subject Index